PURE WATERS

PURE WATERS

Frank Waters and the Quest for the Cosmic

Frank Waters

Edited by Barbara Waters
Foreword by Alexander Blackburn

SWALLOW PRESS / OHIO UNIVERSITY PRESS
Athens

Swallow Press / Ohio University Press, Athens, Ohio 45701
© 2002 by The Frank Waters Foundation

Swallow Press books are printed on acid-free paper ⊗™

10 09 08 07 06 05 04 03 02   5 4 3 2 1

All editorials are from the Taos newspaper *El Crepusculo* (1949–51).
"Notes on Los Angeles" was published in *South Dakota Review* 19, nos. 1–2 (1981).
"Words" was published in *Western American Literature* 3, no. 3 (1968).
"Amazing Mabel" first appeared as the foreword to *Amazing Mabel: Sketches by Mabel Dodge Luhan* by Charmay B. Allred (Santa Fe: One Horse Land and Cattle Company, 1996).
"Symbols and Sacred Mountains" was published in *Phoenix Journal of Transpersonal Anthropology* 6, nos. 1–2 (1982).
"The Regional Imperative" was published in *Sundays in Tutt Library with Frank Waters* by The Hulbert Center for Southwestern Studies (Colorado Springs: The Colorado College, 1988).

Library of Congress Cataloging-in-Publication Data

Waters, Frank, 1902–
     Pure Waters: Frank Waters and the quest for the cosmic /
Frank Waters; edited by Barbara Waters; foreword by Alexander
Blackburn.
     p. cm.
     ISBN 0-8040-1045-5 (acid-free paper) — ISBN 0-8040-1046-3
(pbk.: acid-free paper)
     1. Waters, Frank, 1902—Homes and haunts—Southwestern
States. 2. Southwestern States. I. Waters, Barbara, 1929– II. Title.
     PS3545.A82A6 2002
     818'.5209—dc21
     [B]   2002017660

Dedicated to
Mary Ann Torrence,
Number One Fan of Frank Waters

CONTENTS

viii

Contents

FOREWORD

Frank Waters was born in Colorado Springs, Colorado, on July 25, 1902, and died at his home in Arroyo Seco near Taos, New Mexico, on June 3, 1995. He began his twenty-eight-book career in 1925 with a visionary novel, *The Lizard Woman,* that would be published in 1930 under the title *Fever Pitch* by Horace Liveright, the same New York publisher who was then encouraging another talented young writer, William Faulkner. Now in 2002, with the publication of this centennial volume of uncollected works, Waters's career ought by any critical measure to be considered as one of the most remarkable in the entire history of American letters.

To many of us who knew and read him, Waters was one of the greatest of our writers in the twentieth century, comparable in stature to such contemporaries as Faulkner, Ernest Hemingway, and John Steinbeck. Like them, he wrote novels that are classics. They did not rival him, however, in depth of vision, nor were they philosophers as he was. He achieved mastery as both a novelist and a philosopher, a phenomenon rarely met with either in America or abroad.

His "quest for the cosmic" demanded differing modes of expression, more than one approach—but all approaches were unified by mysticism: the mystic perceives wholeness in everything. He proposed as the evolutionary sanctuary for the psychic life of mankind in the future a new world of consciousness. The proposal was aimed at curing our spiritual condition rather than merely expressing it, which most of his contemporaries did. The fragmented wasteland of the modern age, he realized, called for redemptive vision. Of course, the voice of a visionary may take us aback and put us on guard, but it is an inimitable voice, poetic and plainspoken, humble yet governing in the reign of wonder. The more one reads Waters, the more one accepts the soundness of his judgment; the longer one travels the road to increased awareness, the more one is astonished to discover that he has been there before us.

The literary establishment has taken little notice of him. Readers have discovered him, perhaps millions of them; *Book of the Hopi* and *The Man Who Killed the Deer* are best sellers, and an increasing number of people are being drawn to his other works, most of them available in new editions issued under the imprint of Swallow Press/Ohio University Press. Yet the scholars and editors who are supposed to draw accurate maps of our big territory, American Literature, have never fully recognized this towering genius in the West. Although Western historians and critics acknowledge Waters as a titan, he is seldom accorded even a footnote in the grandiose mega-anthologies published in the East. Long-standing geographical prejudice accounts for some of this neglect: Western writers in general have until recently been overlooked even though the West can claim with considerable justification to have been the most vital literary region in the United States for the past fifty years. The authentic Western experience adumbrated by Waters as early as 1935 in his novel *The Wild Earth's Nobility* does in fact mark the beginning of what is coming to be called a Western Literary Renaissance. But the reason for the East's neglect of Waters is ultimately not geographical but spiritual. An often solitary figure, fully conscious of his times and accordingly estranged from tradition— "standing before a void out of which all things may grow," to borrow a phrase from Jung concerning the truly modern person—Waters was far ahead of those times. Whereas his life spanned the twentieth century, his spiritual quest places him now on the threshold of being recognized as the first great American writer of the twenty-first century.

For those readers coming to Waters for the first time in this present book or after only a random dip in others, a partial tally is in order. An epic trilogy of novels published in the 1930s and redacted as *Pike's Peak* (1971) is comparable at least in reach and in theme to Melville's *Moby Dick*. The novels that deserve a place on the shelf alongside such classics as *The Scarlet Letter* and *Huckleberry Finn* are three: *People of the Valley* (1941), *The Man Who Killed the Deer* (1942), and *The Woman at Otowi Crossing* (1966; revised edition, 1987). The "M" trilogy of philosophical works—*Masked Gods* (1950), *Mexico Mystique* (1975), and *Mountain Dialogues* (1981)—constitutes a monumental exposition of relationships between Amerindian and Mesoamerican mythology and symbology, Eastern religion (especially Tibetan Buddhism), Einsteinian and quantum physics, and depth psychology (especially that of

Jung). *Book of the Hopi* (1963), a penetrating "translation" of the meaning of Hopi Indian ceremonialism, can be read in conjunction with *Pumpkin Seed Point* (1969), subjective reflections altogether calm and Thoreauesque. *The Colorado* (Rivers of America Series, 1946) is swept along by its exuberant prose style and provides insights into Waters's early life. *Flight from Fiesta* (1987) stands in relation to his major novels as *Billy Budd* does to Melville's. Then there are the mavericks: *The Yogi of Cockroach Court* (1947), perhaps the only American novel ever written about a Buddhist among Chinese immigrants in Mexicali; *The Earp Brothers of Tombstone* (1960), a debunking of the Wyatt Earp legend; *To Possess the Land* (1974), the biography of a murdersome Anglo who schemed to take over northern New Mexico; and *Of Time and Change* (1998), posthumously published sketches about Taos artists and writers.

This is a rich book. As one might expect from "uncollecteds," tailings from the mother lode appear in it; but the whole contains treasures, little masterpieces never before published, or republished from buried sources. Waters wrote some of these pieces when he was in his seventies and eighties, yet the prose, as ever, is marked by a warm, alive beauty. The least remarkable of the pieces are seventeen brief editorials dating from 1949–51, when he was editing *El Crepusculo*. In these pieces, he is not taking aim at the cosmic. Still, they convey the spirit of Taos in that period in a voice attuned to "local color" interests in old-fashioned cold remedies, in the changing of the seasons, and in ritual observances of the Pueblo Indians. Here and there one finds beneath their surface ripple some gems too precious not to be assayed:

> . . . thickets of wild plum blossoms heaped like snowdrifts in the sagebrush . . . crossing the pasture like a file of white-blanketed Indians.
> . . . the aspens and the cottonwoods glow butter-yellow.
> . . . a Palomino colt . . . like a jackrabbit mounted on stilts.

Eight speeches and essays reveal Waters in his search for correlations between human and universal destiny. These "planetaries," as I am tempted to call them, cover a wide range of considerations—linguistic, aesthetic, astronomical, even astrological. The essence of the most formidable of them, "Incursions from Outer Space" and "The Mesoamerican Calendar," is distilled for us in "Prelude to Change" (surely a landmark for commencement addresses) and in, above all,

"The Regional Imperative." It is a great American essay. The regional imperative of the title refers to our allegiance to groups, clans, tribes, and nations and to the consequent fragmentation between our conscious and unconscious selves, between our minds and hearts. To unite the world a new way of thinking is needed: the *planetary* imperative. We must regard the entire body of Earth as our one planetary imperative in order to save it from further ravages. Unlike primal peoples, we in the modern world have left out of our theories of evolution the creative thrust of cosmic powers. The evolution of man, Waters argues, is already mysteriously synchronized with that of Earth:

> How alike they are, Earth and man! Each maintains an even body temperature and an equilibrium among the primary elements of water, air, earth, and fire. There can be little wonder that from ancient times man has considered himself the microcosmic image of macrocosmic Earth. Water is the main constituent in both their bodies; blood is man's liquid flow akin to that of water throughout the Earth. Both flows are in tune with the phases of the moon and sensitive to the influences of all planets. Man breathes eighteen times a minute or 25,920 times a day. This relates him to the great 25,920-year cycle of the Precession—the time it takes for the vernal equinox to move through the circle of the zodiac. For every eighteen breaths man takes there are seventy-two beats of the pulse, just as the arc of the ecliptic moves exactly one degree every seventy-two years.

Is the world undergoing the greatest cultural change since the beginning of the Christian era, as Waters contends? Are we emerging to a level of higher consciousness, preparatory to the external transformation of the existing political and economic systems? Part of the answer to these questions lies in contemporary readers' perception of change, for instance in our realization at least since the moon landings that our planet is a fragile speck in the universe. The result of change, according to Waters, will be the virtual creation of a new world.

The hitherto unpublished "Visions of the Good" will flummox critics who no longer think of words as magical or of literature as a measure of a civilization. Waters distinguishes between "horizontal" and "vertical" works of literature, the former well-crafted and often boosted by prizes but lacking "that element which reminds us we are greater than we are." A vertical work of literature, by contrast, "reveals the purpose of our existence, gives us a vision of our potential creativity, and helps to raise our level of consciousness." By what means does vertical literature accomplish this end? It awakens in us, as *Moby Dick* does, "a sense of something transcendental somewhere 'out there' beyond us or 'in here' within us." Specifically, it gives us the sense of nebulous influences: fate, destiny, nemesis, karma.

Now, it would be rash to conclude that Waters's rare venture into criticism amounts to warmed-over Transcendentalism, even though future scholars may press him into its service, the better to fit him into tradition. Serious critics today are in revolt against postmodernism and are demanding that we rediscover a literature that tries to transcend spiritual disabilities—"in order," as Colin Falck argues in *Myth, Truth, and Literature* (Cambridge University Press, 1994) "to re-connect with the most central meanings of human life." Waters, again, is in the vanguard.

I reserve the last of my encomia for the nine personal narratives and sketches in this book. Their beauty, tenderness, and compassion are self-validating, their intimacy compelling.

A few prefatory remarks. Waters's pioneering grandfather, Joseph Dozier (1842–1925), was a distinguished contractor and builder in the Pikes Peak region but succumbed to gold fever and lost the family fortune in mining ventures in Cripple Creek. Frank, who may have been part Indian on the paternal side, was more interested in tracing his dual heritage than in studying engineering, so he dropped out of Colorado College and pursued an informal education in the ways of man and nature in the Wild West. Never an expatriate sipping absinthe in a Left Bank bistro or on a hunt for big game in Africa, he considered the true American experience to be exactly where he was: the Rockies. He would be "the Bard of the Boondocks," as he once jokingly called himself, and borderline poverty would be the price he paid for that commitment. He was a roustabout in the Wyoming oil fields, a lone telephone operative in the vast furnace of Southern Californian deserts, a writer who picked up gigs in Hollywood and who later edited, as already mentioned, a small-town newspaper. He lived in cheap hotels, remote hamlets. Once in 1931, when he had a small grubstake, he traveled alone on horseback for a thousand miles down the spine of the Sierra Madre, where he found peoples who still worshipped the old gods of pre-Columbian Mexico. This was a self-tutored writer who would soon be turning out literary masterpieces at a clip surpassed only, perhaps, by Faulkner. We needn't glorify him, but people of different races and cultures and from all walks of life trusted and loved him; many of them did not know he was a writer.

There's an affectionate anecdote in "Women Who Have Influenced Me Most" about Mrs. Quintana, his neighbor in the old Hispanic village of Arroyo Seco:

> The mountain canyons behind our fields and pastures used to be full of deer. Mrs. Quintana's menfolk ignored the state game laws restricting hunting to a specified open season. All the year around a haunch of deer could be found at their house, and I was often given a venison roast to marinate. One day an Anglo stranger knocked on Mrs. Quintana's door. When she opened it, he asked, "Is this the house of the man who wrote *The Man Who Killed the Deer?*"
>
> Mrs. Quintana didn't know that one of my books bears this title. And her main language is Spanish. She thought a policeman had come to arrest the man who had killed a deer out of season. Hastily denying that the lawbreaker was one of her family, she slammed the door after him. Then she hurried to carry the freshly skinned carcass of a deer to her back pasture, where she burned it.

In this same speech, after confessing to a show-no-emotion upbringing, the author pays tributes to a mother, a teacher, a sister, a friend, a neighbor, a wife. The protagonist of *People of the Valley*, let it be noted, is in her archetypal role the Great Goddess. Waters, we can see, was far from a misogynist male writer.

Reading his "River Trips" sketch, one detects echoes of Joseph Conrad, an early influence. Waters evokes a pristine peace, suggestive of Conrad's Congo, that he found during journeys down the pre–Boulder Dam Colorado River and the Río Usumacinta on the jungle border between Mexico and Guatemala:

> Innumerable flocks of herons floated like spotless white blankets on the muddy brown surface of the river, refusing to be disturbed until we were almost upon them. Then abruptly they rose as if someone had grasped the edge of their feathery blanket and shaken it over our heads.
>
> . . . .
>
> Over all brooded an unbroken silence, the hot hush of the noonday sun. Immobile and silent ourselves, we seemed implanted in a newly created virgin earth.

"The Manby Mystery" narrative, which shows that Waters was a painstaking investigative reporter, is also evidence that he never flinched before the presence of humanity's heart of darkness.

The feelings and meanings that enshrine the spirit are those of the heart's blood, the ones that have absorbed our attention and bestowed on us our awareness. They are, for imaginative artists, the spiritual shrines where the gods abide, those images so imbued with strong emotions as to have the power to crack us open and to fuel the long endeavor of art. In particular, the spirit of place is bound up in the local, the present, ordinary day-to-day of human experience. Place animates a literary work, makes it glow, as Eudora Welty has said, "in a kind of recognizable glory." And so when Waters describes his home in Arroyo Seco, a centuries-old adobe house with nearly fifteen acres of pasture at eight thousand feet of altitude, flanked by the Sangre de Cristo Mountains and full of lofty cottonwoods and aspens, of thickets of wild rose, plum, and chokecherry, everything—man, animals, soil, trees, stones, stars—comes alive. It is all one, all part of the wild earth's nobility.

"The Horses" communicates that power. Here is Waters with Cry-Baby, one of his beloved horses:

> During our long rides through the reservation it always happened; and she seemed to feel it as well as I. We fused into one, and together into all that wildness and beauty of sagebrush, mountain, earth, and sky. There was no differentiation, no sense of movement; all seemed caught up in one timeless unity marked only by the silent, slow, and steady heartbeat through us all.

When he loses Rocket, another beloved horse, he again feels that all is one, all connected, life and death:

> There was an eerie feeling of sadness, of tragedy, in the air. The stars, close and bright in the black sky, glittered with preternatural awareness. The snow packs on the peaks and the snow on the ground gave off a queer muted sheen. And the silence spoke loudest. The whole thing got me: gentle Rocket hiding out there in the dark woods alone, knowing that her time had come. Accepting the mystery of death, I drove home.

Frank Waters rode home for the last time on June 2, 1995. Arriving from winter quarters in Tucson, he looked out upon the whole Taos

Valley. Over there, the abysmal deep of the Río Grande. Ahead, snow-capped Sacred Mountain, at its foot to one side the pueblo reservation, to another side Seco. Scattered about the valley were houses that in evening light resemble, as D. H. Lawrence once observed, crystals. This same vista has inspired generations of artists. The feelings engendered by it have been likened to those of Paul on the road to Damascus. So it must have been for Waters. He was home. He died the next day. His ashes were spread among the aspens and out in the pasture, under the Sacred Mountain's shadow.

ALEXANDER BLACKBURN

INTRODUCTION

For Frank Waters fans, the word "continued" will automatically insert itself before "quest" in the subtitle of this book. They know that his life and writings were one continuous search for cosmic awareness, whether conscious or unconscious. He envisioned a future brightened by an advanced state of human consciousness. He foresaw—and at times experienced—a cosmos or universe distinctive for its order, intuition, harmony, and unity superseding duality. On his granite memorial are carved his words from *The Man Who Killed the Deer*, "We will meet again, as equal parts of one great life." In the subtitle of *Mexico Mystique* he calls this giant step forward "The Coming Sixth World of Consciousness."

Richard Bucke's *Cosmic Consciousness*, published in 1901, strongly influenced Frank from his twenties onward. Bucke contended that four stages of intellect exist. According to him, the lowest is that of the senses, derived from basic "percepts." Next, stemming from more advanced "recepts," is the simple consciousness of animals. With their superior "concepts," human beings have reached the third level, consciousness of self. And a few persons have achieved the final stage—our eventual goal—of cosmic consciousness, or the "intuitive mind."

A century after the book was published, mention of these terms is made here in Frank's speech "Words." Bucke thought that his friend Walt Whitman possessed traits typical of those who have touched upon the highest stage of intellect. Most important are intuition, morality, compassion, spirituality, simplicity, charisma, optimism, oneness with nature, openness to revelation, and freedom from consciousness of self that inhibits creativity. Frank Waters, too, evidenced these qualities in his long search for illumination. They can be sensed in the following pages.

The *order* of the cosmos fascinated Frank, as readers will notice here in the final chapter. This, his favorite essay, is the culmination of his many years spent researching the Mesoamerican calendar and related civilizations. Although it is frequently called the Aztec Calendar, its mathematics actually predate that civilization by centuries. These convoluted calculations originally were based on precise astronomical observations, not astrology. Waters viewed later astrological interpretations from a mytho-psychological perspective. What he truly marveled at was the larger, orderly view that linked age to age from ancient to modern times and beyond, an achievement resonating with the highest level of consciousness. It is not so strange after all to find a strong rational element in a man who was preponderantly, and by heritage, an intuitive. And it will hearten the intuitive to learn that this chapter reads just as well when numbers are merely skimmed as it does when they are carefully studied. It's the wonder that matters.

The human role in a self-inclusive universe is that of learner. Waters always regarded himself as such. As a grown man writing *The Colorado,* for example, he repeatedly referred to himself as "the boy." In *Mountain Dialogues,* chapter by chapter he passed on his learnings to date, several of them mathematically oriented, as he does here. He disliked being called a "mystic," possibly because he saw himself not as a master of the esoteric but as an eternally questing student of the universe.

For change of pace, the essays in this book alternate with speeches and editorials. Frank's so-called essays were often tales that had helped to point his way. His speeches reveal the intricacies of his mind and writing. The editorials selected are the twinkle in his eye, a twinkle noticed by anyone who ever met him. Imagine. In the same book an editorial about pushing a wheelbarrow up Pikes Peak and a speech comparing themes of Buddhism to American Indian religion. This was the complete unabridged Frank Waters: a brilliant, many-faceted enigma.

His essays on Houston Branch, the newspaper *El Crepusculo,* and Dr. Light help us to see how Waters practically and intuitively learned it was best for him to remain a maverick loner. "River Trips," "Notes on Los Angeles," and "The Manby Mystery" demonstrate not only his mastery of descriptive writing but the influence of place upon every aspect of his growth. Waters once wrote, "All of my books, in some way, are about these places which have drawn and held me and about persons who have been affected by their distinctive influences." "The Horses" and "The Guru and the Fox" convey his love of nature and animals, as do several editorials. In his fine speeches "Visions of the

Good," "Prelude to Change," and "The Regional Imperative," he shares with readers part of his greater vision. All is a merging of the human role on earth with one's universal obligations.

Of course Frank had nothing to do with the selection and arrangement of these pages. That my choices are faithful to his originals can be verified in the Frank Waters Room at the University of New Mexico in Albuquerque, where they will be filed with the rest of his original papers and manuscripts. Waters fans and scholars are used to my typing and cautious editing, whether they are aware of it or not, for my husband and I sustained a productive work relationship regarding his writing from 1977 until his death in 1995. Where it has conflicted with current editorial rules, Waters's unique usage generally has been given precedence in this book.

My sincere appreciation extends to Mary Ann Torrence for duplicating the editorials from *El Crepusculo* and encouraging their publication; to Alexander Blackburn, Professor Emeritus, University of Colorado, Colorado Springs, for his astute literary criticism in the foreword; and to Gillian Berchowitz, Senior Editor, and Nancy Basmajian, Manuscript Editor, at Swallow Press/Ohio University Press for efficiently guiding the book through its production process in time for it to appear at the gala celebration in Taos July 25–28, 2002, in honor of the centennial of Frank's birth.

Due to the abrupt departure of a typist working on this manuscript, I had to finish typing it myself. It seemed like old times. Perhaps by chance, the Mesoamerican chapter was completed on July 25, 2001. Elated, I announced to Frank's lingering Presence, "Here is your birthday present, dear. Your favorite chapter—ready for publishing at last!" Several days later when I finished typing his speech "Women Who Have Influenced Me Most," he seemed to reply, "And this is *your* gift." Frank Waters was a generous man. It is our good fortune that he continues to share with us, for our benefit, these gleanings about earthly matters entwined with cosmic imperatives.

Arroyo Seco, New Mexico
BARBARA WATERS

1
River Trips

(Essay)

Slow travel is always the best—the slower the better. Jet flight is not travel at all; one is merely picked up somewhere and set down somewhere else without any sense of the land or sea between. Even automobile travel is too fast. You skim over an interstate paved highway without feeling the changing texture and rhythm of the land. Riding a train used to be an exciting adventure. Especially on the long-gone narrow-gauge lines through the Rockies. The train hurtled through dark tunnels, crept over spider-work trestles, and inched along cliff walls, with massed mountains heaving up on all sides. Travel by horseback, as I did through Mexico, is of course the best.

As a landsman, I know nothing about boats or travel by water. Still, I have taken trips on three rivers: the lower Colorado, the Likiang in China, and the Usumacinta between Mexico and Guatemala. How different they were! And yet they all evoked a common mood and feeling difficult to define. It was as if one were immobile, watching the river unwind, the land unfold. Becalmed in time, high noon gave way to twilight and it to midnight and dawn, like kaleidoscopic images on a screen. The effect was mesmeric. It induced an attitude of complacent calm, a feeling of benign peace. And with this, the realization of our insignificance and impotency to ultimately control the invisible powers of the cosmic flow unwinding slow, indifferent, and majestic before us.

Shortly before construction began on Boulder Dam, I rode the rapids of the upper Colorado down through Grand Canyon to Black Canyon with some engineers. The trip, so commercially popular now, was exciting, spectacular, awesome, and sublime—but not customary river travel. My voyage down the lower Colorado was something else. It was made in 1925 in a small fifty-ton steamer carrying 1,200 fresh cattle hides and fifty Mexican peons from the delta boat landing of El Mayor, down to the mouth of the Colorado, on down the gulf to Santa Rosalia on the coast of Lower California, then across to the port of Guaymas on the mainland of Mexico. The time was mid-August. The stench from the green cattle hides permeated our clothes and sweaty skins. Beset by heat, mosquitoes, and flies, peon families huddled on the deck under the blazing sun. Near the mouth of the river the boat anchored for three days and four nights. The uncovered metal water casks developed a thick green scum from underneath which we dipped stale drinking water. The pails of beans became rancid; we were reduced to eating goat cheese, hard biscuits that exploded tiny puffs of flour when broken, and bitter red coffee three times a day. Still we waited, unmoving. For what?

It came one midnight. A wall of water almost four feet high, clearly visible in the moonlight, swiftly advancing upstream. The massive Cocopah Indian *capitan* had heard it coming. The anchor was hurriedly brought up, the engines started. The little steamer met the blow squarely. She went nose down, deck awash, and came up with a dizzy roll streaming torrents from every passageway. We passengers, the worker families and myself, frightened into an abject mass of humanity clinging to doorposts and deck rails, shivered in abysmal misery, wrang out our clothes, and waited for the sun.

What we had experienced was a tidal bore, a phenomenon encountered in but few river mouths in the world. In fully recounting this experience in my early book *The Colorado,* I described a bore as simply a tidal wave that rushes up a river, opposing in turbulent conflict the current of the river itself. The bores of the Colorado are perhaps the most notable. For here the tidal variation of the Gulf of California varies from twenty-two to thirty-two feet, generating waves that sweep up the river for thirty-seven miles—only to meet the great force of the Colorado itself, the most heavily silt-laden river in the world, sweeping down into the gulf at the rate of two hundred thousand cubic feet per second.

We had been lucky. The river was at its summer low, and the tide of the full moon was past its peak. The fate of the *Topolobampo* only three years before reminded us what we had escaped. She was a little steamer of thirty-six tons, crowded with 125 Mexican peons bound for the cotton-fields of Imperial Valley upriver. On the night of November 18, 1922, she was met by a wall of water fifteen feet high traveling upriver with the speed of an express train. The tidal bore caught the *Topolobampo* squarely abeam and rolled her over like a log. Only thirty-nine passengers survived, and only twenty-one bodies of the eighty-six drowned were dragged out of the mud flats days afterward.

Our own experience was frightening and miserable enough. Yet my memory clings more tenaciously to our uneventful trip downriver before we were engulfed. Why, I can't say; it was so uneventful. Old, foul with hides and reeking in the blazing sun like a garbage tug, our *vapor* crept slowly downstream like a fat beetle crawling down a dusty road.

The delta we were traversing was a strange, wild *terra incognita* of chaparral, swamps, and alkali flats threaded by a dozen channels of the river itself. There were no railroads, no roads. A few cattlemen herded scrubby half-wild cattle on dry stretches, and still wilder shy Cocopah Indians hid in the wilderness. There was plenty of game: groups of wild burros traveling between water holes, wild hogs, mountain wildcats, deer, muskrats, beaver, and boundless flocks of ducks, geese, herons, and gulls.

The river increasingly became inalienably a part of its shores. The chaparral grew more and more dense. Shadows of willows darkened the glades. Lagoons crept under the overhanging foliage and serenely reappeared.

Innumerable flocks of herons floated like spotless white blankets on the muddy brown surface of the river, refusing to be disturbed until we were almost upon them. Then abruptly they rose as if someone had grasped the edge of their feathery blanket and shaken it over our heads. Borne forward along that remote watercourse in an attitude of placid calm, it was as if the doubtful virtues of all our obscure and meaningless lives had been recognized and rewarded with a benign and earthly peace.

Twilight thickened the jungle on each side. Darkness closed it in upon us. To ward off mosquitoes, the families on the deck lighted charcoal braziers and in their faint glow stretched out to sleep. The cry of a night bird rose from the marshes. At dawn returned heat, insects, and the stench of hides. The river had widened, reflecting a sullen muddy aspect that changed our restful mood of the night. The chaparral had retreated on each side. We were approaching a flat, barren tidal plain across which the river wound drunkenly in great curves as if it had lost its way. Slow, indifferent, it crept by us as though we, heirs to power over all the living earth, were no more than an insignificant and unmoving speck upon its muddy surface. It did not know us; and we, with resentful, sun-glazed eyes, stared back upon the river.

Such a trip is impossible now. There are no tidal bores to be encountered. Not one surface drop of the Colorado reaches the gulf. Yet one wonders just how long it can be dammed and bled dry to produce electric power for man's evanescent and often imagined needs. For this great river is essentially a cosmic flow balancing all the forces within the living land, and eventually it must conform to the invisible laws of its nature.

◆

In contrast to my trip down the lower Colorado, my ride up the Likiang River was a Sunday picnic.

The Likiang (or simply Li) River in the southeastern province of Kuangsi is a thread running through China's long past and its most beautiful and unique scenery. The landscape for which it has been famous for centuries became visible as our plane from Canton approached Kweilin, the principal town in the region. High, peaked mountain pinnacles jutting up from both sides of the river extended upriver for nearly a hundred miles. Reminding me of the sharp, jagged rock *picachos* along the lower Colorado at Needles, they loomed up with an aspect at once spectacular, bizarre, and unreal.

Our group in the plane comprised twenty Americans selected by the United States-China Peoples Friendship Association. A geologist in the group explained that these queer "karst" formations were mountains of limestone exposed when weathering had worn away the coarse rock plateau that once covered the region. There was only one other similar karst area, in Yugoslavia.

Kweilin means "acacia," and its wide streets and dusty roads were bordered by acacia trees. The town had been repeatedly bombed by Japanese until it was almost completely destroyed. It has since been rebuilt into a modern city. Unfortunately, it was being industrialized, creating palls of smoke that obscured its pleasant setting. Only after laboriously climbing the 254 stone steps to the summit of Pile Silk Hill would we overlook all Kweilin and the windings of the Likiang River. How beautiful it all was. A jumbled mass of buildings crowded beneath and around those dark jutting pinnacles that lined the banks of the curving river and made of the distant horizon a spectacular wall of spiked peaks.

Formed of soft limestone, these karst mountains contained many caves in which the people of Kweilin had sought refuge during the Japanese bombing raids. One of those we entered was the Reed Flute Cave. It was immense, with numerous high-ceilinged chambers filled with great stalagmites and stalactites and curious limestone formations illumined by colored lamps. Another cavern was the Seven Star Cave with its reputed one thousand figures of Buddha carved in its walls—possibly soon after Buddhism was introduced into China during the second century.

The river with its bizarre background, however, was what fascinated us most. And on a clear October Sunday our wish to see more of it was granted by our Chinese hosts. We were driven in a bus up along the river on a dirt road winding through open fields. How pleasant to get out of the smoke and grime of the city, to see the unspoiled, immemorial land of China. There were no barbed wire fences, no signposts, no screaming billboards.

We stopped at Yan-ti, a tiny village of a dozen adobe houses on the bank of the river, above which rose the ever-present karst pinnacles. Here we boarded what resembled a small Mississippi steamboat of a past era in America. It did not contain an engine of any kind, however, but was pulled on a long hawser by a tug in front. The advantages of this were immediately apparent when we started upriver. There were no vibrations and no noise as our boat had no engine; and the tug was so far ahead, we felt no ripples from it and had an unobstructed view during our passage.

In addition to our group of twenty Americans, a half-dozen German and English guests had been invited by government officials of Communist China. Serving us as guides and interpreters were young Miss Wong and Mr. Yen under the direction of Mrs. Chu, a middle-aged, sharp-eyed, and capable woman. Mao had died scarcely a month before, and China was still closed to all visitors save those invited to see the country. All three of our hosts were dressed in the prescribed dark blue jackets and trousers, in stark contrast to our motley colored shirts and odd pants.

Lounging on the open deck at the bow of the boat, I watched the land unfold. How different it was from the China of immense cities, industrial plants, modern housing developments, crowded hospitals and schools, and rural communes. Here was enduring China. A vast ancient land long swept by war, revolution, and ideological change, but which still showed here its immemorial Chinese placidity and accommodation to outward change. I felt that everything in sight symbolized the indestructibility of China's inner character. Everywhere, on each side, far in front at every turn, rose the forbidding limestone crags and spires, soft and easily molded as the Chinese themselves, which had survived the geological destruction of their hard-rock facades. The Li itself accommodated its course to their seemingly impassable blockades, swinging around and between them, past stretches of open planted fields.

Occasionally we passed one of the houseboats called *sampans,* its shape unchanged for centuries. Squat and weathered, each had a small, central, low-roofed cabin to house its family. A man with pants rolled up to his knees and wearing a big straw hat would be adjusting gear and the square red sail, manning the big sweep, or simply sitting with his fishing gear as the children watched him. This was their life, a life spent on the river. None of them watched us pass. It was as if they, belonging to the past, were unaware of our own present.

Late that afternoon, after a box lunch, we saw the first settlement along the riverbank. The buildings comprised Yang Shan, an ancient junk and sampan trading center. The colorful village occupied the terraces of a steep hill marked by numerous abandoned Buddhist temples and shrines. On one cliff wall was a beautiful Chinese inscription said to have been written in the tenth century by a Sung emperor. Suffering a serious illness, he had made a pilgrimage here and was cured by its serene beauty. On the summit of the hill, overlooking the sweeping bend of the wide river, still stood an ancient bright red pavilion named "Welcoming the River." With its flowing architectural lines blending with the still water below and the blue cloudless sky above, it seemed an ideographic inscription itself confirming the incomparable beauty that once had cured an emperor's illness.

The scene seemed strangely familiar. Painted by generations of long forgotten artists, it appears again and again on old scrolls and wall hangings everywhere. A scraggy karst pinnacle, the gentle river Li, and a gracious pavilion—these are the landscape characters in the drama of China's ancient earth that have endured and will still endure throughout all lesser changes.

The northward-flowing Usumacinta marks for much of its length the boundary between Guatemala and the Mexican state of Chiapas. One of the longest tropical rivers on the continent, it cuts through a dense rainforest of towering mahogany, ceiba, sapodilla, and palm trees choked with growths of bamboo, ferns, vines, and brush. In it lie the temple ruins of the ancient Maya civilization. This also is the homeland of the Lacandones, the last surviving full-blood descendents of the Classic Mayas.

To get here would have been difficult for me without the help of Gertrude "Trudi" Blom, widow of the archeologist Franz Blom. She operated *Na-Bolom* ("at the Sign of the Jaguar"), the Centro de Estudios Scientificos, in San Cristobal de las Casas, Chiapas. In 1950 the couple had established their home here, gradually adding rooms to accommodate archeologists and anthropologists who came to study the Mayan ruins and the Lacandones. During my visit twenty years later, it was the most unusual guesthouse in town. With an excellent library and Trudi's collection of color slides, it offered ample facilities for research and study. Meals were served family style at a table seating twenty to thirty guests. At its head presided Trudi, as we called her, fluent in German, French, Spanish, and English, and shouting and cursing in any of them.

Trudi, then about seventy, was a character. *Na-Bolom* she ruled with dictatorial aplomb, even to prescribing our disposal of used toilet paper. Her secondary role was that of the Great White Goddess of the Lacandones. It was generally constructive. She took them medicines, helped to sell their bows and arrows, and beleaguered the Mexican government to establish this jungle homeland as a reserve. Hence if any visitor wanted to see the Lacandones or the Maya ruins, Trudi, wearing her baggy pants and stout boots, took them.

When I was there, a few of us asked her to arrange a trip. There were five others besides me. I will give them these names: Edgar Smith, a photographer; middle-aged Professor Jones and his wife; and the younger Brown couple, both teachers. Preceded by Trudi and the Browns, the other four of us took off in the plane Trudi usually chartered, a four-passenger Cessna 180. A "jungle pilot" often has to wait hours for the mist to clear from the dank *selva* before taking off. We were fortunate; the morning was clear. The earth below spread out in rolling wooded hills dotted with small clearings in which stood tiny villages of a dozen huts.

Then, below a sea of cumulus clouds formed by the rising mist, appeared the rain forest, a growth so dense it looked like a blanket of moss. Soon I glimpsed a tiny silver rivulet curving through it: the Usumacinta. To travel through the jungle by horseback would have taken two days or more. But in an hour our little plane ducked down through an almost invisible opening to a narrow landing strip in a small clearing beside the river.

Nearby stood a cluster of several partly ruined adobe buildings occupied by a family of caretakers. Trudi and the Brown couple were waiting for us. Trudi was shouting and swearing at a boatman readying a long dugout canoe on the riverbank.

This was Agua Azul, formerly a *central* for mahogany cutters and *chicleros* who gathered chicle, the sap from the *zapote chico*, or sapodilla, for making chewing gum. From here the massive mahogany logs were floated downriver to Tenosique, where they were tied into rafts and floated on down to the Gulf of Mexico for ship loading. Author B. Traven in his well-known "jungle novels" described the inhuman operation of such camps. Indians were enslaved, marched through the jungle, and forced to fell the great mahogany trees, which often reached a height of 150 feet. When they failed to cut their allotted number of tons, Indians were hung up by the thumbs or staked out overnight to be mangled by jaguars.

The mahogany dugout canoe prepared for us was long and sturdy and equipped with an outboard motor. When we had loaded our baggage and seated ourselves, the Mexican boatman started the motor and pushed off downriver. The Usumacinta unwound before us, wide, deep, and placid, but with a strong current. It seemed like a narrow swath cut through an impenetrable forest whose hundred-foot height walled us in on each side. Lofty mahogany trees, giant umbrella-shaped ceibas sacred to the Mayas, red *palo mulatos*, palm and rubber trees. Clumps of bamboo, dense undergrowth entangled in huge ferns and poisonous *mata-palo* vines. Orchids, waist-high begonias, flowers of every color grew everywhere. Each turn of the river revealed a new aspect of lush splendor. We caught glimpses of parrots, always flying in pairs, and tiny deer. Over all brooded an unbroken silence, the hot hush of the noonday sun. Immobile and silent ourselves, we seemed implanted in a newly created virgin earth.

After a few hours the dugout beached on a sandy spit on a wide turn of the river below a twenty-foot-high bank. Up this we climbed to a clearing containing a two-family compound of six or seven *chosas.* All these huts were roofed with thatchings of palm; one had walls of bamboo poles. This center *chosa* was one big room with a four-foot-high, flat-topped fireplace for communal cooking. Children, dogs, pigs, and chickens roamed loose through the compound. Hanging our hammocks in two empty *chosas,* we ate supper by lamplight, balanced ourselves in the hammocks under mosquito nets, and lay listening to the monkeys.

The jungle encroached to the edge of the small clearing. One dared not walk far alone. The ruins of Yaxchilan lay hidden, and next morning we began to seek them. First it was necessary for the head man, who was their caretaker, to cut a path through the dense growth with a machete. Within a few weeks, he told us, it would be overgrown again.

Yaxchilan, embraced by the wide curve of the Usumacinta and isolated deep in the rain forest, must have been, like Palenque, one of the loveliest of all Mayan temple cities. Why it hadn't been preserved and restored like lesser sites is a mystery. The Spanish explorers saw the ruins in 1696. Teobert Maler mapped them in 1897; and many later archeologists studied them, only to leave them to be swallowed up by the jungle, with some of their precious stelae snaked out by thieves. Maler's map shows forty structures rising on terraces to the Acropolis Grande and nearby Acropolis Pequeño.

Now it was almost impossible to detect the architectural plan. The encroaching growth was destroying all temples. Huge trees not only enveloped all buildings, but tree-sized roots and branches grew through roofs, walls, and subterranean chambers, tearing apart the cut stones. Even so, one saw how lovely they must have been. The pyramid temples were not high, but their upper facades and roof-combs were beautifully ornamented with figures in stone and stucco. The stone here is said to be especially hard, so the sculpture was among the best. Yaxchilan is famous for its stone lintels carved in exquisite bas-relief. Lintel 8 records a Calendar Round date of A.D. 755. The huge stelae were equally magnificent. Most of them had fallen and were covered with moss. Others that have been studied had been turned face down to prevent their inscriptions from weathering.

The great temple on the highest terrace was most imposing. In front of the middle doorway lay the decapitated statue of Hachakyum, the ancient Mayan god who made heaven and earth. Here the Lacandones still make pilgrimages to burn copal and offer prayers for the time when the head and body will be reunited. It will mark the destruction of this world and the beginning of a new era, with the rebirth of the old gods and a final flowering of the ancient Maya culture.

The Lacandones also make pilgrimages to Palenque and Bonampak, not far away. Palenque is easily accessible. With its majestic Palacio, its small and exquisite temples, and its pyramidal Temple of Inscriptions containing its underground tomb, it is the finest and best preserved of all the Classic Mayan ruins. Bonampak, hidden in the jungle, was not discovered until 1946 and was still accessible only by chartered plane when I was there. Credit for its discovery is given to Giles Healey, a United Fruit Company scout; but he was led to Bonampak by a Lacandon who promised to show him a sacred Lacandon shrine in the ruins. News of Bonampak's existence spread rapidly.

When I saw it, it was deserted save for a caretaker. The two main structures lay on a hill overlooking a great plaza in which stood a large stela carved in bas-relief. The temple on the right comprised three rooms, all of their walls covered with the now famous fresco paintings. The roof was covered by rusty tin sheeting to protect the murals from drippings of limestone or calcium. The scenes depict preparations for a battle, torture of prisoners, and the dance of victory. Warriors are wearing jaguar skins and towering headdresses of quetzal feathers; ladies in white robes are drawing blood from their tongues; an orchestra is performing with long trumpets, drums, and rattles; a severed head lies below. The temple has been reconstructed and the gorgeously colored paintings faithfully copied in the great national museum in Mexico City.

Yet of these three Usumacinta ruins—Palenque, Yaxchilan, and Bonampak—it was Yaxchilan that struck deepest into my heart. The crumbling ruins of a holy city, a tarnished jewel of classic Maya civilization, a place of brooding mystery.

A few days later we left the jungle clearing at Yaxchilan shortly after midnight for the return trip upriver to Agua Azul. The early start was necessary, for our dugout canoe would be bucking the current, requiring much longer for the trip. From the moment we started, we could feel the strong undercurrent below and the spray in our faces. And now began for me a passage that seemed at once vivid and unreal, timeless as a dream.

The trip down in daylight had revealed at every turn the lofty walls of the rainforest on each side, the dense undergrowth and the profusion of brilliant flowers, glimpses of long-tailed parrots, a small spotted deer. How alive was all this lush splendor! Now in the dark we could see nothing but the pale glint of the river under a quarter-moon that hung suspended over the high, dark walls on each side. How silent it was! An all-pervading silence seemed to muffle the put-put of the outboard motor behind us. Silent, we sat immobile, engulfed in unbroken stillness and darkness. There was no sensation of movement. The river kept unwinding before us as if we ourselves were becalmed. Nor did we move through time. Midnight gave way to dawn like an image on a screen. And now in faint light the silvery-gray curtain of mist shrouded the forest. With sunrise there appeared the tall, bare trunks of the ceibas, the shapes of the great mahogany trees. The colors of flowers screamed forth. Two parrots flew overhead; a jaguar raised its head from the riverbank. It was as if we were witnessing the creation of an original and resplendent new world.

"Pee stop!" yelled Trudi suddenly.

Obediently the Mexican boatman steered the dugout to beach on a gravelly island in the river. We all got out to relieve ourselves and to stretch our cramped legs. It was then I noticed a flower growing on a sandy spit farther out in the river. A single, tall-stemmed, exquisite, lily-like tropical flower whose name I didn't know. Nor did it matter. For something about it struck deeply into my heart. In a few weeks the rainy season would begin. The Usumacinta would swell into a raging torrent that would submerge the sandy spit and the life of this fragile and isolate flower. Perhaps no other human beings had seen or would ever see it again, but its impending fate was of no importance. Proclaiming the fullness of its present moment, it stood there proudly affirming the transcendent life and beauty given it without the need of any human admiration. Like lovely Yaxchilan, it would stand for its own hour before being erased by the wind and the rain of world time. And that, I suddenly realized, was enough to justify the brief life of this fragile blossom, and of Yaxchilan.

So somehow this single flower on a sandy spit in the great Usumacinta epitomized for me the essential meanings of the whole Maya civilization and the organic lifetime of our own technological Western civilization. Each undergoes its own cycle of growth, death, and transformative rebirth. Only our recognition of this universal pattern makes it easier to accept the completeness of our own life cycles.

2

Blame It on the Blossoms

(Editorial—May 11, 1950)

As often happens to the best of mice and men, our mind is not on our business today.

We feel immune to the worthy innovations that are making Taos a more comfortable place to live in. We have no invectives to hurl at Labor, Big Business, or even the Chamber of Commerce. Nothing in the horrible state of world affairs could induce us to preach a tidy little sermon on the injustices of mankind to man.

In our distorted frame of mind, the world looks like the best possible abode for mortal man. Still we know that there comes a time in the Fat Forties when a man must resist the blandishments of nature, and look only at the facts of life seen through the myopic gaze of middle age. Not at the thickets of wild plum blossoms heaped like snowdrifts in the sagebrush . . . crossing the pastures like a file of white-blanketed Indians.

That is probably what threw us off balance this morning. The deplorable necessity of having to walk to work through a country pasture instead of taking a city subway. And being inflicted with the unavoidable sight of that beach of white blossoms flanking the blue pine mountains all the way to the Pueblo.

It could be a touch of May fever. It could be us. But the safest bet is to blame it on those blossoms.

3

Visions of the Good
What Literature Affirms and How

(Excerpted from a speech presented on July 16, 1986, at a writers' conference sponsored by Winona State University, Winona, Minnesota)

ON the assumption that literature affirms something good, we must first ask ourselves what we mean by "LITERATURE" and "GOOD."

Literature, as I see it, comprises narratives in prose, poetic, or dramatic form—not political, social, scientific, and other expositions. It tells a story. The primary or sole purpose of most popular novels and short fiction, and verbal and visual presentations by radio and TV, is to entertain. As someone has said, "We may be the only nation in history to die of giggling."

To be sure, we're also generously treated between commercials to stories showing the horrors of torture and murder. But we don't relate them to reality; the hero usually escapes. These too are merely entertainment.

Literature—which can be spelled with a capital "L" to differentiate it from this lower form of fiction—is something else. I consider it to be that form of narration whose meaning is timeless and universal, and which endures through changing periods of mood and style.

"GOOD" and "BAD." What do we mean by them? They seem to be ever present and relative. What is good for me may be bad for you. It was once considered that a Mohammedan couldn't go to heaven until he had killed a Christian, and that it was a sin for a Christian to murder his neighbor even though the neighbor's cows had broken through the fence into his own cabbage patch. This rule for individuals hasn't held for us collectively. We all—peoples of all races and nations—have been murdering each other by the millions, from the Crusades to the gas chambers of the Holocaust, through two world wars and Viet Nam, to the present worldwide terrorist bombings.

Clearly, universal "GOOD" is not synonymous with ever-changing regional morality.

It was defined by R. A. Schwaller de Lubicz, whose fifteen-year, three-volume study of the ancient Egyptian Temple of Luxor revealed it to be an image of the universe and an architectural figuration of man, showing their harmonic relationship. He believed that the one true measure of a civilization was not the luxuries of a high standard of living it created, but its development of a higher level of consciousness.

The perceptive French biologist Pierre Lecompte du Nouy affirmed that mankind today is not the finished product of evolution, as now generally believed. We are still in the process of "becoming," halfway between our bestial past and divine future. Our evolution so far has taken place unconsciously on the physical plane, he asserted; from now on it must be consciously achieved.

More and more scientific, philosophical, and metaphysical thinkers like Georges Ivanovitch Gurdjieff, Rodney Collin, and Teilhard de Chardin are concluding that the destiny of every live thing within the universe—cells, man, earth, planets, and galaxies—is to become more conscious.

Hence I understand "GOOD" as something that reveals the purpose of our existence, gives us a vision of our potential creativity, and helps to raise our level of consciousness.

If science treats of what *is,* literature is a repository of the past, what Pound called "a lost kind of experience." It reminds us that we are living today without something we once had, and which has been replaced by modern society's belief that the present mundane reality embraces all things possible. Literature is also concerned with what will be in the continuing process of becoming. This glimpse, as it were, of something beyond our temporal existence is the "Vision of the Good" I perceive in that body of literature which affirms or suggests that the world and man, matter, and spirit are one; and that some strange power helps us to direct the course of our lives.

The mythic stories of all races reflect this vision. Those of Egypt, Sumeria, Greece. Of King Arthur and the Knights of the Round Table, and their Quest for the Holy Grail. Grimm's fairy tales, Shakespeare's plays and poetry. Other classic narratives familiar to me are those of the Mayas and Aztecs in the New World. These I will discuss later. Not familiar enough generally are Evangeline Walton's contemporary four novels based on the ancient Welsh *Mabinogion.* They not only recount Druidic magic and wisdom used in the struggle between the supernatural forces of good and evil, but predict a future we see unfolding today.

My favorite reading lately is the series of novels by Arthur W. Upfield featuring Napoleon Bonaparte, a half-caste Aboriginal detective in the outback of Australia. The novels were first published in Australia about fifty years ago. What wonderful stories they tell of the Aboriginals' customs, rituals, and mysterious "dream time." Little wonder these books recently began to be reissued in Great Britain and are now becoming available in the United States.

Their authenticity was confirmed by an Aboriginal who visited us in Taos last summer—Guboo Ted Thomas of the Yuin Tribe, New South Wales. He was well-dressed, educated, and spoke the King's English better than I. The purpose of his trip to America was to enlist support for his people's efforts to halt the destruction of their tribal shrines and sacred landmarks by exploitation of uranium deposits. How familiar this sounded! It is the same problem our Navajos and Hopis face today. Reverence for the land is the same for these peoples continents apart. The land is their culture, their religion, their spirit. It seems to me they all are living the same enduring myth, interconnected on the subterranean level Jung called the collective unconscious.

Among other novels that come most readily to mind are D. H. Lawrence's *The Plumed Serpent,* which fictionally resurrects in Mexico the ancient Aztec religion of Quetzalcoatl, and Carlos Castaneda's first four novels featuring the Yaqui sorcerer Don Juan. There is no such Yaqui as Don Juan. Yet the imaginary Other World he moves in and out of has struck an immediate response from millions of readers. Dostoevski indulges in no such fantasies. But in psychologically and spiritually plumbing the dark depths of his characters, he reveals the light at the end of our human tunnel. In reading Faulkner's long and involved sentences recounting a starkly realistic tale, how often do we seem to feel we have stepped on a high voltage wire. A brilliant flash reveals at once the heaven and hell beyond the tawdry lives of the story's characters, as well as our own; and we realize the compassionate depth of the writer's insights.

Of course there is Herman Melville's *Moby Dick.* The Great White

Whale was more than a whale, as mad Ahab knew. But just what it was, he didn't know. Nor do we know the full meaning of its disturbing symbolism now after a century of psychological probing. The novel, I'm told, sold only one hundred copies during Melville's lifetime and he lived forty years after its publication. There may be an excuse for this neglect. The book, in one minor aspect, was for many people a rather dull exposition of all phases of the whaling industry. Nevertheless, *Moby Dick* is America's greatest novel.

I could continue mentioning other such books which possess the common quality of awakening in us a sense of something transcendental somewhere "out there" beyond us or "in here" within us. It is this virtue which keeps them alive despite their minor faults.

The majority of current novels, it seems to me, are well written, carefully crafted, and sharply observant of our secular life—especially in Manhattan. But they are photographic, pedestrian. They are horizontal novels, without a vertical dimension. Many become best sellers, often Pulitzer Prize winners. But next year they go out of print and are forgotten. For they lack that element which reminds us we are greater than we are.

I would like now to ease into a brief consideration of this element that plays such a significant part in the better forms of literature and in all our lives: the nebulous influence of fate, destiny, nemesis, karma, or whatever we call it.

A curious obsession with this subject distinguishes the work of the noted writer Isak Dinesen. Not only her beloved classics *Out of Africa* and *Seven Gothic Tales,* but all her books seem bathed in the strange dreamlike light of myth. Judith Thurman in her comprehensive and intimate biography of the "Storyteller," as Isak Dinesen called herself, explores this obsession fully. Thurman quotes Thomas Mann as stating that myths provide an answer to "the mystery of the unity of the ego and the world." She adds that this is the same belief incorporated in all the tales of Isak Dinesen. In one of her *Last Tales,* Dinesen herself wrote, "For within the whole universe the story only has the authority to answer that one cry of the heart . . . '*Who am I?*"

She believed in a "divine intention to life," that one was formed by life to pay the price of one's existence in pain, loss, and death. Hence throughout all her writings runs the thread of destiny and nemesis, which she insisted one should courageously embrace. She wrote,

"Nemesis is that thread in the course of events which is determined by the psychic assumption of a person. . . . All of my tales treat Nemisis." And again we read, "One of the forms of perfect joy in life is to be convinced one is fulfilling one's destiny."

Isak Dinesen, as you know, was the pseudonym of Baroness Karen Blixen. Judith Thurman's intimate biography reveals that Dinesen's own life didn't always jibe with her tales. She married a Swedish cousin, Baron Bror von Blixen-Finecke, only to obtain the title of Baroness; and she jealously hung on to it even after their divorce and his remarriage. Imperiously egotistical, she demanded full attention and unreserved loyalty from all her associates. Suffering an incurable illness, she ate little and took pride in being the thinnest person on the world stage. And she died, a famous and rich woman, of malnutrition. What a trying woman she must have been!

The quirks in her persona don't matter. Her magnificent writing does. The literature she achieved seems to me the most deeply concerned with that mysterious influence in our lives.

What is it really—fate, destiny, nemesis, karma, whatever we call it? It is personalized in the witches of *Macbeth,* the three Fates of Greek mythology, in many guises in all fairy tales, objectified in Melville's *Moby Dick,* and impersonalized in the East's concept of karma—that every intent and action causes eventually a compensating effect. In all the literature I've been discussing, this strange influence plays a role in some way.

A search for its meaning leads us into astrology. The origins of astrology lie too far back in prehistory to be found. For long it was believed that the stars were gods, and hence controlled our destiny. This belief is still perpetuated by the spurious "fortune-telling" horoscopes carried in our Sunday newspapers. Modern astrology has outgrown this. It is becoming recognized as a valid form of scientific inquiry into the correspondence between the solar system and the human psyche.

The little I know about it has been gained from the books of my wife Barbara, herself interested in astrology. All astrologers agree that a birth horoscope is at once a "map of the solar system and a map of an individual's psyche at the moment he is born, indicating the nature of his future problems, talents, and mental tendencies." Hence we ourselves, not the stars, are responsible for directing the course of our lives. Stephen Arroyo in his *Astrology, Karma and Transformation* asserts that astrology could well be called a "science of karma," for it enables us to chart our development within our own inherent limits.

The most illuminating books on this theme I've read are those of Liz Greene, a Jungian analyst and a professional astrologer. She also views the solar system as "a symbol of a living energy pattern reflecting at any moment the smaller forms of life within it." And she believes that "the human psyche is also an energy pattern of psychic components which make up the individual." The same forces are manifested simultaneously in both, reflecting their interconnectedness.

The Astrology of Fate voices Ms. Greene's belief that fate, destiny, nemesis, and karma are entwined, acting to balance any overstepping of the boundaries of our natural development, and to restore equilibrium. This law of universal moral order, which guides our continual "becoming" as du Nouy put it and our development of a higher level of consciousness as Schwaller de Lubicz stated, seems to confirm our common impulse toward growth and our attraction to the mysterious, that suggestive element found in the literature I've been discussing.

It's not strange that modern psychology, our newest science, is finding an affinity with the world's oldest: astrology. C. G. Jung, who founded the school of analytical psychology, used astrology and considered the inner self to be an archetype of universal order. His daughter Gret Baumann is also a practicing Jungian analyst in Zurich, Switzerland. When she visited me in Taos several years ago, she told me she based her analyses on the horoscopes of her clients.

Both of these disciplines are concerned with aiding the individual to develop his or her potential creativity; and they are being used by current novelists in their development of characters. They also had a much wider application in the writings of the past, as we shall see.

Literature, mythos, a story. The "GOOD" it affirms is the essence of the oldest and greatest story of all, the story of the creation of our planet and humankind. There are many different versions among all races throughout the world. So devoutly are they believed, they constitute separate, conflicting religions. Let me briefly review one of them, the four-world concept of pre-Columbian America, which is recorded in the oldest written narrative in America: the *Popul Vuh,* the sacred book of the ancient Quiché Mayas in Guatemala. Corresponding narratives written by the Nahuas in Mexico are found in the *Códice Chimalpopoca,* which includes the *Anales de Cuauhtitlan* and the *Leyenda de los Soles.* These are probably unfamiliar to you, but I have no hesitancy in recommending them as great pieces of literature. They relate that there existed four worlds before the present fifth world. Each was destroyed by a catastrophe: the first, according to the Aztecs, by jaguars representing earth; the second by air or winds; the third by fire; and the fourth by water, a great flood.

This creation myth was common throughout all Mesoamerica from Central America to our own Southwest. Here our contemporary Indian tribes still preserve it. The Hopis, among whom I lived for three years, maintain the oldest continuously inhabited settlement in the United States. They observe the four-world myth literally in the rituals, dances, and songs of their dramatic ceremonials. The Zunis regard the four previous worlds as underworlds embodied within the mother of all creation, from whose womb they have been successively reborn. The Navajos, the largest Indian tribe, also recount their emergences from four worlds in a narrative poetic to the highest standard. So you see this creation myth is not merely an anthropological item, but a living pattern.

The most complete development of the myth was made by the Mayas. Perhaps no other people on earth have been so obsessed with the mystery of time. And because the four worlds were created in succession, the factor of time was paramount in determining their dates and durations. Hence about the third century A.D. they developed with a phenomenal knowledge of astronomy, astrology, and mathematics a calendar system more accurate than ours today. It comprised three separate but meshing calendars: a 365-day Solar Calendar, a 260-day Sacred Calendar, and a Venus Calendar based on the 584-day synodic cycle of the planet Venus.

So precise were their calculations that they projected the dates of the creation and destruction of all five worlds. Conceiving time as cyclical, not linear as do we, they plumbed deeper into the past, recording dates four hundred million years ago, and others far into the future. A great wheel with wheels within wheels marking the periods of existence of everything in the universe.

Mayan cosmography and cosmology presents a fourfold mandala form, which as you know is a symbol of psychic wholeness. So certainly it carries a psychological image of the Mayan mind itself. Jung, whom I mentioned affirmed the validity of astrology, wrote in the first volume of his *Collected Works:* "Careful investigation of the unconscious shows that there is a peculiar coincidence with time, which is also the reason why the ancients were able to project the succession of unconsciously perceived inner contents into the determinants of time."

The ancient Mayan concept, of course, coincides with the belief of modern astrology and psychology in the interconnectedness of the solar system and the human psyche. But their projections of all planetary cycles ultimately realigning introduces an idea new to most of us: that the planets, as well as humankind, have yet to achieve full creativity synchronized in the awesome cosmic order.

The Mayas' spiritual insights, even their mode of thought, is lost to the modern world. Yet what little we know of the metaphysical aspect of their vanished civilization is enough to make us wonder if they had attained a higher level of consciousness than our own. I must add that I don't take literally the existence of four previous worlds, however. Rather they seem to me dramatic allegories for the successive stages of mankind's evolutionary development.

This Mayan story seems to pull together the various ideas I've touched upon. It illustrates the "lost kind of experience" described by Pound—that we are living today without something we once had, which has been replaced by our present society's belief that our reality embraces all things possible. It confirms our growing belief that we are still psychically growing. And it provides a firm basis for the concepts of such recent philosophers as Gurdjieff, Collin, and de Chardin that mankind, our global earth, and neighboring planets are all in the process of developing one unified cosmic consciousness. This is an ultimately expanded "Vision of the Good" for every living being.

A dim intuition, an ineffable feeling, an innate awareness of the purpose of the law guiding our existence, which we call fate or destiny, lies in each of us. The higher forms of literature awaken our conscious recognition of it.

I often feel that our materialistic pattern of existence today will be viewed in a distant future as a myth comparable to others in our dark past. But how privileged we are to be living in this exciting hour of the greatest change since the beginning of the Christian era. Experiencing the ending of our present zodiacal age and precessional cycle, and the birth of a new era already beginning to change our way of thinking. More and more, I believe, our Literature will reflect our expanding awareness.

4

The Immortal Drama

(Editorial—April 6, 1950)

O N Easter morning mankind observes the climax of its greatest drama, its most profound Mystery Play, and its most sacred religious ceremonial, the immortal Passion of Our Lord.

The story of the Only Begotten Son returning to His Father through the ordeals of Gethsemane and Calvary is as old as mankind. From our first perception of the annual death and rebirth of nature, the miracle has been expressed in the idioms of all races and creeds.

Long before the advent of Christianity, the worship of the Mother and her dying and rising Son was paralleled by Egypt's Attis-Osiris and the Phrygians' Cybele-Isis. In our own Navajo ceremonialism it is still found in Changing Woman and Monster Slayer.

Another world-religion is built entirely on this motif, on the teaching of Gautama the Buddha that each man may transcend the limits of normal consciousness and attain at-one-ment with the divine.

Even modern psychology reads in the Passion the allegorical necessity for individual consciousness to return and reconcile itself with the unconscious, if man is to attain that psychic wholeness necessary for his further evolutionary development.

Viewed universally in order to be comprehended fully, it is the timeless parable of man's efforts to bring the human body, mind, and heart into cosmic harmony.

None of these interpretations detracts from the faith of the millions who for nearly two thousand years have believed in its literal meaning. For Jesus' Transfiguration, Crucifixion, and Resurrection remain the most human and universal statement of this immemorial, archetypal theme. Through it, more than any other, we have been enabled to glimpse that pattern of psychic achievement embodying the penultimate teachings of Christ and the eventual goal of all mankind.

5

Notes on Los Angeles

(Essay)

In the fall of 1924 I drove out to Los Angeles from the Salt Creek, Wyoming, oil fields with an elderly man who was retiring to live with his daughter in San Diego. Mr. Garth was an old-time Westerner who had been a trapper, horse wrangler, and cowhand, and a guide for one of President Theodore Roosevelt's western jaunts. With the money he had saved, he had bought a little Star roadster for the trip but had difficulty driving it. Hence he persuaded me to accompany him, assuring me I'd find life easy at that end of the rainbow.

"You won't have to buy an overcoat, the weather is so warm. And if you get hungry, all you have to do is pick an orange off the trees along every street."

Our trip through New Mexico was delightful. Highway 66 was an unmarked and unfenced dirt road over which we traveled at some thirty miles an hour. Every evening we turned off to camp in the sage. Mr. Garth, a dead shot with his .22 rifle, was always able to supply a rabbit for the pot. Occasionally another car would come along, and seeing our campfire its occupants would turn off to join us.

Midway through Arizona we faced a prospect neither of us had anticipated. Mr. Garth had assumed I was flush with money from my wages as a roustabout in the oil fields, and I had anticipated he would pay all expenses of the trip in return for my driving the car. Now we discovered that we were running short of money. There was just enough to get us to Los Angeles if we limited ourselves to coffee and doughnuts and cheese sandwiches. Quarreling and grumbling, we drove on.

Then one sunset, from the old mining camp of Oatman on the

desert mountains overlooking the Colorado River, I saw for the first time the Promised Land. Below us unwound the muddy brown river, now reddened by the sinking sun, that I had known as the "Silvery Colorado" in the high Rockies. Across from it stretched away the Mojave Desert, an immense and forbidding expanse of sand, cactus, and parched rock outcrops so unimaginable to the mountain-born. California!

At early dawn we reached Barstow. And there, looming on the horizon like a cardboard cutout, stood the first palm tree I ever saw. Its effect upon me I can't describe. I simply felt that at last I had been transported to a new strange land that held all the promises of the far-off and unreal.

We finally reached Los Angeles. Mr. Garth had not been in the city for many years, and drove into what he remembered as its center—the old Plaza at the north end of Main Street. It was bounded by the historic Mission Church; the Pico House built by the last Mexican governor of California; a trash-filled alley that was later cleaned up and converted to delightful Olivera Street, which housed Mexican cantinas, cafes, and curio shops; and the entrance to Ferguson Alley leading into the maze of Chinatown. The whole area appeared to me curiously decrepit and outmoded, and populated only by Mexicans and Chinese. There were no orange trees bordering the dirty streets.

Nevertheless, I rented a squalid room for four dollars a week in a two-story hotel jutting out on the northwest corner of the plaza. Mr. Garth and I divided our last few dollars, his share being just enough to take him to San Diego. When he left, I confronted the nebulous future.

Hunting a job, I wandered up Main Street—a Skid Row of bars and greasy lunchrooms; flophouses; a boxing arena where every Saturday night Mexicans were matched against Chinese, Negroes against Whites; strip shows like the Burbank Baby Dolls; and a Salvation Army hall. Eventually I reached Sixth Street and turned west. Here I found the new center of a modern city, Pershing Square. It was flanked by the resplendent Biltmore Hotel, the Opera House, tidy shops and restaurants. Well-dressed people thronged the streets and crowded the center of the square to listen to the impassioned oratory of any speaker.

In the evening I retreated down Main Street to my hotel. The rooms were on the second floor. There was no lobby, and for a hotel desk there was a table in the hall. Upon it lay a begrimed ledger in which guests were required to register. This ledger was interesting; it contained so many foreign names: Spanish, Italian, and Chinese. One of them attested to the hotel's dubious respectability: *"Sr. Sin Nombre,"* Mr. Nameless. I then went to Chinatown for my one meal of the day, usually the cheapest bowl of chop suey. After striking up a friendship with a young Chinese named Chang, my meals took on new dimensions. He took me to the cafe of his uncle, who always served us bountifully with chicken, shrimp, pork, and rice. Chinese New Year was celebrated with the dance of a great papier-maché dragon, accompanied by fireworks, and followed by feasts in the Tong houses. As a guest of Chang and his uncle, I made several new friends.

Finally I landed a job as an engineer with the telephone company. On my first payday I went to Santa Monica and for the first time saw the Pacific Ocean. It looked quite unimpressive as I stood on the beach. Yet I felt that at long last I had reached, as had all America, the end of its westward march of empire across the continent.

Los Angeles then, in the Twenties, was indeed the ultimate West, the last frontier. It offered all the rewards of a Promised Land to a generation or more of hardy and foolhardy emigrants from east of the Missouri. What a beautiful and bountiful land spread out in all directions in the clear air. One could see the snow-capped mountains rising beyond the vast flowering orange groves and walnut orchards which stretched eastward to Riverside and San Bernardino. To the southeast lay the Colorado Desert blooming in the spring with a mass of desert flowers, and extending to the oasis of Palm Springs. A few miles west lay the Pacific beaches of Malibu, Redondo Beach, and Long Beach; and one could cross the channel in an hour to Catalina Island for a glass-bottom boat ride. Desert, sea, and mountains, all within a few hours' drive.

Los Angeles itself offered many other Sunday attractions. The Ostrich Farm and Gay's Lion Farm, and the rather naively dramatic presentation of California's history at the Mission Play in San Gabriel. But I found it a more exciting workaday town, with its many different aspects.

For a short time I lived in another hotel on Bunker Hill, reached from Spring Street by a dinky tram car called Angel's Flight. Bunker Hill was far from being a resort for angels. Its great old brick houses and aristocratic wooden mansions had been taken over by prostitutes. The houses were sedate, quiet, and well managed. For the girls largely thrived on the patronage of generous truck drivers and well-heeled, discreet businessmen.

Another place where I lived was a rented room in a family house far out on Pico Street. The landlord's son was a dentistry student who set up his chair in the adjoining room. As it had no electric plug, he ran the cord into my room. So every weekend when he practiced on friends and other students, I endured their agonies through my open door.

For a year I was sent down to the Mexican border to work. When I came back, I moved into a room in a great old manor house with the imposing address of Victoria Park Place, which lay between Pico and Sixteenth Street. This block-square compound was typical of many such squares in west Los Angeles. It was set within the surrounding busy streets, with only one entrance, to isolate it from through traffic. The square was quiet and peaceful, beautifully landscaped with great palms and spacious lawns. The house in which I lived had been converted into a rooming and boarding house by a nervous little Czechoslovakian man named Milo Sedlacek, a former stand-in for a movie star, and his big-boned, heavy American wife. A judge of the District Court occupied the master bedroom on the second floor, and a chorus girl the adjoining room. My own room was on the third floor. Every morning Milo brought up our breakfast trays—a bowl of cereal, orange juice, and coffee. Unfortunately, he could never be persuaded to supply anything but canned milk with the cereal.

The location, however, was advantageous. The Pico Street Yellow Car line, at five cents per passenger, was only three blocks away. But the Red Car line stop was almost at hand, and on it I could whiz downtown for only ten cents. The Yellow Car streetcar system threaded only Los Angeles, while the Red Car Pacific Electric system operated fast trains of several cars that spanned the beach towns of Los Angeles, and on east to Riverside and San Bernardino. It was a marvelous rapid transit system that should have been preserved to alleviate the present congested traffic problem. Unfortunately, the obvious greed of oil companies eager to sell gasoline, combined with short-sighted City Fathers, decreed that the system be replaced by buses.

A few years later I moved to a house in Hollywood I fondly remember. It lay just a block north on Highland, a bit west on Franklin, and up a steep hill—directly across an arroyo from the Japanese Gardens on the opposite hillside, and the roof garden of the Roosevelt

Hotel on Hollywood Boulevard below. It was a little house of redwood planking with a red brick fireplace and an open porch overlooking the arroyo. It had been built piecemeal by a fine carpenter hired by my landlady and her spinster daughter next door.

Here I spent my most pleasant years in Hollywood. The Hollywood Bowl lay just across the hill. There was no need to buy the concert season ticket, which was delivered to every resident in the region. My invited friends and I had only to walk over the hill, spread our blankets in back of the tiers of seats, and enjoy the concerts.

Riding to work in downtown Los Angeles was a daily pleasure. I would walk down Highland to catch a bus on Sunset Boulevard. The bus was a two-decker, and from the top deck I could watch the city spreading out before me. On the way we passed one of the most pleasant and fashionable neighborhoods, Eastlake Park. The lake itself had not yet been cut in two by an overpass, and the district contained some of the best shops in town. The now famous Zona Rosa exclusive shopping area in Mexico City recalls it to my mind.

The Twenties and Thirties, of course, embraced the great era of Hollywood movies. Its ornate picture palaces, like Grauman's Chinese Theater on Hollywood Boulevard, presented premiers of movies featuring Greta Garbo, Gloria Swanson, Mary Pickford, Douglas Fairbanks, and other stars of the period as world-shaking events. In the morning the stars imprinted their footprints in fresh cement blocks in the forecourt. Then in the evening brilliant klieg lights illumined the entrance of the theater as stars, directors, producers, and other notables, attired in formal dress, furs, and jewels, descended from their limousines and walked inside before the multitude of spectators standing on the street outside.

Hollywood Boulevard was a constant show. From Vine Street to Highland it was the "Street of Heartbreaks," paraded each evening by hundreds of young hopefuls who had come to Hollywood with dreams of being discovered—in Schwab's Drug Store perhaps—by a prospective talent scout. Their incentive was another parade, the annual Christmas Parade of countless floats, each bearing a popular movie star. It must be recorded here that the parade began earlier each year until soon it began the day after Thanksgiving. The greatest throngs on the Boulevard I ever saw occurred the night when Prohibition was repealed, in 1933. One massive crowd of laughing, shouting people filled the sidewalks and street.

These were the years of the Great Depression when prices, in retrospect, were ridiculously low. In the large Pig 'n Whistle restaurant, next to the Egyptian Theater on Hollywood Boulevard, you could get a good dinner by ordering the sixty-five-cent Blue Plate Special. In a little cafe around the corner on Highland, down-and-outers could buy a meal for thirty-five cents. A mug of coffee and two doughnuts could be had almost any place for ten cents. In contrast, of course, were expensive places like the Brown Derby frequented by movie and sports notables who came more to be seen than to drink and dine. Musso-Franks on Hollywood Boulevard I considered the best restaurant in Hollywood. Not at all showy, it was justly famous for its fine food rather than for its atmosphere and clientele. Today, so many years later when the Boulevard and all Hollywood have sadly lost their glamour and deteriorated, it still upholds its long reputation.

Fifth Street east of Main Street I came to know through my Uncle Fred. It marked the Japanese section of the city, whose outstanding feature was the huge block-square fruit and vegetable wholesale market. Here at dawn great trucks from Imperial Valley, Riverside, and San Fernando Valley would unload their fresh produce to be bid and bought by wholesale dealers and distributed to retail markets throughout the city before they opened for business. The dealers were predominantly Japanese, excellent judges of produce and shrewd businessmen. Fred, out of work during the Depression, had taken up peddling lottery tickets, horse racing tickets, Japanese lottery tickets, chances of every kind. He was phenomenally successful, being friendly, nonobtrusive, and full of jokes. The Japanese dealers liked and trusted him, and were always ready to take a chance on anything he offered. At the end of their morning's work, they would peel off a roll of bills and buy an entire book of tickets.

One evening they invited us to a ceremonial dinner in one of their lodge rooms. What a wonderful evening it was. Hot *sake* wine, Japanese dishes of every kind, and *geisha* girls for entertainment. A few weeks later I was taken to watch some Japanese judo matches. Every wrestler in turn would approach the Black Belt master, bow deeply, and request the privilege of a fall with him. The master, with miraculous dexterity, would throw him immediately. Then he would summon his opponent and repeat his performance in slow motion. I was surprised to see only one other wrestler who had achieved the distinction of wearing the coveted black belt. He was a white American, a member of the Los Angeles Police Department.

I became acquainted, too, with a lovely Japanese couple who

owned a small fruit and vegetable stand. Uncle Fred and my aunt, and my sister and brother-in-law, always bought their produce from them; it was fresh and artistically displayed. I was away when the United States entered World War II, but my sister wrote me what happened to the couple. With all the Japanese in Los Angeles, they were evicted from their homes, their buildings were confiscated, and they were sent to a concentration camp in Arizona. My sister visited the couple while they were under guard awaiting transportation, and received a letter from them later. They were second-generation Japanese born in Los Angeles, American citizens, and owned their tiny home. It was never restored to them. That they were deprived of their property, livelihood, freedom, and citizenship without warning and redress needs no further comment here.

The south part of town was the Negro section. Down here in a corner beer parlor I met the great Negro composer W. C. Handy, the first to set down the famous blues. He invited me to his room upstairs where we could talk and finish our beers. Watts has since gained disgraceful notoriety for the conditions under which the Negroes were forced to live. Luckily the famous Watts Tower, a unique feat of imagination and construction, escaped condemnation and destruction by warped and vindictive city authorities, largely through the efforts of a dear friend of mine.

Mrs. Kate Steinitz was one of the most remarkable women I've even known. Born in Germany, she had studied art and traveled throughout Europe. Coming to America after her husband died, she met Dr. Elmer Belt, who had developed a passion for the art of Leonardo da Vinci while a medical student. With his later lucrative practice he established a small hospital near Eastlake Park, and began collecting everything about da Vinci he could find. To develop this Elmer Belt Library of Vizcaino, he engaged Mrs. Steinitz, sending her every two years on a tour of Europe with an open purse to buy da Vinci memorabilia—drawings, notes, sketches, letters, everything available. It was a wonderful collection, undoubtedly the most comprehensive in the world.

Dr. Belt was a distinguished man of middle age, with the sparkling eyes of a youth. Interested in everything, he had invited me to give a talk on Indians in the Library. Here I met Mrs. Steinitz. She was then about eighty years old, small and careworn, but with the same irrepressible enthusiasm. Soon after that she telephoned me about the impending destruction of Watts Tower. Worried and indignant, she took me to see the tower and persuaded me to write to the members of the group she was organizing to preserve it. Her efforts were successful. Watts Tower stands today as a scrap iron monument to a lone, unlettered Italian workman thinking of another fabled tower in the Pisa of his homeland—a work of art preserved appropriately by the initiative of the world's authority on the life and work of another, more famous Italian artist.

Mrs. Steinitz I saw often during this fracas. One evening she invited me to dinner in her home. The little house lay in an undistinguished neighborhood, and its furnishings were simple and careworn as she. I forthrightly asked her why she had nothing of Leonardo's in the house. "But I live always in his beauty," she answered. Several years later she visited me in Taos; and knowing how I loved horses, she brought me a gorgeous portfolio of reproductions of all the drawings and sketches Leonardo had made of horses. Inside it she had written a note: "Why is it that there are more horses' behinds than there are horses?"

Enough of these random notes about the Los Angeles I knew in the late Twenties and early Thirties!

It was not a city with a flavor and integrated life of its own like New York, New Orleans, or San Francisco. Merely a hodgepodge of disparate barrios, neighborhoods, and small villages haphazardly spread out over Hell's Half-Acre with no common center or community interest. As such it showed the phenomenal growth it had been undergoing since the first white Americans had begun to pour into this end of all westward trails. A Promised Land, indeed, surrounded by desert, sea, and mountains, imbued with gracious climate, beauty, and inexhaustible treasures for the taking.

The immigrants here were as quick to take advantage of it as they had been everywhere else during their march of empire across the continent. Enterprising and unscrupulous, they began the process of unrestrained commercialization and industrialization that destroyed the very living values that had attracted them.

The changes in Los Angeles since I knew it are almost unbelievable. The orange groves and walnut orchards that extended east to Riverside have been cut down to make room for subdivisions. Bunker Hill and the area around it have been bulldozed for a new City Hall and Civic Center, which is not a civic center. All downtown looks like a deserted ghost town. A modern railway station replaces Chinatown, but few people now ride trains. The Yellow streetcar system is gone, and the great Red Car system now needed so badly for rapid mass transit. The modern freeway network is already incapable of handling the increasing traffic. Hollywood has deteriorated into an outmoded neighborhood. Beverly Hills is now the flourishing business and residential district. Los Angeles has spread out in all directions, solidly filling San Fernando Valley to the north and growing south to San Juan Capistrano. The beaches are polluted. And over all—city, sea, desert, and mountains—lies a thick pall of injurious smog. It is still not a city, though it is still expanding. A fantastic metropolis growing into what may be one of the greatest megalopolises in the world.

The invisible thrust and pull of its phenomenal growth and change permeate the choking air. Certainly it has drawn a multitude of renowned leaders in all fields of culture, art, and religion. And with these the most mixed bag of occultists, psychic mediums, founders of spiritual cults, and popular mystics, along with a new generation of pot-smoking hippies, to be found anywhere.

Anaïs Nin, for one, has written that she has found Los Angeles to be the most stimulating city of new ideas and talented people outside of her native Paris.

Could it be that these new entrepreneurs, experimentalists, and spearheads of the counterculture are confirming it as America's last frontier? If so, we have yet to learn what new and ultimate pattern they will establish.

6

Official Announcement

(Editorial—September 20, 1951)

THIS morning at six o'clock we noticed on the high saddle of the mountain ridge above us, a yellow blur in the spruce-green.

This is worth noting. Here on the slopes of the high Sangre de Cristos the nights have been nippy enough for blankets. There has been frost on the squash vines; the chicken water has been covered with paper ice. But Mother Nature's official announcement of fall is made through the first aspens to turn color.

Now begin the days that every Taoseño loves best. When both the aspens and the cottonwoods glow butter-yellow, the piñon smoke rises fragrant and straight into the chill calm air, and the Indian drums at the Pueblo sound across the pastures the news that the harvest is in and that San Geronimo and fall are here again.

7

The One Great Book of Life

(Speech presented at Henderson District Public Library, Clark County Community College, Nevada, on November 23, 1985)

I T is a pleasure to return to this region. I have known it for many years: before Boulder Dam was built, during the first series of atomic tests, and through frequent visits since.

This is my first time on the Henderson campus of the Clark County Community College, and I feel honored by being included in this program of the Henderson District Public Library. So I would like to preface my talk with a plug for libraries.

Libraries

Libraries always have held an important place in my life and heart. In my childhood there were no TV's and radios. In the evenings after supper, we children sat around the dining room table reading books by the light of a Coleman lamp. Books about people and places far beyond our small neighborhood on Shook's Run in Colorado Springs. Jim Bridger's adventures in the Wild West, Marco Polo's travels in China, Pizarro's conquest of Peru. Fairy tales of all countries. These books we obtained on loan from the children's section of our public library, a walk away. I still remember the shelves of enticing volumes waiting to be devoured.

Such omnivorous, indiscriminate reading was not an escape for children of my generation, but an education. It opened up a world beyond our small confines, stretched our imaginations to embrace the thoughts and feelings of people who had existed long before our time.

In later years when I was traveling throughout the Southwest, researching and writing my own early books, I depended greatly upon local libraries. Still later I was given a grant by the Rockefeller Foundation for research in Mexico and Guatemala into pre-Columbian culture and religion. In addition to visiting all significant archeological sites, I spent much time in the library of the great national museum in Mexico City. Like our own great Library of Congress in Washington, D.C., it was a marvelous place to work. One presented his credentials and passport. Then he was assigned a table and brought priceless Aztec codices and other ancient records to study.

Today the library of the University of New Mexico houses my collection of manuscripts, correspondence, and papers, which are available to researchers, biographers, historians, and students.

The Library, whatever or wherever it is, impartially records our human history—our magnificent achievements and abysmal failures, our dreams of peace and prosperity, and our ghastly blood baths to achieve them.

The Word

The greatest gift to humanity was the Word.

"In the beginning was the Word." So begins the Gospel of St. John in the Judaic-Christian Bible. The Word with which all Became. Whatever it expressed came to pass: deeds, objects, worlds. The birth of language marked the virtual birth of mankind.

The Bantus of Africa, according to Janheinz Jahn, believed that conception and birth were not sufficient to produce a human being, a *Muntu.* The newborn child remained simply a "thing," a *Kintu,* like animals, plants, and stones, until he was given a name. So too the life forces in all things were freed only through the magic power of the Word.

In Tibet and India a word was considered to be a *mantra,* "a tool for thinking"; its sound called forth its content into a state of reality. Hence there developed a system of Mantric Yoga.

The magic and sacred power of the Word. Belief in it is found everywhere in the world.

The art of transcribing spoken words to written form marked one of man's greatest steps toward civilization. He no longer was obliged to depend upon memory to preserve his beliefs; they could be committed to writing. With printing came books—from parchment scrolls and fiber codices to leather-bound editions and mass paperbacks. Books in so many different languages that a word in one did not mean the same thing in another. Books contradicting each other with different religious beliefs and world views. The Word had lost its universal sacred meaning.

We can well believe Lévi-Strauss's assertion that the main function of writing was to make possible the economic enslavement of man rather than his enlightenment. The Anglo usurpation of land from American Indian tribes was largely accomplished because of their different interpretations of the treaties between them. The Anglo newcomers, believing the land was inanimate nature to be bought and sold like any other commodity, held that they were buying outright title to enormous tracts of land. Whereas the Indians, who regarded Mother Earth as a sacred living entity open to all men, believed they were selling only the use of it. This difference of opinion about the nature of Earth has always been the primary cause of conflict as tribe after tribe has been dispossessed of their homelands. And the Indians' main concern today is still the preservation of their remaining reservations against exploitation by the federal government and private interests.

America today, the most powerful and materialistic nation in the world, seems to bear out Lévi-Strauss's assertion. Its phenomenal printing establishment is primarily devoted to selling the products of its manufacturers—to constantly increasing the Gross National Product. One is appalled by the printed matter pouring in upon us. The junk mail we throw away at the post office without reading. Newspapers whose main function is carrying advertisements and advertising supplements. Magazines which depend not on their reading material but on their gorgeous color plates appealing to our extravagant desires for rare furs and exotic perfumes. Even a pictured dish of baked beans carries a brand stamp of social approval. Mass paperbacks crowding the shelves of drugstores and supermarkets sell sex and violence. The Madison Avenue copywriter is the spokesman for the nation. How clever and omnipotent he is! To a bar of soap, a sleek limousine, he imputes emotional properties, sexual imagery. Diplomatic gobbledygook seems dedicated to expanding our foreign markets for them. And the wake of the Ship of State is a stream of empty beer cans.

The Word with its sacred magic power has become synonymous with "Buy"—buy anything, everything, whether we need or want it.

Exploitation of Earth

The production of more and more consumer goods requires, of course, more and more raw materials. These come only from Earth's natural resources—minerals, coal, oil, trees, plants, and so on. Since our march of empire across the continent, we have almost exhausted this nation's treasury of natural resources by leveling great forests, gutting the mountains, ploughing under the grasslands. And our ever-expanding industrial complexes are still destroying vast areas of land by strip-mining; polluting all its surface waters, lakes, rivers, and boundary oceans; and contaminating the very air we breathe.

Such exploitation is not restricted to our America. It has been extended to Central and South America, to the undeveloped countries on all continents, too often with our help. The daily press reports such examples as the spread of acid rain to Canada. The cutting of the great Amazon rain forest to provide grazing for cattle which supply beef for our Big Mac hamburgers. The death of some 2,000 people and injury to more than 200,000 from toxic fumes escaping from a Union Carbide pesticide plant in Bhopal, India. The estimated 375,000 poisonings each year in the Third World from pesticides prohibited in the United States but exported abroad. The spread of desert wastes in Africa due to the replacement of native subsistence farming by huge agribusiness conglomerates choking the land with chemical fertilizer. In short, the ravaging of the entire planet Earth has now reached a level dangerous to human life.

There are two ways of looking at this problem. The view of industry and our federal government is based on political and economic considerations. The ever-present energy crisis, the constantly increasing world population, exhaustion of natural resources, and shortages of food due to natural disasters demand that the output of industrial plants be ever increased. This necessity outweighs the unfavorable side-issues of pollution and contamination. Scientific treatises, economic studies, and political stances amply support this view.

The alternate view is held by a minority of ecologists, naturalists, and environmentalists. It coincides generally with the Indian belief that Earth is a living entity, and that the harmonic relationship between it, the plant, animal, and human kingdoms must be maintained. By destroying these living entities we are alienating ourselves from all nature, of which we too are a part, and thus rupturing our inner selves. Such was the opinion of the Swiss psychologist C. G. Jung, who considered this the great tragedy of our time. This view is supported by a growing number of authoritative books and writings.

How are we to choose between these opposite views, each supported by books, books conflicting with each other? In which of them can we discover the sacred magic Word with which all Became?

Only in the one great book of life, Earth itself.

Mother Earth

Our global Earth is not a book, of course. But the analogy seems apt for the moment because past peoples were able to learn from it, "to read it like a book." Modern mankind no longer learns from Earth, but from books.

If Earth is indeed a living organism like ourselves, it is speaking to us, protesting the destruction of tropical rainforests that supply oxygen to her atmosphere, its pollution by toxic poisons and particulate matter, the contamination of her waters by nuclear wastes, the destruction of much of her surface land. This violation of the harmonic balance between the forces of earth and sky, as she warns us, is resulting in changes of climate, unprecedented floods and droughts, and disruptive changes by earthquakes in the structure of the planet.

How can we halt this worldwide suicidal course?

In a talk last summer in Colorado, I suggested that it would take a full realization of our dire need, a new way of thinking to unite us in one effort as one great body of mankind, if we are to regard the entire body of Earth with a planetary imperative to save it from further ravages. In light of the present political dissensions and social upheavals, such expansion of our perspective might first appear to be a utopian pipe dream. But I think it is inevitable.

Life began on this planet about three billion years ago, and man's slow biological evolution was accompanied by the slow geological evolution of Earth by cataclysmic changes into the conformation of continents and seas we know now. It would seem their evolutionary growths were synchronized to their mutual benefit, so alike they are. Each maintaining an even body temperature and an equilibrium between the primary elements of water, air, earth, and fire in both of their bodies. Little wonder that from ancient times man has been considered the microcosmic image of macrocosmic Earth, both pulsing with the same life pervading the entire universe.

How truly Earth has been the great mother of all her children, the firstborn minerals merging with plants, the plants with animals, and animals with human beings, each higher organism making use of the lower, achieving a harmonious unity. Our Mother Earth is not only man's link with his past, but his hope for the future.

"The Owl of Minerva," it is said, "does not rise until the sun of empire has set." And this is the time when the day of our great empires is ending, when many small nations are facing bankruptcy. It is the time when we are beginning to realize that all peoples and living things obey the same higher laws.

The full expansion of our consciousness to see the world as one living unity, with a planetary imperative to save it from more ruthless plundering, will eventually include each of us. Yet everywhere individuals of every race and nation are already taking this next step in mankind's evolutionary journey. So in this sundown hour let us greet the rise of the owl of wisdom with new confidence in a brighter tomorrow.

8

Science's Rainbow Bridge

(Editorial—January 19, 1950)

THE recent announcement by Princeton University, at the annual meeting of the American Association for the Advancement of Science, that Albert Einstein has completed a new "generalized theory of gravitation" may be the greatest announcement of the century.

All the phenomena of nature are produced by the primordial forces gravitation and electromagnetism.

From their study Max Planck in 1900 developed the Quantum Theory, which defines the inner limits of man's knowledge—of the microcosmic universe, the invisible atom, and all the realities of nature too small to be perceived.

Proceeding from this, Albert Einstein in 1905 developed the Relativity Theory—his now famous Mass-Energy Equation—which defines the outer limits of man's knowledge of the macrocosmic universe, interstellar space, immeasurable time, and all the realities of nature too great to be perceived.

From these two theories of the Little and the Big, of electromagnetism and gravitation, there sprang forty years later the Atomic Bomb—a negative detour on civilization's march to progress.

But for thirty years Einstein has consecrated himself to evolving a new theory, a Unified Field Theory, which would unify all we know of electromagnetism and gravitation, and bridge the microcosmic atom and the macrocosmic universe.

Though his new hypothesis is announced as the "generalized theory of gravitation," scientists believe that it is the definitive Unified Field Theory he has been working on. We do not know yet, scientists say, "because the work is too new, and as yet no one understands it."

But if it proves to be, and is verified by the experiments, it may well be science's Rainbow Bridge. The Rainbow Bridge over which the heroes traveled between earth and sky, according to Navajo mythology.

In today's ensuing Atomic Age, there are still needed, as in the past, both a bridge and laboratory heroes to travel it.

9

Incursions from Outer Space

(Essay)

THE prevailing phenomena of our time—flying saucers, Unidentified Flying Objects, UFOs—remain inexplicable after several decades and thousands of sightings. No one has been able to make heads or tails of their mysterious appearances despite numerous conflicting theories of their nature and origin, and countless books, magazine articles, official and personal reports, movie and television versions.

One of the most popular conjectures is that UFOs are interplanetary vehicles carrying superior beings to reconnoiter Earth, possibly to prepare us for a higher state of existence. The corollary to this supposition is that similar advanced beings from another planet may have visited Earth in the distant past, engendered mankind as we know it today, and established the earliest civilizations.

Erich von Däniken's *Chariots of the Gods* was perhaps the first book to cash in on this belief. It substantiated none of his alleged facts, gave no attribution to his statements; but it presented a view the world was eager to accept. It has been followed by a rash of other, similar conjectures.

Whatever flying saucers may turn out to be, the theories about them are serving a real function; they are bringing to light new facts about ancient vanished civilizations, awakening interest in the planets of our solar system, reminding us of the everlasting mystery of the origin of mankind. More importantly, they help to reveal us to ourselves. This, rather than UFOs themselves, concerns us here.

Zecharia Sitchin's *Twelfth Planet* is a scholarly work which surpasses von Däniken's imaginative generalizations. Sitchin's erudite book, based on an exhaustive study of ancient Sumerian, Akkadian,

and biblical texts, postulates that our planet Earth was first visited as
early as 450,000 years ago by people from a twelfth planet, Marduk,
which orbited Earth every 3,600 years. Through genetic manipulation
and intermarriage with primordial apelike beings, mankind was created about 250,000 years ago, and later established the first world civilization in the Near East, ancient Sumeria. These emissaries who
recurrently visited Earth became the "gods" of the ancient Sumerians
and Akkadians. The postulated twelfth planet is said to have been a
previous planet which disappeared, leaving remnant fragments now
known as asteroids.

A similar theory has been recounted in *The New Soviet Psychic Dis-
coveries* by Henry Gris and William Dick. It was based on the discovery
in the Karakum Desert near Askhabad of numerous tektites, tiny mete-
orites from outer space. They could have come only as rubble ejected
from the thermonuclear explosion and disintegration of a planet in the
solar system. The Soviet academician Sergei Orloff named this ancient
planet Phaeton. It occupied the same position between the orbits of
Mars and Jupiter as the present belt of the asteroids that are the remaining fragments of Phaeton. Also it had surface conditions, air, water, and
gravity much like Earth, giving life to similar human beings, though far
more advanced. Its survivors landed on Earth about 500,000 years ago
and bridged the gap from primordial beings to early man, helping him
to create civilization.

Other similar theories have cropped up in print. A former NASA
space engineer, Josef F. Blumrich, has offered an engineering explanation that the biblical vision of Ezekiel and a chariot with "wheels
within wheels" was a helicopter from a space vehicle, far in advance of
modern technology. Great interest is also being taken in religious ceremonies of the primitive Dogon tribe in Africa, which posit the ancient
arrival on Earth of inhabitants from the remote star Sirius.

All these theories of interplanetary visitors to Earth were, of course,
preceded by the remarkable "Tales of Beelzebub to his Grandson,"
published nearly seventy years ago in the voluminous opus *All and
Everything* by the mystic of Central Asia, Georges Ivanovitch Gurdjieff. He relates visits by a supernormal being on a spaceship to the
planet Earth during successive periods of human history. Beelzebub
and other universal teachers lived for a time in the Near East, Egypt,
Africa, and Europe. They did not create mankind or his various
civilizations, and their religious teachings were soon forgotten or

distorted. Gurdjieff's main purpose apparently was to outline the psychical problems hindering mankind's development according to a universal creative plan.

The later variations of interplanetary invasions from the Twelfth Planet Marduk, the Missing Planet Phaeton, Sirius, the Mysterious Planet X, and others deviate from Gurdjieff's prototypal exposition. They are less philosophical and more rationally specific, postulating the exact methods by which advanced celestial beings created man on Earth, later becoming the gods of myth and legend.

To reconcile these late theories seems impossible, we know so little of antediluvian history. The Soviet theory that Phaeton inhabitants arrived on Earth about 500,000 years ago, a period which was said to coincide with the dawn of Neanderthal Man, "not all that many years prior to the appearance of the creative Cro-Magnon Man," does not agree with Sitchin's theory that the first *Homo sapiens* appeared about 250,000 years ago. Both conflict with anthropological belief that the primitive Neanderthals were suddenly and unaccountably replaced about 30,000 B.C. by the Cro-Magnons, the first true *Homo sapiens,* "thinking man," the ancestors of modern man. To span this gap, Sitchin offers the explanation that a great Deluge occurred about 13,000 B.C., during which most of the human race perished. Its survivors centered in Mesopotamia, beginning agriculture about 11,000 B.C., and founding in 3800 B.C. the great Sumerian civilization, which he says preceded those of the Canaanites, Aryans, Egyptians, Hebrews, and Greeks.

This time scale runs counter to other chronologies and poses many questions. How did the mysterious Cro-Magnons originate, and where did they come from so suddenly? Could they have originated on the controversial continent of Atlantis, where visitors from some other planet had planted the seeds of a great civilization? Then, with the destruction of Atlantis, did many of its survivors flee to the Near East, Egypt, Spain, and Yucatan to perpetuate their culture and religion?

Two eminent scientists, Otto Muck in *The Secret of Atlantis* and R. A. Schwaller de Lubicz in *The Temple in Man,* both assert the existence of Atlantis and present new facts about prehistorical times. According to Plato, our primary source, the catastrophe which sank Atlantis occurred in 9500 B.C. Muck, from a study of Herodotus's Egyptian diary, determines the date should have been 8500 B.C. He fixes the more exact date at 8498 B.C. from a study of the Mayan calendar. This projected earliest Mayan date he believes marks the beginning of the Mayan calendar and the Atlantis catastrophe. One Great Cycle of 5,127 years later, in 3375 B.C., began the Mayans' last and present Great Cycle. (I have customarily used the date of 3113 B.C. as established by other reliable correlations of the Mayan and Gregorian calendars.)

Schwaller de Lubicz refutes the commonly accepted belief that the unification of Upper and Lower Egypt, and the beginning of the First Dynasty, took place between 3100 and 2700 B.C. He establishes the date as being 4240 B.C., which marked the beginning of the first Sothic Year shortly after the start of the Taurus Age in the great Precession of the Equinoxes. He sets no date for the Atlantis catastrophe, but calculates that Egyptian civilization was founded long before the catastrophe occurred, possibly as early as 36,000 B.C.

These various dates contradict the belief derived from the book of Genesis that the biblical deluge took place in 3308 B.C., and Velikovsky's famous theory that the Atlantis catastrophe occurred about 1500 B.C. Just when did the great Deluge occur—in 13,000, 8498, or 1500 B.C.? Was it synonymous with the flood that submerged Atlantis? And do Egyptian, Babylonian, and Mayan calendars, architectural monuments, and hieroglyphic records reflect a common knowledge of the event? How little we know of these past civilizations!

All these theories, despite their discrepancies and contradictions, reflect the relationship between man and the forces of the universe with their rhythmic cycles. More significantly, they reveal the psychological disorder of our present time. Restless and aimless, we are seeking a new approach to spiritual completeness.

C. G. Jung took this view in his book *Flying Saucers: A Modern Myth of Things Seen in the Skies,* published three years before his death in 1961. He considered UFOs as symbols appearing periodically in the past during all such periods of psychological unrest. Their round shapes, which embodied a mandala structure, portrayed the archetype of the self, expressing the totality of the individual, conscious and unconscious. This consistency of form, he thought, was a manifestation of unity and wholeness projected by the unconscious on the outside world.

When ancient man projected on the outside world his unconscious apperception of his inherent totality, he saw the celestial bodies as imbuing numinous forces that he named as gods, each exercising upon him a special influence. And this gave rise to the largest complete round, the zodiacal cycle of heavenly divisions housing their own stars and gods, which corresponded to his own physical and psychical selves. This projection, according to Jung, may account for our belief today. For if the planetary gods of the past once descended by mysterious chariots to our earthly ancestors, why may they not be descending today in the modern, technological chariots we call UFOs?

Meredith Sabine, in a review of several television and movie films from a Jungian perspective, points out that they can be interpreted as dreams of our modern culture, as a "living myth." Outer Space symbolically represents the psychic contents of the unconscious far distant from the conscious world of the ego, the Earth. The films illustrate, on a collective level, the principle of movement from the unconscious toward consciousness, from the ego to the self.

Man's search for spiritual completeness is an ages-long theme. We cannot doubt man's unconscious feeling of a wholeness, a totality, which he has not yet consciously attained. It seems to have been inherent in him since his inception. A realization he had once, has lost, and is still trying to regain. This is the true journey inherent in man's evolutionary Fall: his descent into full physical materiality, and his gradual ascent back into full spirituality.

The long process of evolution may be aided by the invisible influences of the planets themselves, rather than by actual visitors. Gurdjieff from Armenia, Rodney Collin in England, and Guenther Wachsmuth in Germany offer explanations of the celestial influences in comprehensive studies. Collin details their effect upon the glands of the human body over a time scale corresponding to the distances of the planets from the sun. Each planet in turn exercises a predominant influence—Mercury upon the thyroid 15,000 years ago, Venus upon the parathyroid 5000 B.C., Mars upon the adrenals 1000 B.C., and so on. Man's civilizations during these periods reflect in turn the nature of these glandular influences.

Wachsmuth bases his study on the effects of the constellations as they move through the twelve divisions or houses of the zodiac, each representing thirty degrees of the circle of the Earth around the sun, and a period of 2,160 years called an Age. In each period mankind is subjected to the successive influences from the various constellations, and goes through different phases reflected in the symbols of his religion and civilization. The symbol of the bull in the Taurus age, beginning in 4000 B.C., was replaced in 2000 B.C. by that of the ram in the

Aries period, and it in turn by the symbol of the fish at the beginning of the present Pisces period about 1 B.C.

Gurdjieff goes a step further, asserting that cosmic emanations are transmitted by the planets in the solar system, by the constellations in the galaxy of the Milky Way, and by the farthest mysterious creative principle he calls the Absolute.

However different their theories seem, they are essentially alike. All posit the effects upon the psychical-physical body of man and the successive civilizations he creates, of creative forces from the celestial bodies to which he is organically related. It is surprising how closely their chronologies agree.

The "World Clock," the great 25,920-year cycle of the Precession divided into twelve zodiacal "hours" of 2,160 years, is the cosmic timetable. It is the ultimate, prototypal Great Round during which each of the planets and constellations exercises predominant influence upon man, his successive religions and civilizations.

What a majestic, cosmic scope this general theory covers with its development of movement, rhythm, and cyclic periodicity in the life of mankind and the universe alike. In its great pattern earthly man is not dependent upon visitations of planetary beings at each stage of his evolution; he is ruled by cosmic laws governing them as well as himself. In contrast to this great conception, the explanation of the currently viewed UFOs as being terrestrial devices secretly contrived and operated by certain intelligence agencies to promote new social, political, or religious beliefs, appears to be extremely limited. What worldly agency has the wisdom to prescribe the goals of human consciousness?

Jung's psychological theory that UFOs are archetypal symbols of the Great Round expressing the inherent totality of the universal Self toward which man is striving complements the cosmic theory advanced by Gurdjieff, Collin, and Wachsmuth. Jung simply substitutes his postulated collective unconscious, our unknown Inner Space, for the unknown Outer Space. It may well be that in time we will recognize them as synonymous.

Meanwhile we can't deny the possibility that UFOs may turn out to be physically real. Yet even so, their present psychical reality is more important. For they are portents of our ever-expanding consciousness. Whether it will be achieved by Jungian investigations of our Inner Space, or by forces in Outer Space beyond our comprehension, the World Clock will strike the hour of change.

The current Age of Pisces now ending is the twelfth and last age in the present precessional cycle of 25,920 years. A new precessional cycle is about to begin. Can we assume that, having then completed this Great Round of the World Clock, we will have attained completeness of Self? Obviously we can't. According to Collin, the little-known psychic functions of the human pineal gland have yet to be realized. The pineal body is said to be controlled by Neptune, not discovered until 1846. Its predominant influences, with those of Pluto discovered as late as 1930, have still to manifest themselves in the future.

Gurdjieff's metaphysical system agrees with Collin's theory and extends it even further, beyond Pluto to two more undiscovered planets or universal planes from which we already may be experiencing influences to a degree. And Jung's pioneer explorations of Inner Space have yet to be carried by his successors farther into the deeper strata of the collective unconscious where physical and psychical realities unite.

It seems then that man's evolutionary development began far earlier than the present round of the World Clock, and will continue through the next round on a spiral ascent toward our ultimate realization of completeness. It is idle to conjecture archeologically and anthropologically how many rounds man has gone through, how many rounds we have yet to take. The macrocosmic universe is duplicated within our microcosmic selves. These cycles are illimitably large, and their influences inconceivable to our limited human minds.

Faulty and incomplete as the cosmic theories of Gurdjieff, Collin, and Wachsmuth may be, in contrast to the rational theories of Sitchin, Orloff, Blumrich, and others, they offer glimpses of a universal creative plan.

The portents that the World Clock is about to strike the hour of change may well be not phenomena of UFOs themselves, but of the worldwide interest and conjectures they are evoking within mankind.

10

Granny and Sassafras Tea

(Editorial—March 8, 1951)

WITH all the sneezing, coughing, colds and flu, bone aches, and spring fever attacking us at random, we miss Granny more than ever. These fancy new pills don't stand a candle to her wise and simple doctoring.

About this time of year, come February thaws and March tail-twisters, she got down to business. No more buckwheat cakes; they heated the blood. A body's blood needed thinning. Granny used sassafras tea. For stubborn cases there was sulphur and molasses. Windows could be opened a mite at night. To keep your feet warm, Granny slipped between cold sheets a hot brick wrapped in flannel. Sage tea was another dandy remedy. Nothing was more soothing to a sore throat than a cold compress on the outside, and a hoarhound drop melting on the inside. A hot mustard foot bath helped to draw the blood from the head.

No, antihistamine pills, serum injections, and making believe the body doesn't change with the seasons have taken all the fun out of catching cold. We don't need one nowadays to get orange juice and ice cream. Granny knew better. She had what it takes to adjust a fellow's living apparatus to the coming of the first robin.

11

Words

(Paper delivered at the annual meeting of the Western Literature Association in Colorado Springs, Colorado, in October 1968)

W HEN Dr. J. Golden Taylor informed me that the Governing Board of the Western Literature Association wished to appoint me as an Honorary Life Member in the Association, I was beset with some qualms. If I now accept this honor, more gratefully than gracefully I'm afraid, it is because it has forced me to attempt to account for my reservations.

For after having been a professional writer for many years, I'm just beginning to realize what a dangerous game I have been so inadequately playing in writing words, and more words about words, and still more words about words written by others about words. I question my own assent to becoming a life member in a literary association unless I realign my sights on what must surely be the common aim of us all.

This writing, criticizing, reviewing, lecturing—this hawking of words, to put it crudely—is more than a craft whose products occasionally achieve the dimensions of art. It is a magic, as often black as white. And so I feel like a sorcerer's apprentice who, after mastering a few little tricks, views with trepidation his initiation into the esoteric mysteries of the trade.

To the black race of Africa the word was a sacred and powerful magic. Janheinz Jahn defines it by the Bantu word *Nommo* as the vital force that gave life to everything through the power of the word. The Bantus believed that conception and birth were not sufficient to produce a human being, a *Muntu*. The newborn child remained simply a "thing," a *Kintu* like animals, plants, and stones, until he was designated with a name. So too the life forces in all things were freed only through the power of the word, which could be conjured by man. No crops would grow, no woodcarving could take proper shape, unless called forth by the word.

Black Africa below the Sahara, about which we yet know so little, did not develop a written language. It relied upon the audible language of the drum, a communication medium subtle, swift, and far-carrying. This was expressed not by a Morse code of sorts as we commonly suppose, but by a complex system of pitch, tonality, modulation, and rhythm. The "Divine Drummer" was trained from childhood on specially prepared drums, and was accorded the highest privileges of tribal rank. He possessed the magic power of the word.

The brown and yellow races of Asia believed, as did the black race of Africa, that the whole universe was penetrated by a common and unlimited life force. Out of this emerged those limited individual entities of our temporal world when given form, *Rupa,* and defined by name or word, *Nama.* The word was a *Mantra,* a "tool for thinking"; its sound called forth its content into a state of reality. Hence there developed in India a system of Mantra Yoga, and in Tibet not only the word but every letter in the alphabet was a sacred symbol.

This impersonal spirit of life the red race of the Americas called by various tribal names, such as *Orenda* by the Iroquois, *Wakan* by the Sioux, and *huaca* by the Incas. From its revelations through dreams and visions, warriors, mountains, and rivers derived their ceremonial names. The words imbued power, and were seldom spoken.

"In the Beginning was the Word." So begins the Gospel of St. John in the Judaic-Christian Bible of the white race. The Word with which all Became. Whatever it expressed came to pass: deeds, acts, worlds. The birth of language was the birth of humanity.

We explain this in our scientific terminology as the transition of percepts, or registrations of bodily sense impressions, into generalized or common recepts as mankind emerged into simple consciousness. Then the work of accumulation began on a higher plane. Hundreds of recepts were combined into a composite concept, a word, a name, which like an algebraic sign stood for the thing itself. Henceforth self-conscious man took possession of the world with the word.

Indo-European dominance of the world in modern times is of course a remarkable phenomenon. Its languages, particularly English, reflect our materialistic ideology. The early reverence for the sacred magic of the word gave way to the compulsion to practical economics.

The French ethnographer Lévi-Strauss asserts that the rise of handwriting was immediately related to the establishment of cities and empires, the organization of men into political systems, and the formation of classes and castes. Its main function was to make possible the enslavement of man rather than the enlightenment of man.

In Africa, European colonialism took over, beginning the exportation of up to a million slaves a year. The acoustical phonetic language of the drum was abolished by law and replaced with a foreign optical script, rupturing traditional thought forms.

European domination of America followed the same procedure. The usurpation of lands from American Indians and the virtual extermination of tribe after tribe was largely accomplished with the use of the word as an economic weapon. So-called "Treaty Chiefs" or "Whiskey Chiefs" appointed by government land commissioners were induced with whiskey to sign treaties giving up their tribal lands. Yet even then the government's word in treaties drawn for "as long as the grass shall grow" was violated as a matter of economic expediency so that the pitiful remnants of the great tribes could be deported and dispossessed again and again—as was the Delaware tribe, five times.

The helpless Indians observed simply, "White men speak from the head, not the heart."

We too are aware of our own duplicity. If any people have the gift of gab, it is we. Our language reflects it. We speak with split tongues; our tongues wag on both ends; we double-talk, smooth-talk, sweet-talk.

And so today English-speaking America, the culminating apex of Indo-European civilization, dominates the world with the materialistic ideology reflected by its language. There is no doubt as to the magic of its power. But we must question whether it is a black magic we are practicing and perpetuating.

Now I don't want to drum out too blatantly a theme obvious to us all. Especially on this eve of national elections when every candidate poses as all things to all people. Ben Jonson long ago expressed it succinctly: "Language most shows a man; speak that I may know thee."

We have only to read the advertisements which comprise 60 percent or more of the column inches of every newspaper. To listen to the radio and TV commercials, to the stock market quotations, which take up a third of all news reports for the simple reason we are not as interested in what is happening throughout the world as we are in how the events are influencing the New York Stock Exchange. The Village Crier, the Divine Drummer, has been replaced with the Madison Avenue spokesman for the nation. How clever and omnipotent he is! To a bar of soap he imputes emotional properties, our physical desires, sexual imagery. And diplomatic gobbledygook seems dedicated to expanding our foreign markets for it.

Little wonder that Semitic, Russian, Chinese, African, and other peoples are mystified by our view of the world as no more than a business arena. Their own languages impose upon them far different views. As Edward Sapir says: "Human beings do not live in the objective world alone . . . but are very much at the mercy of the particular language which has become the medium of expression for their society. . . . The 'real world' is to a large extent built up on the language habits of the group."

That the picture of the universe differs in different languages, and that our very manner of thinking depends on language, Benjamin Lee Whorf called the principle of linguistic relativity. "The linguistic system of each language is not merely a reproducing instrument for voicing ideas, but is itself a shaper of ideas, the program and guide for the individual's thinking," he asserts. "The concepts of time and matter aren't given in the same form by experience to all men, but depend upon the nature of the language through which they have been developed. . . . Newtonian time and matter are not intuitions. They are recepts from culture and language. That is where Newton got them."

The Word with which we Became. We are not only saying what we are; we are what we are saying.

Whorf, a great linguist, studied not only Latin, Greek, Hebrew, Chinese, and Russian. His special field was the Amerindian languages: Aztec, Mayan, and particularly Hopi. He concluded that there are no "primitive" languages; many of them so called functioned on a higher plane of rationality than those of civilized men, the African and American Indian languages far outdistancing the European languages in their logical discriminations of causation, dynamic quality, and directness of experience.

Like most American Indian languages, Hopi sentences are not divided into subjects and predicates. In English we say, "The light flashed." "Light" is the subject, "flashed" the predicate. The Hopi says simply, *"rehpi"*—"flash"—for the entire phenomenon. For what is it but the light and the flash combined, synonymous subject and verb? "English compared to Hopi," says Whorf, "is like a bludgeon compared to a rapier."

The language of the Chichewa, related to that of the Zulu in Africa, has two past tenses: one for past events influencing the present, and one for past events without present results. A past objectively recorded in external situations, as distinguished from a past subjectively recorded only in the psyche. This subtle difference, not made in English, presents a view of time different from ours.

A far different view is seen by the Hopis in Arizona. I have been particularly interested in this tribe, and have written at some length about its beliefs. Hence I don't want to risk boring you with repetitious observations. Let me recall to you only that the Hopi language does not have our three-tense system of past, present, future. Time to the Hopis is not a flowing horizontal stream, but a deep still pool of duration holding all that has been and will be—as does the unconscious. So in Hopi there is no time and space, no velocity, no kinematic action; only intensity, a factor we do not include in English.

Clyde Kluckhohn, the eminent anthropologist who studied the Navajos extensively, reached similar conclusions. English and Navajo operate in different worlds. One must know the Navajo linguistic structure to know the Navajo world view.

If these Navajo, Hopi, and indeed all American Indian pictures of the universe seem to us abstract, metaphysical, and incomprehensible, how much more so are those of the great philosophical-religious systems of the Far East.

There are no English equivalents for the Sanskrit words *Sat, Chit,* and *Ananda,* which can be roughly taken to mean "Being," "Consciousness," and "Bliss." These are said to be the three predictables or attributes of the one infinite life-force and consciousness embodying to some degree all finite entities in nature, and which correspond to the *Nommo* of the Bantu and the *Orenda* of the Iroquois.

We do not admit the existence of such an infinite conscious power functioning in finite stones, trees, and animals, in ourselves. Consciousness to us is only the wakeful consciousness of the individual human mind, whether it operates as a function of the physical organ of the brain, or independently.

But to the peoples of India, Tibet, China, and Japan our consciousness is unconscious. For consciousness is an observer, a cognizer, a knower of that beyond itself; it is a subject requiring an object to be known. Within a greatly restricted finite field it so functions. But as this field of perception necessarily expands, our limited personal consciousness becomes helpless. Unable to know its limitations, or itself, it becomes the object of *Chit,* the one infinite consciousness that is the ultimate subject and supreme knower.

From this original source derives the word, reflected in turn through mind and thought. But with this we get into deep water far beyond the sounding of these casual comments.

So there are great differences between the conceptions of the inner and the outer universe of man held by Western psychologists and Eastern metaphysicists. We here do not seem too eager to reconcile them. As Lévi-Strauss suggests, we are too engrossed in employing words for the purpose of economically enslaving rather than enlightening man. The early reverence for the word as the focus of energy and embodiment of the spirit is forgotten. And with the constant barrage of words indiscriminately hurled at the public through all possible mass media, Western culture and language have reached, in Whorf's opinion, a dead end whose name is Babel.

Is it foreseeable that we will succeed in enforcing our language on all the rest of the world, and with it our limited, objective, and economic view of nature and the universe?

Or do we have a capacity for growth large enough to encompass the abstract and subjective views of the outer and inner universes of man as reflected by the languages of other peoples and cultures?

Nebulous as these brief comments here may sound, I hope their intent at least may be pertinent to the members of a society whose stock in trade is words. The function of the Western Literature Association is, I take it, to encourage the development of literature in and of the American West. And literature, if we accept Webster's definition, is writings distinguished from works merely technical or erudite, and from journalistic and other ephemeral literary writings.

This is a tall order for a comparatively new organization whose major sphere of interest is one section of the country. Yet there is no cause for us to sit uneasy in the saddle. Certainly this vast heartland of a continent can boast of a long tradition of Literature with a capital "L." The ritual prayers, recitations, chants, songs, and poetry of the Navajos and Apaches, the Zunis, Hopis, and other Pueblo Indian tribes are *belles lettres* by the highest standards. Even though they are now relegated to dusty shelves of Smithsonian reports, they still preserve the magic power of the word.

More and more modern literature will come, is already coming, as we raise our sights to it. But it will not be produced by a promulgation of concepts limited to our present, generally accepted view of the world. We can no longer keep concocting mechanical tales of stereotyped Redskins, Cowboys, Bad Men, and Pioneers for the avid consumption of eastern readers and Hollywood agents. What excuse is there for seriously reviewing such books simply because they are new? Nor can we afford the time to constantly rehash in academic treatises outworn historical documents, squabble about obscurely written paragraphs, append lengthy footnotes to chance phrases. We have better work to do.

The past and the future lie in the ever-living *now*. Whatever there is anywhere, everywhere, is right here at our hand. The immortal verities of time, space, and nature still assert themselves. Even though the mighty waters of the Colorado and the Rio Grande no longer reach the sea, the flow of the spirit can never be dammed.

I have the distinctly uneasy feeling that the many uninformed pages of words I have written, and the brief words I am speaking now, may in some measure contribute more to our general confusion than to our enlightenment. Yet I hope that I will not in the future sell short the golden coins of our realm. I would like to bite them between my teeth, ring each one on the hard pavement of reality, and make sure that their exchange purchases to the last cent their ultimate worth.

Words, words, words! Each has shape and color, sound and fragrance, a music and a meaning, all its own. How sharp and curt they are, how long and alliterative, how melodious and mysterious! They roll like the drum-thunder of hoofs from off the horizon; they swoop down like hawks to rend with bared talons; they purr from firelit pages, smooth the wrinkles from sleepless nights. But ever they speak as foci for unmeasured power with the mystery of their divine origin.

The same old words, but words which still can be conjured as vital expressions of universal human experience if we are magicians adept enough to recognize their original sacredness and potent energy. Words whose power, by our more judicious use, can remake us into better images of what we really are.

12

Hurray for the Common Cold

(Editorial—December 29, 1949)

CHEER up; this isn't going to be solemn.

It's just that it rather pleased us to hear that the American Medical Association recently announced that it had made no headway at all against the common cold. Also to realize that there had been no report at all from the General Electric Company, which some time ago put a vast sum of money aside for research into this malady. The company stated at the time, rather resentfully, it seemed to us, that it lost we don't know how many man-hours of work each year because of the common cold.

Could it be, we wonder, that common man doesn't really want to be cured of the common cold? That every so often he just wants to get away from it all, get away from the office, or the duty of making more man-hours of profit for General Electric? That the sniffles are his last refuge, his citadel? Why, when the modern doctor believes that malady after malady derives from a mental state, doesn't he think this of the common cold?

We advise GE and the AMA to give up their campaigns. They won't catch their germ or their man. He will be safe at home with the Kleenex box within reach, the orange juice or hot toddy on call, and the attentive wife, hovering around the bedside, asking him if he is warm enough.

13

Houston Branch

(Essay)

BILL Branch was the most creative, prolific writer I've known. The paradox is that nothing he wrote was ever published. His output was limited to Hollywood films. This is not disparaging. For Bill arrived there during the Hollywood Gold Rush when the movie industry was clamoring for talent of every kind and creating a name and an era of opulence that have not been equaled.

Bill had a natural aptitude for all phases of theatrical production. As a young man from somewhere back East, he had left home and school to manage successive small theatrical troupes touring the countryside. He concocted the skits, arranged the programs, laid out itineraries, and held reins on the cast. It was inevitable that, as an ambitious entrepreneur, he blew into Hollywood during its heydays—the days of famous stars, directors, and producers calling for writers and stories to supply what seemed an inexhaustible demand. And Bill had plenty to offer.

He was endowed with a great imagination and a sure dramatic instinct. Loving people, he was a shrewd judge of character, having an observant eye for their mannerisms and idiosyncrasies. Unschooled as he was, he was an omnivorous reader with an infallible memory. There were few histories of peoples, nations, and war campaigns he didn't know, and his accumulated library was impressive.

Almost immediately he sold one story, then another. Up to the time I met him, he had sold to the studios—on a rough guess—about 150 original stories. Some of these were mere narrative outlines or plots sketched on a few pages. As he became better known, he had only to recount them to a star performer, director, or producer. The stories themselves, however, were not general ideas or hazy outlines. They were fully thought out, tightly constructed. Later he was often engaged to develop them into screenplays. This didn't appeal to him; he preferred to work at home and sell the original story idea for more money. He was, in short, a creative writer.

I met him in Hollywood about 1940 when I was broke and trying to find a job. He telephoned to introduce himself, saying that he had read a couple of my books and had a proposition that might make us both some money. Next day he came to my one-room apartment bringing the narrative outline of a story entitled *River Lady*. He had sold it for $15,000 to a film producer with the provision that it first be published as a novel, which would of course help to advertise the film. Bill offered to pay me $1,000 for writing it as a novel and then get for me the job of helping him write the screenplay at a salary of $500 per week.

Bill had just been married and needed the money. I also needed the thousand dollars. But I was hesitant to attempt to write a novel about timber cutting on the upper Mississippi and rafting logs downriver just after the Civil War in a part of the country I'd never seen. Nevertheless, we called on the producer, Jack Skirball of Republic Studio, a former Jewish rabbi who had produced a very successful play on Broadway and was now producing films in Hollywood. He assured me I could do a good novelization, and Bill's price was secure.

Development of the sketchy outline of *River Lady* required a lot of work: the addition of characters, scenes, subplots; the creation of atmosphere, descriptions, characterization; the inclusion of timber cutting details in the northern woods and rafting of the logs. To supply me with all this information, Bill came often to see me.

He was a big man, weighing about 250 pounds. A gourmet, he loved to eat at only the finest restaurants. He did not drink, and smoked in his ever-present pipe only Dunhill tobacco imported from England. High-strung, he turned on music the instant he entered the house. I also met his wife, an attractive young girl who soon left him.

I finished the novelization of *River Lady* in short order, a purely commercial book I was not proud of. It was published in 1942 and later in a British edition. Republic Pictures immediately laid plans to produce the film version. Clark Gable was to play the leading role, joined by Barbara Stanwyck. As the upper Mississippi had been long denuded of forests, a small town and an expanse of timberland along the

Columbia River was leased to serve as the setting, along with a Mississippi steamboat as the "River Lady." But by then World War II was escalating. Gable entered the air force, and the projected film was abandoned. Years later the rights were resold for the sad production of a third-rate film based on only the first few chapters. Bill Branch, however, was inordinately proud of the book, which showed his name as a joint author. He carried a dust-jacket to show his friends, and hung an advertising poster on the wall of his library.

A few years later Bill presented MGM producers with the virtually unknown story of the *Shenandoah,* the only ship in the Confederate Navy that had sailed around the Horn and up into the Arctic and destroyed the Union whaling fleet. The producers tentatively accepted the story, offering him $5,000 in advance to research the facts and to write it as a novel.

World War II had just ended. I had been released from a government job in Washington, D.C., and was in New York, anxious to return home to Taos. Late one afternoon he telephoned me at my hotel, enthusiastically recounting the story, and proposing we collaborate in developing it as we had *River Lady.* The story, which he had titled *Diamond Head,* was dramatic and exciting; but I didn't want to work on it. What did I know about the Civil War and sailing ships? My longest ocean voyage had been from the port of Los Angeles to Catalina Island. Besides, I wanted to go home and resume my own work.

Early next morning I was awakened by a telephone call from Bill's Hollywood agent, Dave Diamond, who had flown into New York during the night and was waiting for me in the lobby. These persistent, resourceful Hollywood agents! I went downstairs, and during breakfast with him Diamond half-persuaded me to agree to Bill's proposition. The other half-persuasion, I insisted, must come from my publishers, Farrar and Straus. We took a taxi to see John Farrar. Diamond glowingly presented his pitch on the great novel and film possibilities of *Diamond Head.*

"What do you think about it, Frank?" John Farrar asked me.

"I suppose I could write it if Branch did all the research for it," I answered. "But would you publish such a novel?"

"I'll publish it if you'll write it, Frank."

Diamond grinned. "That's it, then. I'll speak for Branch. Can you give me a note of agreement to present to the MGM producers, Mr. Farrar?"

That was it, indeed; I was committed to another collaboration with Bill.

I flew to Hollywood to talk over the project with him. Things had been going well for him. He had married again, a beautiful unspoiled girl named Jeanie. Also he had bought a house on a hillside along the Hollywood Strip, as it was then known, which overlooked at night the twinkling lights of Los Angeles. The house itself was large and beautifully furnished. All his life Bill had admired and coveted Chinese art. So now, in a lush period, he had bought from Gump's in San Francisco a porcelain Ming horse to set on the mantel above the fireplace.

Diamond Head, novelized and filmed, he was sure would bring us in a jackpot. Development of the story would require much work from both of us. The $5,000 advance we would split between us. With his share Bill would do all the research, sending me the material in Taos where I would write the book.

A couple of weeks later Bill and Jeanie set forth on a combination research and honeymoon trip, and stopped off in New Mexico to see me. I met them at the airport in Albuquerque and drove them up to Taos. Bill had spared no expense in outfitting them both in new clothes, packed in so many bags, suitcases, hat and shoe boxes that I could hardly squeeze them into the back of my old Ford coupe. All went well on the long drive until we came to the steep grade up from Pilar. The overloaded car simply couldn't make it. Bill was forced to unload his 250 pounds and walk up the final hill of a horseshoe curve. In Taos, I wanted to drive them up into a couple of mountain canyons to see the high aspens turning yellow. Bill promptly balked, afraid of being stuck again. Also he was eager to get along with their trip. So I soon drove them back to Albuquerque and saw them away on the plane.

The first leg of his journey was down South to research the background of the Confederate States during the Civil War and their desperate need to stop the flow of whale oil that lighted the Union's cities, supplied its factories and ships, and greased the wheels of its supply trains and ammunition wagons. Now from the Confederate Museum and historical papers at Richmond, Virginia, there began to come to me copies of official documents and reports, commissioned officer rolls of the Confederate States Navy, the personal account of the voyage of the *Shenandoah* by its executive officer, and a photograph of the actual flag carried at the peak of the ship. Not content with this, Bill sent me descriptions and photographs of many great plantation homes.

From Richmond the Branches flew north to the old home ports of the whaling fleet. From the Bourne Whaling Museum in New Bedford, Massachusetts, the Peabody Museum in Salem, and from Mystic, Connecticut, he sent me blueprints of whaling ships, handbooks on sailing vessels, and logs of voyages. And still more material flowed in from the century-old Boston marine house of James Bliss & Company, and the public library in New York.

Topping off all this information, I received an old map of Honolulu, a guidebook to Iolani Palace, and a history of Hawaii and its native rulers from Kamehameha I to Lilioukalani. What a thorough research scholar Bill was! We had collected enough material for a documentary history. And what an exploit it was, this fabulous 58,000-mile voyage of a single Confederate ship following the route of the Union's whaling fleet down the Atlantic, around the Horn to the rendezvous at Honolulu, and up into the Arctic where it destroyed thirty-two vessels and captured thirty-eight of the fleet. Virtually unknown, buried in the musty files of a tragic Lost Cause, it proved that fact is stranger than fiction.

Utterly fascinated by it, I spent the winter retracing the voyage of the *Shenandoah* in my home, eight thousand feet high in the Sangre de Cristo mountains of New Mexico. While a blizzard hurled snow against the windowpane, I saw outside the great ocean waves breaking against the bow of the ship. Mountain pines were transformed into tropical palms. What a lot I learned about the migration routes of whales. I began to feel more comfortable aboard ship, walking to the bow and stern instead of to the front and back. But how to write this as a fictional romance posed difficulties. Bill, upon returning home, sent me the outline of two love affairs, and kept sending suggestions for new characters, scenes, and events. Some of these were too outrageously contrived, too old-fashioned. And I became aware that he, as all writers, had distinctive personal likes and predilections that were reflected in his stories. For one thing, he had an ankle fetish. He characterized a woman by a well-turned ankle. Not a beautiful face or gorgeous hair, not even a silken leg or dimpled knee. Only the glimpse of a neat ankle protruding from her skirts. None of his characters were drawn in the round. They were either villainously bad, or nobly good. His forte was contriving romantic encounters to maintain suspense and keep the story line progressing. If one could only make the improbable seem possible, the implausible sound convincing!

By spring I had finished the novel, and took the manuscript to him in Hollywood. We went through it carefully, cutting and rewriting, and sent it to Farrar in New York. The novel was published in 1948, followed by a Dell paperback edition, a British edition, and a French translation.

But in Hollywood the wind had changed. The MGM producers had lost interest in the story by now, and simply wrote off the negligible advance paid us. A few years later another company produced a picture under the title *Diamond Head.* The story was entirely different, and it was obvious the producers were trying to cash in on the reader audience provided by the success of our own novel under the same title. There was nothing we could do about it; titles, unlike stories, cannot be copyrighted.

The failure of MGM to produce the film was disastrous for Bill. He had put all his best efforts for several years into *Diamond Head;* and without income from other stories, he was running short of money. Jeanie had given birth to a baby daughter—this with the upkeep of his large house was incurring expenses he couldn't meet. Aside from this expedient problem was the more serious problem of his career as a Hollywood filmwriter. The Gold Rush days were over, when a freelance writer like Bill could sell stories offhand to any studio. The big studios were becoming more particular, putting under contract the authors of best-selling books which had established wide reader audiences. It mattered little what the subjects were. Successive staff writers could convert them into some sort of film. Bill, as I have said, had never been content to be a staff scriptwriter. Nor with his innate dramatic instinct, directional ability, and theatrical background had he followed the customary rise in the movie industry from writer to director to producer, combining and utilizing all these interwoven functions. Why? Simply, as he told me, because he refused to get up in the morning and punch a time clock. He was a free man, a creative writer, able to work when and how he chose.

But times were changing. Hollywood itself was changing. And public tastes were changing. Romantic love stories were no longer the fashion, even with Clark Gable in the leading role. The film stories were more realistic, had a sharper, harder line. And in this emerging new era Bill desperately needed a production from a major studio to re-establish if not insure his standing. *Diamond Head* did not provide it. To the contrary, it signaled the end of his filmwriting career.

In a last-ditch struggle against the inevitable, he sketched out a couple of excellent, timely stories, and I developed them into narrative outlines that aroused no interest. Then I returned to Taos to resume my own work. My movie fling was over, like those of so many lost souls trudging up and down Hollywood Boulevard, the Street of Heartbreaks, hoping to discover the pot of gold at the end of the rainbow.

Not for several years did I see Bill again. He had sold his big house on the hillside for a nominal sum, and it had just been resold for an unbelievably higher price. Jeanie and his daughter he had moved into a comfortable apartment in a street below it. He himself was installed in a nearby apartment where he could work undisturbed. One of its rooms he had converted into a library holding his thousands of books. Here, day after day, he sat smoking his favorite Dunhill tobacco. It came in small round tins, which he ordered by the carton. His hat still had a feather stuck in its band. He wore the same English tweed jacket with leather-patched sleeves. And he was still creating those wonderful adventure-romances which had once made him professionally famous and now were disregarded.

Shortly afterward Jeanie collapsed from a sudden fatal heart attack. Where Bill found a home for his daughter I don't know. When I visited him sometime later, he had given up Hollywood and was working as a public relations consultant for a large manufacturing company up in San Fernando Valley. During the evening I spent with him in his apartment nearby, he showed me some of the brochures and publicity releases he was writing. Photographs of the plant and its products, descriptions extolling their excellence. Sales pitches in technical jargon. Unbelievably dull. He had aged, his hair had thinned, his face seemed drawn. Only his blue eyes still contained their twinkle.

"Not as exciting as rafting logs down the Mississippi, or dancing at the Royal Hawaiian Ball given by King Kamehameha in his palace, is it?"

"And I don't see any trim ankles peeking out from petticoats," I ventured.

He let out a booming laugh. "Well, they were good tries even though our sails were shot down, hey!"

That was the last time I ever saw him.

Several years later, however, he telephoned me at Fort Collins where he had tracked me down during the time I was teaching a course in Western American Literature at Colorado State University. He was in Boston, working on public relations for another company of some kind. That, he said, was immaterial. What he had in mind was a truly great project that would benefit the whole country and make us famous, perhaps infamous. His voice was vibrant and enthusiastic. The project was a book that would be an indictment of American medical practices. It would be based on an actual case history, with full documentation. Ignoring my objections, he mailed me the bulky manuscript that had been brought him.

The details of the case I don't remember now. It involved a wealthy and evidently brilliant businessman, whose wife had become seriously ill and was taken to a leading hospital. Here she soon died, apparently due to incorrect treatment of her illness. Subsequently, her husband investigated every aspect of the case. All this material, fully documented, he recorded in the lengthy manuscript he had given Bill, asking him to find a writer to prepare it as a book for publication.

The case was shocking, indeed, and it aroused my full sympathy. Yet for many reasons it was a project I could not tackle. I so telephoned Bill and returned the manuscript. He was disappointed, but I thought not too surprised; and we parted with the hope that someday we could get together again.

With mixed feelings, I hung up the telephone receiver. How could Bill, after his years of writing romance-adventure yarns, have been drawn into such a sad, horribly realistic exposé of American medical practices—if indeed a publisher could be found for the book? And how miserable he must be punching a time clock and grinding out dull publicity releases in cold and conservative Boston, so far away from the bright lights and tinsel wrappings of Hollywood. Yet Bill was still Bill, forever an entrepreneur attuned to high drama, with sympathy and love for people of every kind. Perhaps his own disappointments, disillusions, and sufferings had widened his perception of the misfortunes and tragedies suffered everywhere, even in Boston.

That telephone call was my last contact with him. When he died I don't know. I mourn his passing as a close friend and co-worker whose jovial companionship long gave me enjoyment and enriched my life.

14

June in January

(Editorial—January 26, 1950)

As if lending her efforts to rejuvenate an old song in this season of hit-tune revivals, Mother Nature has crossed up the weather forecasters and surprised us with a bit of June in January.

All last week we strutted around in shirt-sleeves. Mama was able to catch up with the wash, and aired the blankets in the hot sun. Red-breasted robins in red willows were betrayed into prematurely voicing the rites of spring. Even a few surviving flies awakened to buzz against warm windowpanes. Symptoms of spring fever broke out up and down the Rio Grande.

Drily giving credence to these undisputed miracles, the weather bureau officially announced that the temperature of sixty degrees in Santa Fe last Friday set a record for the warmest January 20 since 1879.

We aren't going out on a limb to insist that it will last. But for the brief period of revival, we can safely hum it's June in January, ta-da-ta-dum, in tune with all nature and the weather.

15

Women Who Have
Influenced Me Most

(Speech presented at a luncheon honoring Colorado College's Women's Educational Society on September 23, 1988)

TODAY Colorado College is celebrating the one hundredth year of its Women's Educational Society under the theme of "Women Helping Women." It's about time women begin to help themselves, instead of continually caring for others.

Some years ago I wrote the biography of the little wife of a stalwart six-shooter marshal of Tombstone. *Time Magazine* in its review of the book included a photo of her. The caption read: "The woman behind the man behind the gun." It seems appropriate that today I express my debt to the women who have influenced me most with a similar thought: "The women behind the man behind my pen."

My Mother—May Ione Dozier Waters

As portrayed in my Colorado trilogy, *Pike's Peak,* Mother was the eldest of six sisters and a brother; she was therefore expected to take care of them all. To everyone's surprise, she married late in life and for a few years experienced happiness in her own home on El Paso Street here in Colorado Springs across from the Santa Fe Railroad embankment, which was later something of a slum area but has since been spruced up.

After my father died when I was twelve, we moved into my grandfather's nearby house at 435 East Bijou Street. My divorced Aunt Matt also left her two small children here while she ran candy stores in a succession of mining towns in the Rocky Mountains. Thus Mother had to raise Aunt Matt's children, my younger sister, and I; care for my grand-parents; and do most of the work in the ungainly three-story house. She never remarried, devoting much of the rest of her life to unremitting drudgery.

I remember her unceasing love, devotion, and tolerance. We loved her but took her for granted. Not until after her death have I appreciated her great, lasting influence upon me.

The historic plaque now on the door of that house should read, "A crazy family once lived here."

My Teacher—Miss Ruth Jocelyn Wattles

When I was thirteen or fourteen, Miss Wattles helped me write my first published story, for *Columbia Sayings and Doings,* our little school paper. We pupils at Columbia Grade School, which my grandfather had built, were an unruly lot. Miss Wattles didn't discipline us. But if we behaved all day, she would read us stories from the mythologies of all countries. Alternating with these she read excerpts of letters from her cousin, the wife of a trader on the remote Navajo Reservation. A few years later Miss Wattles had them published in *Harper's* magazine, then as a book under the title *Desert Wife* by her cousin Hilda Faunce. In 1981 I had the privilege of writing the introduction for a new printing of this book.

Miss Wattles later taught English at Colorado State University until she died. While I was teaching there in 1966, I called on her. When she opened the door, I said to her, "Why, Miss Wattles. You haven't changed a bit in fifty-four years!" She quickly replied, "You haven't either, Frank, but now you're wearing long pants!"

She was a loved friend and a great teacher, who introduced me to mythology—a wonderful world frequently unknown to young people nowadays with their television stories of sex and violence. And Miss Wattles started me on my writing career, such as it has been.

My Sister—Naomi Dozier Arnell

I could never repay the debt I owe Naomi for her love, constant encouragement, and lasting influence.

She, my brother-in-law, Carl, and my little niece, Susie, lived in Los Angeles during the many years I was moving to one town after another in the Southwest, living in cheap motels and makeshift bed-rooms, doing research, and writing most of my published books. I wrote the earlier ones in ink on yellow, blue, or green legal-size paper, which I found easier on my eyes. As I finished each chapter, I sent it to Naomi to type and keep until the book was completed. She would then mail the manuscript back to me for editing before I sent it with a devout prayer to a publisher.

Every one of my books was an immediate flop. Not until later did they gain a measure of attention and were translated into several other languages. Naomi was never discouraged by their initial failures, and her constant encouragement kept me writing. She was a small, fey woman with remarkable intuitions. She gave me sound advice, and edi-torial help. I often felt that without her, I would never write another book. All this, of course, was in addition to our personal relationship. From childhood, we were always very close, as I was later with Carl and Susie. Tragically for us, Naomi died in 1969, leaving us with her enduring influence.

67

Women Who Have Influenced Me Most

My Friend—Mabel Dodge Luhan

Hers was a familiar name in America and Europe when I first came to Taos, New Mexico, almost fifty years ago. Everybody seemed to know the facts of Mabel's life—as a hostess in her villa in Italy and her salon in New York, her relationships with four husbands and several lovers, and her unaccountable move to the backward village of Taos where she married Tony Lujan, a Taos Pueblo Indian wearing hair braids and a blanket. Here she built a twenty-three-room house on the edge of the reservation.

Mabel wrote it all in her four volumes of *Intimate Memories*, em-bellished by public gossip and controversy. The consensus was that she was a willful, selfish, and capricious woman.

I was hesitant to meet such a famous woman when I was taken to a large party she was giving for a hundred guests in her Big House. Our meeting dispelled my uneasiness. A rather short and compactly built woman in her fifties, she greeted me with warm friendliness and the loveliest voice I've ever heard. Tony and I hit it off at once. Thus began our intimate friendship that lasted until their deaths almost twenty-five years later.

I lived in two of their smaller houses or "studios" for short periods, drove with them to Mexico where I had been before, visited them in New York, and saw them in Los Angeles while I was living there. Among her few close friends Mabel was warm and generous. She was immune to opinions of others, and had the knack of always putting her worst foot forward among them.

Tony was like an elder brother to me, or a ceremonial uncle, in the Indian way. What bound me to Mabel, this sophisticated woman of the world, I don't know. She enlarged my perspective as a regional Westerner by introducing me to men and women who had achieved fame in all fields, opening a world of wealth and power. "Take a good look at it," she told me. "It's falling to pieces. I know. I was part of it."

She devoutly believed that Western civilization could be transformed by adopting the inner values of Indian society, a belief that was widely ridiculed. Searching for her own inner values, she had collected a great library of books on philosophy, psychology, and religion, some of which she gave me to read. "But don't believe any of them," she cautioned me. "You've got to discover your own inner self." Mabel was not an intellectual; she probably didn't understand all the books she read. But independently convinced fifty years ago that our civilization was dying, she was hunting the roots of her own being.

It was this look at the great materialistic world of crumbling wealth and power, and the greater inner world, that expanded my own limited perspective and influenced me permanently.

Mabel died in 1962 at the age of eighty-three, and was buried in Taos's historic Kit Carson Cemetery. Tony died a year later. His own Indian people carried his body from the hospital to the Pueblo graveyard; I was the only Anglo to attend his burial. Wrapped in his Chief blanket, his best beaded moccasins on his feet, his body was simply lowered into his Mother Earth.

My Neighbor—Mrs. Alicia Quintana

In contrast to Mabel was Mrs. Quintana, my close neighbor in the little Hispanic village of Arroyo Seco, on the slope of the mountains above Taos.

When I bought my old adobe and fifteen acres of land in 1947, I was the only Anglo resident here. Mrs. Quintana was the undisputed matriarch of Arroyo Seco. Largely through her influence I was accepted in the community. Her husband was a teacher, as she had been, and later a sheepherder grazing his flock in the mountain valleys above us. Her three sons were strong and muscular, but Mrs. Quintana outworked them all, including her daughters. During the years I lived here alone, she looked after me with care and devotion. She always addressed me as "Mr. Waters," as I called her "Mrs. Quintana."

I think she could never understand why a man would spend most of the day pecking at a maquina in the house. A man's place was outdoors all day.

I could tell stories about her, her customs, her kindnesses, her belief in brujas or witches, for the rest of the afternoon. But some of these have been written in one of my books, so there's no need to repeat them. The Quintanas probably could write a better book about me! One amusing incident I will recount.

The mountain canyons behind our fields and pastures used to be full of deer. Mrs. Quintana's menfolk ignored the state game laws restricting hunting to a specified open season. All the year around a haunch of deer could be found at their house, and I was often given a venison roast to marinate. One day an Anglo stranger knocked on Mrs. Quintana's door. When she opened it, he asked, "Is this the house of the man who wrote *The Man Who Killed the Deer?*"

Mrs. Quintana didn't know that one of my books bears this title. And her main language is Spanish. She thought a policeman had come to arrest the man who had killed a deer out of season. Hastily denying that the lawbreaker was one of her family, she slammed the door after him. Then she hurried to carry the freshly skinned carcass of a deer to her back pasture, where she burned it.

Mrs. Quintana is a descendent of the Martinez family who once owned the enormous Martinez Grant awarded to the first Spanish settlers in Taos Valley. Overtly she betrays no sign of her aristocratic heritage, but carries on the traditional life that has enabled her people to endure centuries of isolation in the wilderness. She used to make her own soap in a great kettle, bake her own bread in a woodstove, grow and preserve her own fruits and vegetables.

Today, at ninety-three, she still works in the garden and tends to her large flock of chickens. Whenever I sit at my maquina daydreaming of fame and fortune and a thousand things I don't need or really want, the sight of her coming in the door jerks me back down to the eternal living earth of which she—and all of us—are a part.

My Wife—Barbara

In looking back over the years, it seems that at every stage of my life a woman has been there to aid my slow growth toward maturity of heart and mind. These I've mentioned are only isolated examples.

I have saved these few remarks about my wife, Barbara, to the last. Not only because she is the last one chronologically, but because she has most nurtured my delayed development.

I am somewhat leery of appearing to be a husband singing sentimental praises of his wife, so I'm a little reluctant to talk about her. She is here; and when you meet her, she will speak for herself. In the meantime, I'll be as objective as I can.

For all her youthful appearance, Barbara is the mother of two grown sons from a former marriage, and grandmother of two. Bursting with vitality, she loves to hike and ride horseback in the mountains and desert. With plants, birds, wild animals, rattlesnakes, our own horses, dogs, and cats she has a rare affinity. This earthy quality of course endears her to Mrs. Quintana, who taught her to roast green chiles in a woodstove oven.

The physical help Barbara gives me daily is immeasurable. She is my right leg, left eye, and my guilty conscience. But she has another side, mental and spiritual, which is more significant.

For many years Barbara taught English to high school juniors and seniors, has a B.A. degree, and an M.A. in journalism. This enabled her to help me in typing and editing my own manuscripts and reading galley proofs. Her own writing of books for young people reflects her love of animals, a high sense of humor, and imagination. I'm looking forward to their eventual publication.

Since retiring from teaching, she has just graduated with another M.A. from a small select psychotherapy program at the University of Arizona. This two-year course was arduous and comprehensive, involving studies in physiology and all major psychologies, and personal counseling of nearly one hundred clients. Her final dissertation comprised over two hundred pages, which some day will be published. How she ever managed this press of work, in addition to cooking meals and doing housework, I don't know.

Barbara is now beginning her private practice. Her special field will interest you members of the Women's Educational Society—to help women regain their self-esteem. As I mentioned in my talk last evening, our society has always regarded women as inferior. Only fairly recently have women asserted their natural equality with men on all levels. Yet there still are numbers of divorced women, single mothers, and widows who are destitute and untrained for jobs, have lost their sense of self-worth, and are desperately seeking help.

The effect of this misguided view has been just as disastrous to men. As a Westerner brought up on the belief of male supremacy—like "the man behind the gun" I mentioned earlier, who ignored the woman behind or beside him—I did not acknowledge the influence of women. A woman's proper place was in the bedroom and the kitchen. And I was taught to repress any displays of the so-called feminine qualities of love, tenderness, and compassion in my own dual nature. It just wasn't manly.

Barbara today is patiently unlocking these hidden qualities in me with her love and daily care, expanding my inner perspective and spiritual growth.

So let me proudly introduce her to you now. My admiration embraces not only my wife, but all women, everywhere.

16

Amazing Mabel

(Foreword to the 1996 first edition of Amazing Mabel:
Sketches by Mabel Dodge Luhan)

I AM indebted to Forrest Fenn for sharing with me samples of Mabel
Luhan's sketches. They are a great surprise. In all the time I knew her,
I didn't know she was doing these truthful and spontaneous drawings.
Her notes and letters possessed these same qualities, however, and in
the same way, she used to surprise her friends by her selection of dinner guests, invitations to call at the house, selection of places to go on
her daily rides. As in her art and writing, her choices seemed spontaneous, depending upon her mood.

Mabel had a quick, observant eye and an artist's hand. These
sketches reveal also the wide interest she took in all types of persons. A
major aspect of her personality resonated to people.

Mabel's chief role was that of catalyst. As a celebrated hostess at the
Villa Curonia in Florence, in her salon at 23 Fifth Avenue in New York,
at Croton-on-Hudson, and in her Big House in Taos, she displayed
her talent for drawing together anarchists and artists, business and political figures, psychologists, columnists, novelists, dancers, actors, so-
cialites, strikers, and muckrakers—the most disparate persons
imaginable. If the object of bringing them together, her "compulsion
to meddle" in other people's lives, was to see what happened, many
things did. Curious friendships and new bursts of creativity resulted as
well as divorces and feuds.

Yet Mabel was not a social butterfly flitting aimlessly from one
gathering to another. One sensed her growing awareness of the world
in which she had been trying to play a part and always feeling unre-

lated, "a world that was on a decline so rapid one could see people one knew dropping to pieces day by day, a dying world with no one appearing to save it, a decadent, unhappy world where the bright, hot, rainbow flashes of corruption were the only light high spots."

She began to feel that the European-American civilization of which she was an inherent part, with its false values and superficial attitudes, its greed and corruption, had reached a dead end like other civilizations of the past. As she confided to me, she had resolved to record it fully, as in Proust's vast *Remembrance of Things Past,* without sparing her personal experiences. This, to me, was an illuminating statement of purpose. It revealed that the four published volumes of the *Intimate Memories* were more than the casual jottings of an egotistical exhibitionist, which was how they were regarded by some. Her drawings, too, can be viewed as part of this ambitious endeavor fully to report her time.

In *Edge of Taos Desert* Mabel comments on one facet of her involvement with others: "In order to lose the sense of death and isolation that was my solitary mode of being, how often I had flung myself into fictitious relationships in order to escape the conviction that I was nothing in myself! I had called it love, when at its best it had been a certain chemical magnetism motivated by curiosity, the curiosity of the damned seeking the chance of salvation. This combination of magnetism and curiosity was a potent one. It had enabled me to know and understand people."

Taos was always slightly in awe of Mabel. More than anyone else—including the Chamber of Commerce—she established the town's international fame by drawing to it a continual stream of famous persons from all walks of life throughout this country and Europe. This small backward village took on a cosmopolitan tinge. One could meet here notable figures impossible to meet in the many closed circles in New York.

Mabel had no interest in people of the so-called middle class, only in the rich and notable and the talented artists and in the poorer Indians and Hispanic residents. Her close friends included the old gambler and stage driver John Dunn; Ralph Meyers, the noted Indian trader; and Eve and John Young-Hunter, the Scottish portrait artist. And every year she gave a tea party for the aging old-timers in town.

Her frequent large parties in the Big House were great events.

House and grounds swarmed with guests. In the big tiled dining room was seated an orchestra of Hispanic musicians. Outside on the flagstone *portal,* Indians danced to the beat of a belly-drum. Ample drinks and food were served by attendants. Guests included visiting notables, all the artists in town, Hispanic and Indian friends. Not invited were members of the business community, town officials, and merchants. Their omission aroused a deep, repressed resentment, which in later years emerged in a movement to run a proposed bypass through her property, destroying her own Big House. This did not take place, fortunately.

In her later years when I knew her, Mabel always perversely put her worst foot forward, adding to the gossip about her. Only her close friends knew her less obvious virtues. She was as generous and thoughtful as she was willful and selfish. She was noted for placing a high priority on advancement of the arts. Her public gifts of a large tract of land and a hospital, along with a collection of Persian miniature paintings, Hispanic *santos,* and several thousand rare, first-edition and popular books to the Harwood Library, as well as a bandstand in the plaza, were well known. Few knew of the money, food, clothing, and personal help she constantly gave to those in need. As Claire Morrill reported, "Her reticence was somehow reserved for her virtues."

Mabel was too many persons in one for others to find a common denominator. She was a woman whose complexity roused storms of controversy throughout her life, but whose private virtues have outlasted her public faults in the memories of those who loved her and knew her best. This collection of her sketches will most certainly increase our respect and continuing interest in the woman who was Taos's most famous person in her time, a writer, an artist, and a friend.

17
Time for Staying Still

(Editorial—December 22, 1949)

Now being observed at Taos Pueblo is the Time for Staying Still. In accordance with tradition, all the people move back into the Pueblo from their summer homes in the fields. The plaza is barred to ironshod hoofs and wagon-wheels. There must be no noisy sweeping, no wood-chopping within the walls. It is the interregnum between the annual death and rebirth of Our Mother Earth, a period of quiet gestation.

We need not stretch our imaginations too much to conjure the benefits to the world at large if we too observed such a tradition. Not for forty days. But for only one hour.

What devilish havoc that hour might play with our illusion that we are controlling the stream of life! The competitive scramble for wealth and power stopped. Cars stalled on the highways. Trains dead on their tracks. Lights, radios, and power turned off, crowds immobile on street corners. Congressmen holding their tongues for once. Soviet leader Vishinsky frozen in a tirade. The United Nations caught like a cold congregation in the middle of a preacher's prayer.

Yet for that hour the illusion of our egotistic self-importance would be dispelled. We might feel in the stillness the swish of our earth-planet rotating about its axis at the rate of one thousand miles an hour, and revolving around the sun twenty miles per second. There might come to us the deeper rhythm of our solar system moving within the immensities of interstellar space. In the ghastly silence we might hear the crash of falling snowflakes, the roar of sap running through cold trees, the terrified shrieks of our imprisoned consciences. We might even become aware, in 1949, that mankind is still dependent for survival upon ancient verities not controlled by our technological sciences.

It always has been in such individual Times of Staying Still that there have come to all the creative personalities of history the intimations of the great religions, philosophies, and world-movements which have benefited mankind. It was at such a time, nearly two thousand years ago, that there appeared to three lone wayfarers on a desolate December plain that star of faith which we have followed since.

Out of another Time for Staying Still as our neighbors observe here, there will appear again perhaps a new symbolic star, that renewed faith for which we all are seeking to lead us through the ever-noisier, ever-faster ensuing Atomic Age.

18

The Manby Mystery

(Essay)

THAT Manby! He enacted for us in his life the great myth of all
America and with his death left an unsolved mystery. Woven from the
spirit and texture of the land itself, our own greed and fears, his story
is as relevant today as when I first heard it many years ago. Even now,
after having written a book about his incredible life and mysterious
death, I find in it a disturbing element of the unknown that exists in
us all.

When I first arrived in Taos, Manby was the prime subject of
wild conjectures at dinner tables, bars, and street corners. A few years
before, on July 3, 1929, his headless body had been discovered in his
nineteen-room hacienda near the central plaza. The gate in the high
adobe wall was locked and bolted from inside. So was the door to his
bedroom. Inside on a cot lay the old man's decapitated body. Crouching on the floor was his German police dog, Lobo. The investigating
group of men, who had gained entrance to the house through the back
patio, then discovered Manby's head in another bedroom down the
hall. Most of the face was obliterated.

A coroner's jury immediately pronounced that Manby had died
from natural causes and that Lobo had gnawed off his master's head.
Within an hour the group had placed the head and torso in a wooden
box and buried it at the back of his property.

This did not settle the matter. Pertinent questions were being
asked. If the dissolute old recluse had been murdered, as seemed likely,
how had his murderer entered the house through the locked gate and
bedroom door, and how had the door been locked from the inside
when he left? Was it possible that Lobo had chewed off Manby's head

and carried it to another room? Some persons claimed that the body found was not Manby's; he had substituted another body and disappeared. Others swore they had seen Manby after his alleged body had been buried. One reliable artist was positive he had seen Manby during a visit to Italy.

All this persistent speculation led to an official investigation, with international complications, authorized by Governor Dillon of New Mexico. The background facts it unearthed hit front pages from New York to Los Angeles: theft of a large Spanish land grant, a legal contract drawn for the disposal of $827,000,000, a suit for breach of promise, a secret society terrorizing the town, and three more unsolved murders. Detective Martin in charge summarized his findings in a report to the governor. He stated that Manby had been murdered and named four chief suspects. "I do not see any mystery to the A. R. Manby case. If less publicity, less talk, and more work was done, the guilty party could be brought to justice without much time." With his report he submitted a bill of $750 for his services and incurred expenses to date. Inexplicably, Governor Dillon dropped the case, and Detective Martin was never paid.

Evidently more was involved than Manby's murder. Rumors and speculation continued in Taos for a time, then suddenly stopped. Spud Johnson in his little weekly news sheet, *The Horsefly*, ventured some comments of his own. Next morning he found under his door a scribbled note reading, "Keep your nose out of the Manby business if you know what's good for you." Obviously there were persons in town who meant to keep hidden the truth of Manby's murder. Nevertheless, it still cast a dark and silent shadow over the poor Hispanic villagers, the Indians at the Pueblo, Anglo merchants and artists alike. All, in some way, had been involved in Manby's incredible life and mysterious death.

Not until 1960 did I undertake to clear up for myself some of its puzzling ramifications. Little was known about Manby. A few magazine articles and a chapter in a book of unsolved murders had been written; all proved to be inaccurate. Dr. Myra Ellen Jenkins, head of the New Mexico State Archives, had given several talks, mainly about Manby's unscrupulous legal and business dealings, but knew nothing about his personal life. And that was all. It was clear that my task would demand research on the course of his entire life, and documentation of each fact unearthed.

I began the task slowly and with caution, remembering the note Spud Johnson had found under his door. My part-time research took nearly twelve years. The book I wrote from it, I realized at once, could not be cast in the form of a novel. The source material was too astounding and bizarre to be believed as fiction. It had to be presented as a factual, documented biography of Arthur Rochford Manby, son of a country squire and church rector in Morecambe, England.

Immigrating to America in 1883, at the age of twenty-four, Manby arrived in the Territory of New Mexico. Here he bought four sections of land in Vermejo Park, which lay in the wilderness of the immense, historic Maxwell Land Grant. Sending for his two brothers, he began raising cattle. They were not popular with their neighbors in the settlement of Castle Rock. One morning, in a quarrel over water rights, Manby and his brother Jocelyn shot and killed Dan Griffin. Both were indicted for murder. While awaiting trial, the controversy over the ownership of the Maxwell Land Grant came to a head. The Maxwell Land Grant Company was fraudulently claiming two million acres, and preparing to evict all settlers as trespassers. It induced the governor to organize a militia armed with eviction orders. The force was captained by Jim Masterson, brother of the already infamous Bat Masterson, a trigger-happy crony of Wyatt Earp in Tombstone, Arizona. Sending for more gunmen from Dodge City, he marched them into Raton to terrorize the citizens who resented the Company's eviction of settlers.

Manby allied himself with Masterson's gang as they rioted down the street, breaking store windows, assaulting men, and terrifying women and children. Early next morning Raton citizens organized a force of six hundred vigilantes, who captured all of Masterson's gang and marched them to the Colorado line with orders never to come back. Manby and two other members of the militia were excepted as they were bona fide residents of New Mexico. Manby claimed that he was out of town during the rioting; but George Curry, who later was elected governor of New Mexico, positively identified him as a member of Masterson's militia.

Things quieted down, and Manby and his brother Jocelyn were brought to trial for the killing of Griffin. Manby's alliance with the forces of the Maxwell Land Grant stood him in good stead. He secured its chief lawyer, Thomas Benton Catron, to defend them. Catron was the most powerful figure in the Territory: United States attorney general for New Mexico, head of the Santa Fe Ring which exercised political domination over all New Mexico, and owner of all or parts of thirty-one land grants stolen from their Spanish or Mexican grantees. The outcome of the trial was never in doubt. Manby and his brother were pronounced not guilty.

Manby's first two years in New Mexico were an auspicious beginning of his career. He had killed his first man and had been exonerated. He had learned how easy it was in this lawless land to give vent to the violence and will to power within him. And more important, he had learned from the immense Maxwell Land Grant where power and money lay. In land! In millions of acres to be seized if one knew how.

Done with ranching, he moved up into the mining district of Moreno Valley. Here, with Jocelyn and his partner, he filed on four mining claims. Then, in a trip down to Taos, he heard of an old Spanish land grant nearby, which had been given in 1716 to Antonio Martinez in accordance with the will of His Majesty, the King of Spain. Ownership of the old grant had been ignored until 1848 when Mexico, which had achieved its independence from Spain, was forced to cede all New Mexico to the United States. The Congress in 1891 then established a Court of Private Land Claims to determine the validity of the grants. A court hearing in Santa Fe had just been concluded, Manby heard. Four men had showed up to claim the old grant for sixty-eight heirs of Antonio Martinez. The judges ruled that they had no definite proof that they were the rightful heirs. Moreover, no one knew how large the grant was; although it was believed to comprise some sixty-one thousand acres, its boundaries were uncertain. Hence until all these facts were known, the court could not confirm the title.

Manby immediately hired a horse and rode out to the grant. It lay not far away, an immense expanse of sagebrush stretching from the Rio Grande on the west to the Sangre de Cristo Mountains on the north and east. Within it lived the alleged Spanish heirs of Antonio Martinez in a couple of bedraggled villages, Arroyo Hondo and Arroyo Seco, which had been founded in 1745. The Antonio Martinez Grant! Sixty-one thousand acres or more of beautiful, unclaimed wilderness, his for the taking. The kingdom he had come to America to win.

This was the major turning in Manby's life, the focus of all his efforts for the next twenty-two years. The methods by which he acquired the land were ruthless, devious, and corrupt. He persuaded the county treasurer to put up for sale 25,400 acres for delinquent taxes. This tract—one-fourth of the whole grant—Manby obtained for $179.24. It was just as easy to obtain from storekeepers in town the names of poor Hispanic farmers and sheepherders who owed unpaid bills for supplies. He would then go to them, say he had paid the bills, and threaten to put them in jail unless they repaid him with their land. By enlisting the aid of an unscrupulous judge, manipulating the uninformed county officials, and constantly harassing the poor Hispanic settlers, he gradually increased his holdings.

Meanwhile, he built a large nineteen-room adobe hacienda and began buying other property in town. Sending to London for his oldest brother, Eardley, a retired major in the British army, Manby showed him the land he was acquiring—bigger than the boroughs of Morecambe, Lancaster, and the valley of the Lune. A virtual empire with gold, timber, grazing, and farmlands. The major was impressed, loaned him money, and promised to raise more in England.

During this time Manby began to court a young Hispanic girl named Circilia, daughter of the aristocratic Juan de los Reyes Santistevan. Don Juan, the most influential merchant in Taos, had established the only bank in the county and had served twice in the state legislatures. Unfortunately, he was now deeply in debt and appealed for help to Manby, whom he viewed as a future son-in-law. Manby advised him to go into bankruptcy and to turn over all his holdings to him to liquidate. Don Juan accordingly assigned everything he owned to Manby: twenty-one pieces of real estate, store merchandise, twenty thousand head of sheep, seventy-five thousand pounds of wool, and other assets. Manby persuaded nominal friends to appraise all these holdings at the lowest possible value, then put them up for sale and bought them himself through dummy purchasers. Don Juan was ruined, and Circilia dropped from Manby's graces.

Still more money was required to develop the Grant. Manby incorporated the Taos Valley Land Company and began to offer shares to prospective buyers back East. They included Alexander Prescott in Maryland, who came with his wife and daughter to inspect the Grant. Manby promptly fell in love with the sixteen-year-old daughter, Edith S. Prescott, nicknamed Pinky. A month later, in March 1907, they were married. A year later she gave birth to a baby daughter who died soon after birth. Manby was not too disturbed. The Prescotts were clamoring for return of their money. Pinky fled to Colorado. Here in June 1909 she was granted a divorce on grounds of cruelty, with an alimony of $1,700 that Manby never paid.

A few years later Manby fell in love with Miss Margaret Waddell, a cultured Scotswoman who had come to Santa Fe to retire. Manby brought her up to Taos to see his large estate and told her of his plans to erect back of his hacienda a magnificent resort hotel, which would serve all the people he would bring in to settle on the Grant he was developing. He and Miss Waddell became engaged, and she turned over to him some $10,000 of her savings. She also proudly showed him the exquisite trousseau she was having made. Manby did not press the marriage. To hasten building of the resort hotel, Miss Waddell raised more money to give him in return for stock in the venture he promised her. Finally reduced to pawning her mother's jewelry and her own, she filed suit against him for breach of promise and fraudulently obtaining her savings. The suit dragged on for years and was finally dropped at Manby's death.

None of these personal relationships seemed to bother Manby. He was completely engrossed in stalling the Prescotts' demands, combating the suits of other creditors, organizing one land company after another through manipulations of stock, in a legal tangle never completely unraveled. But on May 20, 1913, the day finally came for which he had worked twenty-two years. The court awarded him full ownership of the Antonio Martinez Grant. All his! All 61,605 acres!

Just three years later, on June 6, 1916, he lost it. Overwhelmed as Manby and his many paper companies were by debts that may have totaled anywhere from one-quarter to one-half million dollars, the same court decreed that the Grant be publicly auctioned to the highest bidder—as it was.

From then on until his death or disappearance in 1929, his life became that of a dissolute recluse, his unbalanced mind spinning fantasies which took shape in a secret society that terrorized the town. This, in outline, was the course of Manby's life. Unearthing the details was an exhausting job. Yet it showed me that no man's life can be completely hidden. Everything he does leaves somewhere, somehow, a record of his thought and character that eventually comes to light. I had almost finished my research before learning anything about Manby's background in England. Then I happened to meet Steve Peters, working as a bartender in Santa Fe, who gave me his own notes on the Manby family history. He generously took me to meet Mrs. Edith Kearney, whose grandmother was Manby's sister. Mrs. Kearney gave me a full account and several photographs. How timely! She died shortly after our meeting. I was able, with the help of the English artist Don Perceval, to obtain the family genealogy and marriage and birth certificates from the London General Register Office.

That Manby first had settled on a ranch in Vermejo Park was generally unknown. Not until I talked with Frank "Bunny" Alpers in Cimarron about the Maxwell Land Grant did I learn of the killing of Dan Griffin by Manby and Jocelyn. I found it duly reported in the Raton and Las Vegas newspapers, which gave different dates for the killing. In addition to Manby's published statement at his preliminary hearing, details of the Griffin feud and killing had been presented in full by the defendants and witnesses. The Colfax County Courthouse had a record that this testimony had been filed, but the papers had been stolen. Frank Brookshire, a rancher and close friend of the clerk, managed to obtain for me a copy of the original sixty-page transcript of the case, taken down in early Pitman shorthand. This style of shorthand has been replaced; and after five years' search I was unable to find anyone able to transcribe it, including the Shorthand Reporters Association in Madison, Wisconsin. If ever transcribed, it may reveal a hidden aspect of the case not presented at the trial exonerating Manby and Jocelyn.

Documenting Manby's acquisition of the Grant was of course the most tedious job. It involved tracing down patents, warranty, mortgage, quit claim and receivers' deeds, titles, certificates of incorporation, public notices, receipts, powers of attorney, contracts, and promissory notes. All these were transcribed in ink in great, musty, leather-bound books of official records kept in the vaults of the old Taos County courthouse. Without the help of Milton Spotts and Robert Montoya, accomplished abstractors, it would have been impossible to find them.

Manby's theft of the relatively small Antonio Martinez Grant throws into focus the usurpation of 275 other Spanish and Mexican land grants after the Territory of New Mexico had been annexed by the United States in 1848. Ownership of the land was assured to the grantees and their descendents by the Treaty of Guadalupe Hidalgo, which guaranteed that the property of Mexican citizens would be "inviolably respected." Hence a Court of Private Land Claims was established to investigate all claims. Some sixty-four land grants comprising some nine million acres were confirmed by Congress, and eighty-two New Mexico grants embracing almost two million acres were confirmed by the Court of Private Land Claims. But with American occupancy came a horde of greedy land speculators, cattle and railroad companies, and unscrupulous lawyers and politicians, who took over the land.

Not until recently has this history of chicanery been exposed by Malcolm Ebright's Center for Land Grant Studies. Its first comprehensive study details the way the great Tierra Amarilla Land Grant of 584,515 acres was stolen from its real owners, the pioneer grantees. Studies of other grants are under way.

This wholesale theft of land from its Spanish owners had its national parallel in the Anglo-American march of empire from the Atlantic to the Pacific when all Indian tribes were dispossessed of their homelands and herded into reservations. During recent years a federal Indian Claims Commission has awarded millions of dollars to many tribes in reparation for lands illegally taken from them. Mr. Ebright suggests the establishment of a Hispanic Claims Commission to make restitution to grant owners in New Mexico.

With the ever-increasing population, nothing of course can be done about the land itself. Land, the ultimate source of our wealth, our very existence, is becoming ever more scarce and expensive. Yet it is still being exploited by powerful private interests with the backing of federal agencies. Manby is still alive today in the swarm of real estate hustlers in his lost kingdom and all Taos County, putting Manby's methods to shame.

Seen in this larger perspective, it is not remarkable that Manby was a transplanted Englishman who carried on the tradition of his countrymen. For it was the Anglo, more than the Spanish, French, and Portuguese, who began to possess the land from the day the first Pilgrim Fathers stepped down from Plymouth Rock. An impoverished people suffering feudal restrictions, they viewed America as a vast expanse of free land for them to take and colonize, giving birth to the richest, most powerful, and most materialistic nation on earth, and to the myth that dominates it today—that property rights must take supersedence over all human rights. This is the great myth that Manby personalized for us in his time.

Yet he held high hopes of colonizing his kingdom by founding in it several tidy towns and villages, establishing a health resort like Morecambe at Manby Hot Springs on the Rio Grande, building a twelve-mile promenade along the rim of the spectacular gorge, and a great avenue encircling the entire valley before its natural beauty was destroyed. His own lilac garden attested to his green thumb. A man of culture, with a discerning eye, he appreciated paintings. And to a few rare persons he sometimes revealed a sensitive, kindly streak that ran through his violent nature.

Manby's acquisition of the Grant is an extroverted history of economic and social importance documented by official records. His introverted personal life and character can be viewed only as a psychological mystery. There are no factual records to illuminate it. No antecedents in the genealogy of his distinguished, clerical English family can account for his deviation as a curious black sheep. Even to his immediate family he was a mystery. Who knows what karmic predispositions, what dark forces may erupt from the deep well of the unconscious in any of us? One might regard him as a man who adopted the mask of the outer personality with its transient materialistic values, repressing the inner essence, the universal, unchanging spiritual Self of all existence. Or as a man finally possessed by his "shadow," the negative repressed part of the dual nature of every man.

From the day he lost his kingdom, it possessed him completely. He became a recluse, shutting himself in his dusty hacienda behind locked gates and doors. Life had played a miserable trick on him; and in case it still held danger for him, he slept every night in a different room. Constantly he concocted fantastic schemes to get even with his invisible enemies and to obtain enough money to win back his rightful kingdom.

His one trusted friend was his own beloved Princess, Teracita Ferguson, daughter of a Spanish woman and a raw-boned Scottish miner, Columbus Ferguson. Manby had met the family up at the gold camp of Elizabethtown where Ferguson with two partners, Stone and Wilkerson, were working two claims, the Mystic and Ajax. Neither working produced more than a living wage although they lay near the fabulous Aztec mine on Mount Baldy. Shortly after Manby arrived, Stone was found dead, his body mutilated. He was replaced as a partner by Manby. Then the Aztec mine closed down; it couldn't be made to pay because of high-grading—the theft of its high grade ore. At the same time the Mystic began to show rich samples of gold, which Manby shipped to a smelter at El Paso, to avoid talk.

Meanwhile, he had fallen in love with Teracita, and persuaded Ferguson to move down to Taos from the high mountains. Here he arranged for them to buy a tourist camp. It lay up Taos Canyon, a short horseback ride from Manby's house. Often in the evening he rode his black horse, Nigger, up to see her. His own Princess Teracita! The only woman he ever really loved. There was no doubt she returned his affection. She gave birth to three children, each baptized with the name of Ferguson.

Money! Enough to buy back his lost kingdom. Where was he to get it? Hearing of an immensely wealthy man, Dr. Victor C. Thorne in New York, Manby began writing him. Page after page in his bold handwriting proposed fantastic schemes for Thorne to finance. Sales of an alleged original Van Dyck painting, construction of a resort hotel at Manby Hot Springs, organization of La Bajada Sheep Company, mining seven million dollars' worth of copper ore, cutting ten million feet of timber. . . .

Then on September 28, 1921, Wilkerson showed up at Teracita's tourist court, followed by Manby and a young man named Salazar. Where Wilkerson had been since Ferguson had given up the Mystic mine, he didn't explain; but he was dressed in new clothes and carried a lot of money. Marguerita Tafoya was working in the house as a servant girl, taking care of old Ferguson and Teracita's children. She put the children to bed, served supper to the grownups, then went to bed. Next morning she noticed a bulky mattress on the floor. Underneath it lay the body of Wilkerson with a mass of blood on the left breast. Then Salazar came in and carried the body out to a pickup. Manby and Ferguson drove away with them.

Badly frightened and not daring to talk, Marguerita Tafoya quit her job and moved away. Old Ferguson began to have delusions, screaming something about Wilkerson's head and endlessly repeating the date of September 28. He was taken to the insane asylum at Las Vegas and kept for several months. Then he was returned to Teracita's tourist camp, a white-headed mumbling old man.

Manby himself deteriorated rapidly. On sleepless nights he read his favorite book: H. G. Wells's 1908 novel *The War in the Air*, which prophesied the collapse of modern civilization after a worldwide war of new flying machines. This grim tale of horror reflected Manby's own bloody anger against the world.

It was then, in the winter of 1923–24, that people in Taos became aware of a secret organization supposedly vital to the safety of the entire country. Its name was the "United States Secret and Civil Service Society, Self-Supporting Branch." Manby had organized it, Teracita was its president, and secret meetings were held in the front room of her house. Manby would receive the members, then ask Teracita to step into the back room to receive orders from the secret agents who directed the Society's activities. In a few minutes she would return to send various members on strange missions, or to collect a large sum of money from each member. Failure to pay was punishable by death. Manby in the orchard would show them how, going through the motions of knifing a victim, slashing off his head, stamping on his body.

The Society grew too large to hold meetings. Written instructions to individual members were delivered through the "Grapevine Messenger Service" by Carmen Duran, who was believed to have committed several highway robberies. In addition to large cash payments, the Society now demanded first mortgages on houses and titles to real estate. Although few members knew who the others were, they included prominent professionals and businessmen. One of them was Alvin Burch, a middle-aged man with five children, who owned a prosperous mercantile store. His son-in-law Cecil Ross, suspecting that the Society was a bunco game for fleecing money and property out of its members, joined the Society. Then realizing he was unable to cope with it, he resigned. That evening Special Messenger Carmen Duran came to see him. "Nobody leaves the Society. That means old Burch, his son Clyde, and you. Or you know what you'll get!"

The Society was not only a fantasy spun by a disordered mind. It was a hard economic and social fact. Like witchcraft, it thrived on suspicion. No one knew whether his brother or neighbor was a member, but suspected them both.

Alvin Burch finally realized he had been fleeced out of some $60,000 and demanded return of his money. Yet he was gullible enough to grasp at a preposterous chance to recoup his loss. Teracita asserted she was about to receive $827,000,000 collected for her as damages by the Society. This sum she was authorizing the Society to pay to Burch to put in trust for her and her children. Burch's compensation as trustee was to be $1,000,000. Accepting from Manby a federal gold certificate for this amount, Burch drove to the Denver Mint to cash it. The certificate was such a spurious forgery that the officials merely laughed at him and made no effort to arrest him.

Teracita promptly went to the respectable legal firm of Downer and Keleher in Albuquerque to recover the $827,000,000 entrusted to Burch. One of their lawyers persuaded her to believe Burch had actually received $817,000, and he filed suit against Burch in 1928.

Manby meanwhile had been able to borrow some money from Thorne, giving him as collateral his own home property, Manby Hot Springs, and Teracita's interest in the Mystic Mine.

And then it happened. Teracita stopped coming to prepare his supper each evening, and Special Messenger Carmen Duran began demanding money without Manby's knowledge. Then Duran moved into the court as her common-law husband, and ordered the dirty old man to keep away. Betrayed! By his adored Princess Teracita. By the Society. He was now sixty-nine years old. Wracked by jealousy, with no one to look after him, shunned and despised, what would happen to him?

It happened, of course, sometime late in June 1929, and a few days later his decapitated body was found in his locked room. Full details of these preposterous events were revealed to me by many sources. The most important were the results of the investigations made by Detective Bill Martin, hired by Governor Dillon to clear up the mystery of Manby's death. I had met by chance his widow, who had married Captain C. O. Ward, a retired navy officer living in Santa Fe. She was immensely proud of her former husband, with good reason, and had written his biography. Born in Switzerland, Martin had come to New Mexico and set up the Martin Detective Bureau. Fearless and talented, he had become the chief investigator for the state police. Within eight years he had investigated 174 murders, obtaining 160 convictions. Captain and Mrs. Ward generously opened up their storeroom and gave me copies of Martin's official reports to Governor Dillon and his own personal files. These included portions of a voluminous diary kept by Manby and many letters.

With this as a guide, I checked the Governor Dillon Letter File in the State Archives, and drove down to Encino to interview ex-governor Dillon, who was operating a little country store beside the railroad tracks. He could give no reason why the state couldn't afford the few hundred dollars to pay Martin and to clear up the case.

I also interviewed ex-attorney general M. A. Otero, who gave no explanation why Martin's voluminous reports on the case had never been admitted in court as evidence.

My most pleasant interview was with that great New Mexico historian and lawyer W. A. Keleher in Albuquerque. I had just found in the Taos County Records that his law firm had indeed filed in 1928 Teracita's suit against Burch for $817,000. "How was it possible," I asked him, "that such a notable legal firm as yours could believe a small storekeeper like Burch could keep such a sum hidden in an old boot?" Keleher, a courtly, elderly man, laughed and took me to lunch at the country club. There he explained that he and his partner had selected a young member of the firm, D. T. Kingsbury, to handle the case. Teracita had insisted the Society had turned over to Burch $827,000,000, but Kingsbury had persuaded her to file suit for only $817,000. "You must remember, Frank," Keleher told me, "that a lawyer doesn't pass judgment on any case brought to him. That is for the court to decide. And no matter how unusual it is, it may prove valid. Strange things happen."

Another letter file then tumbled into my lap—eighteen letters from Manby to Dr. Thorne. Written in his scrawled handwriting, they outlined all his fantastic schemes and attempts to borrow money. One of them was his prospectus for developing Manby Hot Springs. It was illustrated by his pencil and colored crayon drawings of the Rio Grande Gorge and ancient Indian markings on the sides of the spring. The letter file was casually loaned to me by Miss Helen Williams, a middle-aged woman whose connection with the case I was soon to learn. Elmer Burch, Cecil Ross, and many others gave me valuable information.

It was amazing how so much evidence now came unbidden to me after working for so many years without telling anyone what I was doing. But if I had found that Manby, secretive as he was, had left somewhere a record of his activities, I now discovered that my own supposedly secret research was well known. I was walking through the plaza one noon when a group of schoolboys passed me, one of them yelling, "Hey, Mr. Waters! When is your book about Manby going to be published?"

It seemed that now, after many years, time and circumstance had lifted the dark and heavy weight of fear and secrecy surrounding Manby's death.

Shortly after his death, Princess Teracita and Grapevine Messenger Carmen Duran, both of whom Detective Martin believed to be prime suspects in Manby's murder, were convicted of burglarizing and then setting fire to the home of the noted portrait painter John Young-Hunter and his wife. Teracita was sentenced to prison for a term of from four to six years, and Carmen Duran was given from seven to ten years. Teracita was paroled after serving five months and returned to Taos; but Duran had kept out of town, at least out of sight. Now in 1971 he had returned, and he died on May 14. Was it he, I wondered, who had slipped the threatening notes under Martin's and Spud Johnson's doors? In any case, he was now dead and the lid seemed lifted from the case although the mystery was not solved.

There remained the one person who undoubtedly knew more about Manby's gruesome murder than anyone—Teracita. According to Martin's reconstruction of the case in his report to Governor Dillon, Manby was called to Teracita's house on the night of July 1, 1929. There he was given poisoned whiskey, and several blows on the head, by a woman and a man. Knowing that poison could be easily detected, they decided to cut off his head so as to bring a quicker decomposition of his body. When this was done, on July 2 they, with the help of one or two other men, drove the remains to Manby's house with keys to gain admittance. Next day one of the murderers informed the authorities of Manby's death. How did this man know about it? There was no way for anyone to know about it, to see through bolted gates and locked doors. The deputy sheriff arrived, unable to gain admittance until the house was opened by one of the murderers who had unlocked the door. Martin in conclusion listed four prime suspects: Teracita, Carmen and George Duran, and George Ferguson. His report, of course, went unheeded.

Teracita I had known and liked for many years. Always a fey woman, she read fortunes from cards, a crystal ball, or palms. Among her devoted clients was Mrs. Kibbey Couse, wife of the son of the famous artist. Kibbey had left her and her three children in Taos while he worked on a government contract in New Jersey. As she had no car, I often drove her and Tinka Fechin, her closest friend, for a reading from Teracita. The Princess, when I called upon her, was still sharp-eyed, affable, and close-mouthed. She admitted having sued Burch, but knew nothing about the existence of the United States Secret and Civil Service Society. As for Manby, he was a fine, misunderstood man who had been like a grandfather, an uncle to her. A gang of crooks had ruined him, killed him. It seemed impossible not to believe her until she said the gang had burned the courthouse in order to destroy all records of his and their activities. I left, still liking this fey, black-haired, black-eyed woman of Spain. But this was all I could get out of her. She died a few years later, carrying the mystery of Manby's death to her grave.

There was still one more source of information, Dr. Thorne. He had come in 1930 to a federal court hearing in Albuquerque to foreclose on the mortgage he held on Manby's property. The court granted him a judgment of some $12,000, ordering a foreclosure sale to be held on January 12, 1931. Thorne instead took over the property. Four years later Miss Helen Williams arrived in Taos to manage Manby's house for Dr. Thorne. Middle-aged, capable, and close-mouthed, she employed a crew of gardeners to put the weedy garden and park in shape; and plumbers, electricians, masons, and carpenters to rebuild and modernize the large house; even a corps of engineers from Denver to install the first central heating plant in town. "Don't stint on money," she said Dr. Thorne had told her. "Don't ask what anything costs. Just send me the bills."

When the house was completely remodeled and furnished, a housekeeper, maid, and cook were moved in. Then Miss Williams threw open the door to "Thorne House."

Its purpose was to serve the community. Dinners were served to invited guests. Organizations were invited to discuss their affairs. Bedrooms were offered to visiting artists until they could establish themselves. The only guest it lacked was the mysterious Dr. Thorne, who never showed up at all.

All Taos was perplexed. Why should a New York financier who didn't know Taos, which he never visited and in which he had no friends, spend a half-million dollars at least to remodel the old Manby hacienda to serve the community? The only likely explanation was that the mysterious Dr. Thorne was Manby with a new name, a fistful of money, and a bad conscience. Miss Williams was of little help. She said only that she was a friend of Dr. Thorne, who had requested her to serve as his representative in Taos, as he had heart trouble and could not stand the high altitude.

A few years later I was visiting Mabel and Tony Lujan in New York. Mabel one afternoon happened to run into Miss Williams on the street and invited her to dinner. "I can't come. Dr. Thorne is in town to discuss some business with me."

"So much the better!" replied Mabel. "Bring him along."

That evening I was sitting with Mabel and her guests in her One Fifth Avenue tower apartment, talking as usual about Manby and the mysterious Dr. Thorne. "Of course Dr. Thorne's Manby!" said one. "So naturally he won't show up."

At that moment Dr. Thorne, without ringing the bell, stepped in with Miss Williams at his heels. Making a little bow, he said humorously, "Well, you can see I'm not Mr. Manby!"

Indeed, he wasn't. He was years younger, shorter, lightly built, with a sharp mind and quick humor. Everyone laughed. Thorne did not explain his purpose in creating Thorne House nor why he never went to see it. But just the same, he seemed to have been provided with a dossier on everyone in Taos. There was not a person mentioned, not a rumor, he didn't know fully. He even knew I was working on a book about the Colorado River, and mentioned an old out-of-print source-book on its delta. "I'll send it to you," he said. The next morning, at eight o'clock, a special messenger arrived with a copy.

Nevertheless, the close relationship of Manby and Thorne was still a mystery. According to Miss Williams, it was Thorne's intention to leave a trust fund to finance the operation of Thorne House. But in 1948 he dropped dead after a sudden heart attack, without amending his will to that effect. Thorne House was sold for $45,000 to the Taos Art Association. Dr. Thorne, however, left $100,000 to Miss Williams to manage it for the benefit of the community as the Taos Foundation. More was added to it from time to time, enabling the foundation to donate $125,000 to the Embudo Hospital for building a new wing. It loaned money to medical and business school students, made donations to needy persons needing new teeth, and every Christmas supplied schoolchildren with shirts, jeans, and galoshes.

Miss Williams herself remained a shadowy figure until her death. A closer relationship of Thorne and Manby, of Thorne and herself, which undoubtedly existed, she never acknowledged. In her later years she became curiously touchy and irascible whenever anyone mentioned Manby's murder.

And so his death remains today, with all its unpursued ramifications and unanswered questions, a mystery that is yet to be solved.

19

Good for Fred!

(Editorial—March 16, 1950)

EFFECTIVE next month the Santa Fe's California Limited will stop for meals at the Harvey Houses in Albuquerque, Gallup, Winslow, Williams, and Seligman.

Soon as it stops, the deep-toned restaurant gong will start ringing. Passengers will tumble out of cars, sprint up the brick platform. Soup will be steaming on dining room tables. Marble horseshoe lunch-counters will be piled high with their famous ham sandwiches wrapped in tissue and tied with blue-paper bands. Shiny coffee urns will be fragrantly smoking. Afterwards you can stroll out for a look around, with a smug sense of unhurry and well-being.

Nothing revives our nostalgia for the leisurely, colorful past like this rejuvenation of an old custom. Or restores our equilibrium more, in this frenetic age of hurtling breathlessly and blindly across continent.

For an era the Fred Harvey House stood out as both a symbol and a practical institution. A functional part of its regional background, it was the only true inn of the Southwest and in the Southwest tradition.

The destruction of beautiful El Ortiz at Lamy, the closing of the Castañeda at Las Vegas, and the dreary deterioration of the Harvey House at Needles—with the innovation of auto, plane, and nonstop superspeed train travel—almost spelled the end of the Fred Harvey system.

But with this return to its grassroots, and its solicitation of more leisurely travel through the scenic Indian country of the Southwest, the tradition of the Harvey House may be perpetuated for another generation.

Good for Fred!

20

Symbols and Sacred Mountains
Comparable Themes in Buddhism and American Indian Religion

(Annual W. Y. Evans-Wentz Lecture, presented at Stanford University, California, on May 5, 1981)

It is a privilege and a pleasure to meet with you at this annual lecture honoring Walter Y. Evans-Wentz. It provides me with an opportunity to attest to his great contribution to world culture and religion, and to acknowledge the help he gave me during our seventeen years of friendship.

As you know, he received from Stanford University his B.A. and M.A. degrees, a doctorate in literature from the University of Rennes in France, and from Oxford University the degrees of B.Sc. and Doctor of Science in Comparative Religion. These academic attainments were but mileposts marking his way toward a lifelong devotion to psychic and spiritual matters.

For four years he did psychic research among the Celtic peoples of the British Isles and Brittany, resulting in his book *The Fairy-Faith in Celtic Countries*. In Egypt he studied for three years the ancient funeral rites described in the *Egyptian Book of the Dead*, and followed that with travel through Ceylon, India, and Tibet. This led him into an intensive study of Tibetan Buddhism. On this he became a world authority with the eventual publication of those now well-known, ancient treatises, which he edited and annotated: *The Tibetan Book of the Dead, Tibet's Great Yogi Milarepa, Tibetan Yoga and Secret Doctrines,* and *The Tibetan Book of the Great Liberation.*

Dr. Evans-Wentz himself embraced the faith of Mahayana Buddhism and settled in India, buying property in Almora, Kumaon Province. Here he lived in an *ashram* on Kasar Devi, planning to develop it into a research center for Eastern religious philosophies. The outbreak of the Second World War put an end to his efforts. He returned to the United States, settling in San Diego.

He had inherited a large ranch of some five thousand acres lying on the international border of California and Baja California. It embraced Mount Tecate, known to surrounding Indian tribes as the sacred mountain of Cuchama, on whose summit young men had undergone initiation into the sacred rites of their people. Dr. Evans-Wentz became interested in the traditions concerning it, and in the religion of American Indians.

My correspondence with him began about this time—in 1947 to be more exact. I wrote him that I had discovered in the first volumes of his Tibetan series many parallels to the esoteric beliefs and rituals of the Pueblos and Navajos which I was recounting in my own writings. Dr. Evans-Wentz in turn found other similarities in my published books. As he wrote me, "You have gone deeply into the esotericism; and the parallels which you point out with Oriental religions are well founded . . . I am astonished with the fundamental similarity." So our friendship was founded on a mutual interest.

It developed further when he began preparing a book on Cuchama and other sacred mountains throughout the world. Familiar as he was with those in the East, he knew little about those in America and asked me for information about them. I met him in San Diego, accompanied him to Cuchama, and was given his manuscript to read as he developed it over the years.

Unfortunately, Dr. Evans-Wentz died in 1965, at the age of eighty-seven, bequeathing the unpublished manuscript to Stanford University. It has been my privilege, with Dr. Charles L. Adams of the University of Nevada, Las Vegas, to edit it for publication under the title *Cuchama and Sacred Mountains,* now released under the joint imprint of Swallow Press and Ohio University Press.

There are many aspects of Indian America's native religion with correspondences in Buddhism. Mesoamerica, or Indian America as I term it, embraces that vast area from our own Southwest down through Mexico and Guatemala, whose tribes, ancient and contemporary, observed many common religious beliefs. One of the few I shall briefly develop here, with their Buddhist similarities, is the veneration of sacred mountains. On this I shall peg my first remarks.

Sacred Mountains

Mt. Meru in the Himalayan range is the spiritual heart of two of the world's oldest civilizations, India and China. According to the cosmography of Hindu and Tibetan Buddhism, it is the axial core of the cosmos. It is eighty thousand miles high and eighty thousand miles deep, containing within it four realms, one above another. Surmounting them is the supreme heaven, the vestibule to Nirvana. If man's psychophysical organism is a microcosmic pattern of the universe, his spinal column represents Mt. Meru. And likewise he is crowned by the highest center of consciousness, the thousand-petaled lotus of the mind.

And just as man's various centers of consciousness branch out from his psycho-physical spinal column, so Mt. Meru extends in girdles of seven mountains and seven oceans to four worlds in outer space. Spreading out like a four-petaled lotus blossom, these four worlds are oriented to the primary directions and bear directional colors. Mt. Kailas, twenty-two thousand feet high, bears the name of the metaphysical Mt. Meru, but it is only its material image.

A striking parallel in the American Southwest is the Encircled Mountain, which stands in the center of the cosmography of the Navajo Indians. It is surrounded by four lesser mountains that mark its boundaries: the San Francisco peaks in Arizona, the holy mountain of the west; Mt. Taylor, in New Mexico, the holy mountain of the south; Wheeler Peak, the holy mountain of the east; and a peak in the San Juan or La Plata range in Colorado, the sacred mountain of the north. The location of the Encircled Mountain is marked by a small peak, but the Encircled Mountain itself is invisible. Being the axial core of the whole universe, it existed before the First People emerged from the lower worlds, and spans a time and space beyond our earth-dimensional comprehension. This is its metaphysical reality.

They have other similarities. The sides and outer worlds of both Mt. Meru and the Encircled Mountain bear the same directional colors: white on the east, blue on the south, red on the west, and either green or yellow on the north. Below each mountain the cosmos spreads out like a four-petaled flower, a lotus. Each of the world-petals is protected by a Lokapala or World Guardian, as each of the Navajos' holy mountains is guarded by a Talking God. And this today in a Navajo sand-painting is the symbol of the great axial rock—a four-petaled flower, like a Buddhist lotus.

In ancient China the Taoists regarded five mountains as sacred. When the Buddhists entered China in the second century, they designated four more of particular sanctity. All were oriented to the cardinal directions. To these nine sacred mountains millions of pilgrims came for centuries to climb their steep trails, to pray, and to deposit offerings. Mt. Omei, ten thousand feet high, is one of the most beautiful. From its base to its summit are more than seventy monasteries and temples.

Dr. Evans-Wentz regarded such sacred mountains as repositories of psychic power upon which man could draw. He paid tribute to those Himalayan peaks near his home, and once walked barefoot around Arunachala in South India.

In Japan, early in the seventh century A.D., there developed *Shugendo*—the "Way"—by which human beings could attain the spiritual powers inherent in the mountains by pilgrimages and rituals. The meaning and purpose of Shugendo are made clear by the derivation of its name: *Shu*—beginning enlightenment of a pilgrim's inherent divine nature; *gen*—his innate realization; and *do*—his attainment of what Buddhists call *nirvana* and the Japanese *nehan*. The pilgrim, beginning his climb up the mountain, was considered to be "entering the mountain, leaving this world for the other world," finally attaining spiritual rebirth on its summit. Mt. Haguro with thirty-three temples was the most important of the 134 sacred mountains in Japan. Shugendo was officially proscribed in 1872, but since then has been rejuvenated.

In ancient Mexico the Aztecs held an elaborate ceremony to honor the towering mountains of Popocatepetl, the "Smoking Mountain," and Ixtaccihuatl, the "Sleeping Woman," during the annual "Feast of the Mountains." Villagers made small images of amaranth seed to represent the mountains. Then the little dough images were decapitated and eaten. Following this, a great procession carried four richly dressed children, with gifts of precious stones, to the tops of the mountains. Here fires were lighted, incense burned, and the children sacrificed. The sixteenth-century Dominican friar Diego Duran makes this comment: "It should not be considered that the mountains were held to be gods or worshipped as such. The aim was to pray from that high place to the Almighty, the Lord of Created Things, the Lord by Whom They Lived." It seems clear that here as throughout the world, sacred mountains were not worshipped as deities, but regarded as places of access to the divine power of Creation. Popocatepetl and Ixtaccihuatl still today hold many shrines, all above twelve thousand feet altitude, and a ceremony is held at them each year.

To these examples in Tibet, China, India, Japan, and Mexico could be added more in South America and Africa. And in line with this mode of thought, it was from Mt. Sinai that Moses brought down the Ten Commandments, and the gods of ancient Greece were said to live on Mount Olympus.

So too today the home of the Hopi spiritual beings, the kachinas, is on the San Francisco peaks in Arizona. And my home neighbors, the Indians of Taos Pueblo in New Mexico, still make annual pilgrimages up their Sacred Mountain, only a horseback ride from my own adobe, to conduct ceremonies never witnessed by a white man. Also current today is the reverence for sacred mountains observed by the Chamulas and Zinacantecos of southern Mexico whom I visited a few years ago. They follow the ancient Mayan custom of erecting crosses at the foot and on the summit of sacred mountains. Here they deposit offerings of flowers, chickens, and rum, and burn candles and incense. The cross has no Christian meaning for them, but marks the meeting place between them and their ancestral Mayan gods.

Always, everywhere, sacred mountains have served as places of communication between men and their gods.

Psychological Interpretation

We may well ask the origin of this world belief. Apparently it has a sound psychological foundation, rather than being a primitive folk belief. The modern psychologist Mimi Lobell, in her study of spatial archetypes, equates the emergence of the mountain out of the sea of chaos with the rise of the ego and self-consciousness from the womb-cavern of the unconscious. There began in world history the era of mountain-venerating and pyramid-building civilizations in which reverence for the Earth Mother gave way to that for the Sky Father, and patriarchal replaced matriarchal patterns. This was reflected in the social stratification of different castes, with a divine ruler at the apex of the social pyramid. Yet eventually the ego in turn experienced spiritual enlightenment, which again related it to the mother of all creation, the unconscious. Hence the function of the sacred mountain was to enable man to surmount his worldly existence at its summit, and achieve transcendental unity with the universe.

A manmade stone pyramid and even the body of man were in effect sacred mountains. On the summit of a sacred mountain, at the apex of a pyramid, or in the mind-center of a human pyramid, man sought an expansion of his spiritual consciousness.

American Destruction

If the relationship between mountains and mankind is so universal and deeply rooted, our disregard of them in the United States needs little comment here. No reverence is given to those once held sacred by our indigenous Indian tribes, for the very reason that the tribes themselves were decimated and almost obliterated during our march of empire across the continent. Most of those still remaining are being exploited for industrial gain. As a result, we have bought the physical energy derived from their gold, oil, coal, and uranium at the expense of the psychical energy so equally necessary. Becoming spiritually bankrupt, we are beginning to learn that our relationship to the earth includes a psychical as well as a physical ecology.

The Tibetan Book of the Dead

Let me now descend from the mountaintop to the deepest pit of Hell.

The Tibetan Book of the Dead, the first of Dr. Evans-Wentz's Tibetan series, was committed to writing in the eighth century A.D. The ancient treatise was translated from Sanskrit by Lama Kazi Dawa-Samdup, edited and annotated by Dr. Evans-Wentz, and published in 1927 by Oxford University Press.

It is similar to the *Egyptian Book of the Dead,* and its teachings are generally subscribed to by most peoples throughout the East. It is founded upon the Doctrine of Reincarnation.

Orthodox Christianity asserts that man has only two existences: one short life span on this earth, followed by an eternal existence in a sublime Heaven or in an abysmal Hell. The Doctrine of Reincarnation, to the contrary, posits an after-death period on the Bardo plane.

Here the deceased, the "soul" or causal nexus, passes forty-nine days before being reincarnated in another human body on the earth plane.

The period reflects the Buddhistic belief in forty-nine stages of man's physical evolution. These are recapitulated after death, accompanied by forty-nine stages of psychical evolution. During them the deceased experiences the karmic results of his past earthly life. He is beset by thundering sounds and by different colors representing the constituent elements of his earthly body: fire, air, water, and earth. Each element has mental and emotional attributes. Peaceful Deities help him. Wrathful Deities menace him. None of them is real. They are but hallucinations, thought forms created by karmic reflections of the deceased's good deeds and bad deeds, dormant lusts and desires, during his earthly incarnation. They thus comprise a "Book of Judgement" from which he passes sentence upon himself, his predilections determining his need to be reincarnated for another earthly existence.

Only a few persons, like enlightened yogis, recognize these hallucinations for what they are, and see the one blinding light as the Clear Light of Reality, of the formless Void. They then outstrip the normal process of evolution, attaining Enlightenment and Emancipation from the Wheel of Life, and achieving transformation into a higher spiritual plane.

Hence the Sanskrit name for the *Tibetan Book of the Dead*, the *Bardo Thodol*, is "Liberation by Hearing and Seeing on the After-Death Plane." Dr. Evans-Wentz regarded it as not only a mystical manual for guidance through the after-death plane, but a guide to us in life.

The Zuni Shalako

In the great Shalako ceremonial of Zuni Pueblo in New Mexico, we have a reminder of the symbolic forty-nine days that the soul of the deceased spends on the Bardo plane.

These forty-nine days, as previously mentioned, represent the forty-nine stages of man's physical and psychical evolution. As the Hindus explain, there are seven degrees of Maya within the phenomenal Sangsara, represented by seven worlds; and there are seven stages of evolution in each, making forty-nine active existences from amoeba to man.

The great Shalako ritual is a forty-nine-day ceremonial featuring the annual return to Zuni of the Shalako kachinas or spirit beings.

Preparations to receive them have been made all year. A new house has been built for each. The family hosts have gone into debt to purchase cattle and sheep, which will be butchered to feed the crowd of guests; hundreds of loaves of bread have been baked.

In October, on the morning of the tenth month of planting prayer sticks at the full of the moon, the kachina priests receive a cotton string tied in forty-nine knots, one to be untied each following morning. During the ensuing days they rejuvenate the kachina masks, ritually feed them with cornmeal, and hold secret observances in the kivas. On the fortieth day the first kachinas appear in the plaza. They are the Koyemshi, the Mudheads, their heads and bodies covered with pinkish clay, their faces grotesque, pitifully deformed. Another group of kachinas march in on the forty-fourth day. They are led by the Rain God of the North, called Long Horn from the great horn protruding from his mask, and which signifies long life. On the forty-eighth day come the little Fire God, the Rain God of the South, the warriors of the East and West, the war brothers of the Zenith and Nadir.

All kachinas make the rounds of the pueblo, leaving prayer sticks on the thresholds of the ceremonial houses. The little Fire God climbs up a ladder to the flat roof where he leaves two more, male and female. Then all of them enter the house and bless it with long poetic prayers.

By dusk all is ready. In cold, darkness, and silence, the waiting Zunis and spectators stand facing the freezing river and its causeway of stones and sticks.

At last the six Shalakos come, tall spectral shapes gliding across the causeway. Shapeless, armless bodies, eight to ten feet tall, draped with white kirtles embroidered in red, green, and black. Each enormous head mask is colored turquoise and surmounted by a crest of eagle feathers raying like the sun. From their gargoyle faces protrude bulging ball eyes, up-curving horns hung with red feathers, and long, wooden, clacking beaks. Huge anthropomorphic figures, part beast, part bird, part man.

Each is conducted to the house prepared for him and seated in the "valuable place," beside the altar. Here for hours he recites a long, prescribed ritual address. Then from midnight until dawn he dances in the great, lofty room before the crowd of squatting spectators. It is one of the greatest Pueblo ceremonials, and one of the most unique rituals in the world.

What does it mean?

From the arrival of the early Spanish priests it has received more observation and interpretations than perhaps any single Pueblo ceremonial. It has been anthropologically classified as a war ceremonial, a hunt ceremonial, a ceremonial for longevity and for fertility and reproduction. It may indeed contain all these elements. Yet above all these explanations, it seems to me that the ceremonial's period of forty-nine days, its concern for the return of the spirits of the dead, their ritual feeding, and the Shalakos' own long recitals, combine into the one predominating motif of the meaning of death.

The kachinas are of course the spirits of the dead; of all the plant, animal, and human forms; of the color directions. The inner forms of all the forces of life. Wherefore their masks of horn, snout, beak, and abstract design to represent all aspects of life, as the composite Shalako. From where have they come? The Zuni Creation Myth tells us there have been four previous worlds from which man has been successively reborn to continue his journey on the Road of Life. Their names are significant. The first underworld was the "Place of Generation." The second, "dark as the night," was called the "Umbilical Womb" or "Place of Gestation." The third world-cave was lighter, "like a valley in starlight," and was named the "Vaginal Womb" or "Place of Sex Generation." For here peoples and things began to multiply apart in kind. In the fourth world-cave—the "Womb of Parturition"—it was "light like the dawning," and men began to perceive according to their natures. And finally into this great upper "World of Light and Knowledge or Seeing" mankind emerged, first blinded by the light and glory of the Sun Father, then looking for the first time at one another.

I will have more to say later about this four-world concept. It is introduced here simply to show that the Zunis' Road of Life leads up through these four underworlds and also mirrors man's evolutionary development on the way. This is visually shown by the progressive kachinas as they appear, from the first unformed and deformed Mudheads.

And why have the Shalakos returned? Simply to recount in hourslong recitals their own journey to their yet earth-bound fellow travelers whom they have preceded, and to assure them that death does not interrupt the continuity of their journey. Breath is the symbol of life, and inhaling an act of ritual blessing. Wherefore during the recital all

in the room inhale, holding up their hands before their nostrils to par-
take of the essence of the sacred prayer:

> . . . That clasping one another tight,
> Holding one another fast,
> We may finish our roads together;
> That this may be, I add to your breath now . . .
> May our roads be fulfilled.
> May we grow old,
> May our people's roads all be fulfilled . . .

So the Shalakos dance and pray with their people. At dawn they stop
dancing. Long Horn clambers up to the roof. Facing east, he unties the
last knot, the forty-ninth in his string. The Shalakos, escorted by
singers back across the frozen causeway, then make their transition
back to the spirit realm.

The winter solstice is at hand. All fires in the pueblo are extinguished. The whole earth dies. But from this ceremonial the people
know that it all is simply a withdrawal, that life will be renewed with
freshness, vigor, and a deep sense of its continuous flow.

Borgia Codex

That the *Tibetan Book of the Dead* had a remarkable parallel in prehistoric Mesoamerica I didn't discover until a few years ago when I was
given a Rockefeller Foundation grant for research into the religion and
culture of the ancient Toltecs, Aztecs, and Mayas. What a Christmas
present from Santa Claus it seemed to me! I had not applied for a
grant. The Foundation simply suggested I apply for one, and granted
it immediately. A *permiso* from the Mexican and Guatemalan governments gave me free access to all archeological and anthropological
sites. So for six months I had a wonderful time visiting all the great
ruins of ancient cities and pyramids.

I then spent some time in the impressive library of the National
Museum of Anthropology in Mexico City, which permitted me to pe-
ruse the documents of a vanished civilization.

Among the most important is the *Borgia Codex*. It has become the
property of the Vatican, where it now reposes. In 1898 the Duke of
Loubat financed a reproduction in colored photoengraving, and the

great German scholar Eduard Seler was engaged to interpret it. His two-volume commentary in German was published in 1904. Not until 1963 was it translated into Spanish, and it has not yet been translated into English.

The *Borgia Codex* itself is a screen fold of seventy-six paintings. Their gorgeous color and design make it the most beautiful of all codices. Its ritualistic content makes it also the most complex and esoteric of all those known.

The pictorial account of Quetzalcoatl's apotheosis comprises its most essential and esoteric section. It describes, in Seler's words, "*El Viaje de Venus por el Inferno*" or "The Journey of Venus through the Underworld." Venus, of course, is equated with the mythical Nahuatl god Quetzalcoatl who was transformed into the planet.

Quetzalcoatl was the culture hero believed to have brought the arts of civilization to Mexico about the time of Christ. His name reflects his world duality: *Quetzal*—a brilliantly colored bird, and *coatl*—a serpent; literally the Plumed Serpent. The religion he established spread from the American Southwest to Central America, and lasted for nearly one thousand years.

As the ruler of Teotihuacan, the City of the Gods, Quetzalcoatl was wise, good, and chaste. Then evil companions induced him to drink pulque. Afterward he slept with his sister, Xochiquetzal, goddess of love and beauty. Upon awakening he lamented that he had become drunk, forgotten his chastity, and committed incest. In expiation, he disposed of all his kingly riches, went to the seacoast, and built a great fire. Then he cast himself into the flames.

After his physical body was consumed, he went underground to the Land of the Dead. Days later he was transformed into the planet Venus, the Morning Star, the Lord of Dawn. Thereafter he astronomically repeated his ritual journey: first appearing in the western sky as the Evening Star, disappearing underground, and then reappearing in the eastern sky as the Morning Star to unite with the rising sun.

This is the astronomical interpretation of the myth given by most scholars. But its hermetic meaning also seems clear. It is an expression of the universal doctrine of sin and redemption, of death and rebirth, the transfiguration of matter into spirit, of man into god.

Quetzalcoatl's tribulations in the Land of the Dead curiously parallel the experiences of the deceased on the Bardo plane as described in the *Tibetan Book of the Dead*. He traverses the four regions of sin and death: the East, North, West, and South. How frightening are the scenes! Queer hieroglyphs, strange images, barbaric Demons of Darkness. Quetzalcoatl then enters the deepest pit of hell. Two roads lead into it, one black and one red. May I ask you to remember these two roads? We shall refer to them later.

We now see two Quetzalcoatls: one black, destined to live, and one red, destined to die. His division into two beings can be best understood by the Buddhist doctrine of karma and rebirth. For although a man may have consciously repressed or inhibited all his base instincts during his lifetime on earth, he carries them into the after-death state. What is necessary before he emerges into full spirituality, then, is that these karmic propensities or predispositions be extinguished on the unconscious level as well as on the conscious. This is what is happening to Quetzalcoatl. He is divided into all manifestations of his mental, emotional, and spiritual components according to the karmic propensities of his being.

There follows a painting of the red Quetzalcoatl stretched out on the sacrificial stone, his heart being torn out. Appropriately, the one who executes the sacrifice is the black Quetzalcoatl destined to live. Now the black Quetzalcoatl, the enduring spiritual principle, is resurrected. He drinks the water of renewal and is transformed into a hummingbird perching in a flowering tree. The hummingbird was the Aztec symbol of rebirth. The flowering tree was, of course, the Tree of Life of many world mythologies and religions. And now in the last painting is shown Quetzalcoatl ascending at last in the eastern sky as the Morning Star, the Lord of Dawn.

The *Borgia Codex* is a significant document of Indian America, with the greatest of all themes—death and transfiguration.

The Four Worlds

I don't want to impose on your time by enumerating many minor aspects of American Indian religion which correspond to Mahayana Buddhism. But there is one more fundamental religious belief which I'd like to develop for you.

This is the concept of four previous worlds mentioned in the Zuni Shalako ritual. Commonly held throughout all Indian America, it was the foundation of ancient Aztec and Mayan thought in Mexico, and of the Andean Incas in South America. And it is perpetuated today by the

Pueblos and Navajos in our Southwest who still affirm the previous existence of four successive worlds.

Especially to the Hopis, among whom I lived for three years, this cosmological concept is a living reality. To them, creation of the world and man did not take place just once, at a prescribed time. Creation was a long continuum of events during which one world was destroyed and replaced by another. And each time a portion of humanity escaped destruction to emerge in the succeeding world. All of the Hopis' nine major ceremonials with their rituals, dances, and songs dramatically enact and recount their literal Emergences from each of the preceding worlds. I wish I had time to develop these for you. They comprise the most profound, indigenous Mystery Plays of America.

Buddhism develops this concept in psychological detail. It traces the evolution of man through the mineral, plant, animal, and human kingdoms associated with the four primary elements of fire, water, air, and earth. From the fire element man derived his life heat. From the air his breath of life. From water his life stream, his blood. And from the earth the solid substances of his body. But man is more than a physical organism. Hence he also derives corresponding psychical qualities. With fire, an aggregate of feelings. With air, volition. With water, consciousness. And with earth, touch. But with these he also receives corresponding passions. Fire and feelings give rise to his passion of attachment and lust. Air and volition, the passion of envy. Water and consciousness, anger. And earth and touch, egoism.

This will remind you of the previously quoted belief that when man's physical body dies, he still carries into the after-death state these psychical attributes, which must be resolved before he attains higher consciousness in a fifth state or world.

This brings us back again to ancient Indian America. The Aztecs' famous Calendar Stone depicts the four previous suns or worlds, which also represented the four elements, earth, air, fire, and water. In the center is the symbol of the Fifth Sun, termed the Sun of Movement because it was the unifying center of the four preceding suns. Yet within the Fifth Sun lay another synthesizing center, the soul of man. For only in the movement taking place in man's own heart could the opposing forces be reconciled.

The idea of movement also suggests the great cycles in which the various suns or worlds perish and are succeeded in each case by another.

The Mayas developed this idea most completely in terms of time. Like the Aztecs, they held that there had existed four previous worlds, each destroyed by a catastrophe, and that the present world was the fifth. No other people have been so obsessed with time. With mathematical and astronomical precision they measured timeless time from a *tun* of 360 days up to an *alau'tun* of 60 million years. Their most common cycles ranged from 52 years to 5,200 years. This last Great Cycle measured the duration of each of the five successive worlds. Their overall duration totaled approximately 26,000 years, the length of the great cycle of the Precession of the Equinoxes—the time required for the Vernal Equinox to move through the twelve space-and-time divisions of the great circle of the Ecliptic.

The Mayas' last Great Cycle was regarded as the duration of the present Fifth World. The astronomer-priests projected its beginning back to 3113 B.C. and projected its end to A.D. 2011. What an astounding prediction to have been made in Indian America about fifteen hundred years ago! And how closely it is paralleled by the present well-known Hopi Prophecy, which assures our present world will soon be destroyed.

I don't believe myself that an engulfing catastrophe will overtake this planet. I prefer to believe that the four previous worlds were dramatic allegories for the stages of man's ever-evolving consciousness. Symbols of cosmic changes taking place in rhythmic cycles that relate the inner life of man to his vast outer world.

Conclusion

I hope these few outstanding aspects of Mesoamerican Indian religion illustrate their similarity with the significant beliefs of esoteric Buddhism in sacred mountains, after-death experiences, the four elements and four worlds, which represent the stages of man's expanding consciousness. Clearly they all spring from a common source, far back in time, deep in mankind's common unconscious.

What significance do they have for us today in materialistic and rationalistic America? In partial answer to this I shall end these observations by briefly recounting a vision given a nine-year-old Plains Indian boy in 1872. He held it to be so sacred that he did not reveal it in full detail until 1931, when he was a destitute old man. He was the Oglala

Sioux holy man Black Elk, and his vision as recorded by John C. Nei-
hardt is one of the finest pieces of American Indian literature.

Black Elk in this vision had been transported to meet the Higher
Powers above. In a series of dramatic experiences he was conducted to
the four horizontal directions of the Sioux "hoop" or nation on two
roads, one black and one red. These I hope will remind you of the
black and red roads that the divided Quetzalcoatl traveled in the Land
of the Dead. Black Elk as he traveled saw behind him ghostly generations of his tribe, embodied in the element of past time.

Now ahead of him rose four "ascents" whose vertical dimensions
suggest the element of future time. So it was. On each ascent he saw
the troubles of his people below steadily increasing. His vision foretold
the campaign of U.S. cavalry troops against the Sioux nation, ending
with the infamous massacre at Wounded Knee in 1890. When he
reached the summit of the third ascent, the nation's hoop was broken,
the buffalo had been destroyed, and the people herded into reservations were starving. A terrible storm was coming, the winds of war
fighting like wild beasts about him—foretelling a century more of injustices and prejudices his people would suffer as a racial minority.

And then begins the eloquent passage describing the climax of
Black Elk's Great Vision in *Black Elk Speaks:*

> Then I was standing on the highest mountain of them all, and round
> about me was the whole hoop of the world. And while I stood there,
> I saw more than I can tell and I understood more than I saw; for I was
> seeing in a sacred manner the shapes of all things in the spirit and the
> shapes of all shapes as they must live together as one being. And I saw
> that the sacred hoop of my people was one of many hoops that made
> one circle, wide as daylight and starlight, and in the center grew one
> mighty tree to shelter all the children of one mother and one father.
> And I saw that it was holy.

Who can doubt that this simple and illiterate American Indian boy
had attained the divine Illumination and Experience of Totality
achieved by Buddhist holy men and other world saints and sages?

I don't think I'm walking upon the sands of surmise when I com-
pare his four ascents with the four worlds and eras we have discussed.
A surer footing is found in Black Elk's own statement in 1931 that he
believed we were now hearing the winds of war fighting like wild
beasts, and that something bad was going to happen to the world.

Certainly today ours is a period of war, revolution, and worldwide change. The twelfth and last zodiacal age, that of Pisces, is ending; and with it the present great precessional cycle of 25,920 years.

What lies ahead? If Higher Powers are governing the evolution of all life throughout the universe, we must believe that sometime we too will stand on the highest mountain of all, and see below the hoops of all nations, and in the center the Flowering Tree sheltering all us children of one mother and father. Dr. Evans-Wentz affirms the truth of this Great Vision by dedicating Cuchama as a mighty monument to symbolize the inherent religious unity of the East and West, of all mankind.

21

Tombstone Travesty

(Editorial—February 9, 1950)

GOVERNOR Garvey of Arizona has proclaimed this to be "Tombstone Restoration Week." The celebration hails the restoration of Tombstone by the Tombstone Restoration Commission, beginning March 1, as the "Williamsburg Restoration Project of the Southwest."

Wooden sidewalks of the '80s will replace the present ones of cement. False Leadville fronts will be put back on store buildings. The famous old Bird Cage Theater, where Lottie Crabtree sang, and Ed Schieffelin's King Solomon Lodge, will be restored.

Laudable as the project is, there are indications that several steps may defeat its purpose. One of them is the probable glorification of the Earps' shooting of the Clantons with reconstruction of the O.K. Corral. Another is the printing of a special edition of the weekly *Epitaph,* "Tombstone's only newspaper," for distribution throughout the U.S.

Wyatt Earp and his gunmen were, of course, tinhorn outlaws operating under the protection of tin badges as marshals of law. They were finally run out of Arizona when President Arthur threatened to declare martial law unless the territory was cleaned up.

The notorious *Epitaph* was their mouthpiece. It was not "Tombstone's only newspaper." The *Nugget* was also currently published, and it was the only newspaper that fearlessly printed the full testimony during the farcical J. P. trial, which cleared the Earp gang of murder.

Glorification of these early Western exhibitionist gangsters, forerunners of Al Capone, is neither in accord with the facts in my manuscript on file in the Arizona Pioneers Historical Society, nor with public sentiment throughout the Southwest.

More to the point would be recognition of pioneer Sheriff John Slaughter, who cleaned up the Tombstone area. Of the late Jeff Milton, a noted peace officer who died there. And of the hundreds of hardy, unsung pioneers who made possible the Southwest of today.

Else the Tombstone Restoration, as a Hollywood set, will but perpetuate the Tombstone Travesty as seen by the authentic citizens of that time.

22

A Misadventure

(Essay)

N ED was about ten years old then, scrawny and high-strung. He lived next door to me in Placita, on the outskirts of Taos. His family's name was Bright, and Ned was a chip off the old block in more than name. But bright as he was, he was mischievous, downright obstreperous. His constant pranks didn't endear him to me.

He was, however, something of a pet to Dr. Gertrude Light, an unmarried, childless, and careworn woman of sixty or more. Not too much was known about her, remarkable and loved as she was. Apparently she had received early medical schooling in Europe, worked in Russia, and was the first woman doctor to graduate from Johns Hopkins. When she began her practice, she found doors closed to her; for in those days women practitioners were regarded with disfavor. Perhaps that is why she eventually landed in the backward village of Taos, only to encounter the same prejudice. The town's two doctors were young and inexperienced, without her sound medical and surgical qualifications. But they controlled the small hospital and refused to admit her patients. Nevertheless, Dr. Light built up a practice among Spanish-American villagers too poor to afford large doctors' fees and hospital costs. None minded her occasional vagueness and brief lapses from work. Gradually she became more widely known for her devoted care and profound knowledge of the illnesses and rare diseases of children.

Soon after I arrived in Taos, she diagnosed unusual illnesses in four impoverished children from outlying communities and appealed to hospitals in Santa Fe and Albuquerque to accept them without charge. All declined. So Dr. Light finally persuaded a large hospital in Denver to take them in. She appealed to me now to drive them there in her old Ford sedan. She also insisted on taking Ned. "He's never seen a big city, and he's such a bright boy the experience will be a great adventure for him."

Early one morning she, Ned, and I started out. Our first stop was at the village of Questa to pick up two of the ailing children. They were waiting for us with their parents, neighbors, and the parish priest. Both were girls swathed to the eyes in the blue-black *rebozos* worn by their mothers and grandmothers before them. Each had been given a little paper sack of hard candies and some pennies. Neither spoke English. When they had been properly blessed by the priest and cried over by their mothers, we drove on to Costilla and the old Spanish town of San Luis in Colorado. Here we picked up the other two children patiently waiting with their families. They were boys wearing dirty little shirts and pants, both of them barefoot. Their pale faces betrayed both anticipation of the adventure ahead and fear of the unknown.

Ned and the two boys sat in the front seat beside me. Dr. Light sat behind with the girls. One of them, who had a bad heart, she cradled on her bony lap with smelling salts and a bottle of oxygen in case they were needed when we crossed La Veta Pass.

Safely over the Pass, we stopped at a restaurant in Walsenburg to give the children lunch. "Take the boys into the bathroom, Frank," Dr. Light instructed me. "Then bring them back for a bowl of soup and some ice cream."

What wonderful, excited little children they were in their shabby clothes, the girls clutching the pennies they had been given to spend on their great adventure into the unknown! None of the children had tasted ice cream. Neither of the boys had ever seen a modern toilet; one boy kept flushing this miracle over and over again. Ned, of course, superciliously refused to use it.

We reached Pueblo, Colorado, in midafternoon. Dr. Light had telephoned ahead to a Catholic school, and the Sisters in attendance served us cookies and milk.

The long drive by now was beginning to tell on the ailing children. They were worn out, and kept asking, "Where can we spend our pennies?" Dr. Light answered them cheerfully. "It won't be long now. You'll see the high Daniels and Fisher Tower in the Big City soon." Ned was restless, bored, squirming in his seat.

Not until dark did we reach the great hospital in east Denver. The novelty of an automobile ride had worn off for the children. They were homesick for their little adobe homes, frightened by the aspect of the great looming hospital, and petulant because they had been given no opportunity to spend their pennies. It took all of Dr. Light's warm assurances to persuade them to accompany her into the great building.

Ned and I were left alone in the parking lot. He was suffering badly, not having let water all day. Sympathizing with him for the first time, I led him out on the dark lawn. "Here, now you can pee, Ned." He kept straining and piteously crying, "I can't and it hurts!" I took him farther out to stand at a tree. "Pee, Ned!" I demanded. "If you don't, I'm going to take you into the hospital and Dr. Light will stick a long nasty tube up you and draw your water out!"

Ned, frightened by this prospect, finally urinated.

Dr. Light upon her return to the car directed me to drive downtown to a hotel where we could spend the night. We passed the grand old Brown Palace to which my father and grandfather had taken me as a child during mining conventions. Farther west lay the area that had been the downtown heart of Denver. It lay between Seventeenth and Fifteenth Streets, on Curtis, Champa, and Arapahoe. Curtis had been the Great White Way of movie palaces and Bauer's famous Ice Cream Parlor where we used to take our best girls for ice cream sodas. On Fifteenth Street the antiquarian Fred Rosenstock had opened his celebrated Bargain Book Store. Nearby stood the historic Windsor Hotel in whose lobby one could see fabulous characters of history and legend.

The section that we now entered was ill-lit and dreary. Times had changed; the business section had moved east. The movie palaces were closed and dark. Historic old Windsor Hotel was becoming a cheap lodging house. Dr. Light seemed oblivious to these changes. Evidently she too was living in the past.

"I remember the hotel I always stayed in. Modest and comfortable. And so conveniently located. On Seventeenth Street, just a short walk from the Union Railroad Station."

This building was easy to find. It was a decrepit three-story hotel she had known in its better days. Here we secured separate rooms for her, Ned, and myself. The windows were streaked with soot, the curtains grimy, the wallpaper faded. Not an aspect to rejuvenate our wearied spirits.

Nearby was a dreary all-night bar and lunchroom where Dr. Light and I went for a catch-as-can sandwich. Ned refused to go with us; all he wanted for supper was a half-dozen candy bars. These Dr. Light brought back to him with a pint of whiskey for herself.

Next morning she said cheerfully, "Now, Frank, I'm going to the hospital to see the children. While I'm gone, you must show Ned his first big city. What an adventure it will be for him!"

In my memory the details of that morning merge into a confused chaos. I walked him uptown to peer up at the Daniels and Fisher Tower, the highest building in the city. He promptly lost himself in the crowds. Then streetcars caught his fancy. He would break away from me, hop on the front end of one without paying a fare, then run to the rear door and get out only to board another. Pursuing him was like trying to chase a jackrabbit through the sage. He would disappear on one corner and pop up on another.

Then, when I thought I'd completely lost him, I glimpsed him standing in front of the Gano Downs men's clothing store, whose famous concave windows gave the illusion there was no barrier between the sidewalk observer and the displayed articles of clothing. Puzzled, Ned tried to solve the mystery. By the time I caught up with him he had dashed inside the store. Evading the pursuit of the clerks and myself, he hid in racks of men's suits, and crawled beneath them to other racks.

Just how this chaos ended I don't remember, save that Ned and I wound up at the hotel about noon to meet Dr. Light. His pranks did not disturb her. "He's just a little boy who's been in a big city for the first time. What a fabulous adventure it has been for him!"

We began the long drive home immediately. This time Ned was put in the back seat. Dr. Light sat with me in front, for we hadn't had any chance for conversation during the trip up.

The drive was long and arduous, and it was dark when we approached Walsenburg, the western turnoff to La Veta Pass and the southward road into New Mexico.

Suddenly Dr. Light said in a mild, unexcited voice, "Frank, Ned's gone."

I jammed on the brakes, stopped the car, and looked behind me. Ned was not in the back seat. Obviously, he had opened the door of the car and jumped out. The narrow highway here skirted a deep rocky arroyo into which he may have fallen. I jumped out and explored with a flashlight, expecting to find his mutilated body. Then suddenly, from far behind the car, sounded Ned's frantic cry.

"Don't go off without me! Wait for me!"

Dr. Light and I ran back up the highway. My flashlight picked up his small body limping toward us. "I've lost my shoe!" he wailed. Then we noticed that his face was covered with blood. We led him to the car and stretched him out on the back seat so Dr. Light could examine him. "My shoe! I've lost my shoe!" he kept repeating.

I ran back up the highway to hunt his missing shoe. What had happened seemed clear. The impact of Ned's body hitting the pavement from the moving car had curiously torn off one of his shoes, but I couldn't find it on the highway or down in the arroyo. Fortunately, a strong wind blowing dust that often obscured the road had slowed the speed of the car. Had I been driving faster, Ned might well have been killed.

As it was, Dr. Light's worn face showed an anxiety that she kept out of her voice. She had wiped the blood off his face and found it was trickling from a cut in his head. His shirt and pants had been almost torn off, revealing a bloody shoulder and one thigh where the skin had been scraped clean. "Any broken bones?" I asked. "I think not. Just the head injury. Of course, the light here is insufficient. We must go to the doctor in Walsenburg."

"Where's my shoe? I've lost my shoe." Ned's voice was weak and sleepy; he was feeling the shock.

"It may require a stitch or two," Dr. Light said quietly. "That'll fix you up, Ned."

We reached Walsenburg about nine o'clock. The town was old, small, and dark. The corner drugstore was open, and the obliging druggist telephoned the only doctor in town to come down to his nearby office. Into it we half-carried Ned and stretched him out on the only table. The physician was a perfect example of a good country doctor. He was middle-aged, warm and human, and competent to his limited capacity. His examination of Ned revealed no broken bones. The skin abrasions on shoulder and leg, bloody as they looked, were superficial; they could be treated and bandaged. The head injury was another matter.

The doctor cut off some of Ned's matted, bloody hair and carefully inspected the gash. "A few stitches will do, Dr. Light, as you suggested." He began to lay out the tools of his trade.

And now began a prolonged technical, medical dialogue between him and Dr. Light that I could not understand. During it she revealed the comprehensive medical and surgical training she had received in Europe. "How do you know this is merely a scalp wound? Are you sure the skull hasn't been fractured beneath it? There is one test, without x-rays, prescribed in Vienna thirty years ago." Dr. Light went on to explain it in brilliant detail. "The shock of such an injury is reflected throughout the whole physical organism. Undoubtedly, it is accompanied by psychological reactions long after the local physical injury is said to be healed. I quote the experiments made in Berlin and in London, with which you're no doubt familiar. What can we do now to ensure that these effects are not prolonged? May I offer the suggestion that . . ."

Silently nodding assent, the man efficiently went about his business of stitching up the nasty gash in Ned's head. It was apparent that Dr. Light, completely unnerved, was unconsciously projecting all her past experience upon a problem too simple to need it. She became more and more compulsively vague.

Then, as he finished sewing up the gash in Ned's head, some instinct for the need to regain her self-control asserted itself. She drew the doctor aside to the corner. In answer to her entreaties, he simply put his arm across her shoulders and shook his head with an emphatic NO. Was she asking for drugs of some kind? I never knew. But he took her into the drugstore, which had remained open for anything we needed. Returning with a quart of bourbon whiskey, Dr. Light calmed down.

All three of us took Ned to the small run-down hotel next door, and put him in a room to sleep off his ordeal. Dr. Light and I retired to our respective tawdry rooms. I was completely exhausted by the events of the trip: my sympathy with the four impoverished children taken from their homes, the antics of Ned in Denver, his accident, and the revelation of Dr. Light's lapse. My heart, I noticed, was beating with a vastly accelerated pulse. I felt decidedly undone.

A knock sounded on the door, and Dr. Light came in. Her face showed the acute physiological and psychological strain she had undergone. She plunked down on the table the quart bottle of whiskey. "You need a drink, Frank." I poured into a glass a modest drink and pushed the bottle toward her. Without hesitation she filled her own glass almost full, and emptied it neatly in one deep swallow. Then, grabbing up the bottle, she went back to her own room.

Worried about her, I went into her room next morning. She was still in bed, and the whiskey bottle on her dresser was empty. Ned in his room was awake. His head was bandaged, as were his shoulder, leg, and the foot from which the shoe had been torn off. Yet he asked cheerfully, "When do we get up?"

"As soon as Dr. Light wakes up. I'll call you."

Eventually Dr. Light came out, and we roused Ned to take breakfast with us. "You promised to buy me a new pair of shoes and anything else I wanted!" he insisted. "Yes, I promised," said Dr. Light, "and Frank will take you out now."

Her worried look reflected her dread of the telephone call to Ned's mother, Mrs. Meriam Bright, that she had to make. We listened to her conversation. "Now Meriam, don't be alarmed. I promised to bring Ned home last night, if possible; but we've had a slight accident which will delay us until tomorrow. No, not serious. So when you see Ned with a bandage or two, you must not be worried. A very minor mishap which has been well taken care of . . ."

I then took Ned to the general merchandise store around the corner and bought him a new pair of shoes. This wasn't enough. "Dr. Light promised to buy me anything else I wanted!" We went through the clothing department, the toy department. The only thing Ned wanted was a pair of roller skates. On these, bandaged as he was, he skated back to the hotel and then to the doctor's office.

The physician was exasperated. "Get this boy off these skates and put him to bed for the rest of the day!" His main concern was for our leader. "Dr. Light, you need rest and complete relaxation. All this has been a severe ordeal. Come back into my office and I'll prescribe something for you."

Next day we drove back to Taos and delivered Ned to his mother, who was much relieved after Dr. Light's telephone call. I went home, feeling that Ned's great adventure had turned into a misadventure for us all. Dr. Light, as she drove off, I was more uneasy about.

Ned's injuries healed rapidly. Dr. Light resumed her practice as usual, but with more frequent, curious lapses. I began to feel that our trip to Denver somehow had marked a turning point in her life.

A few months later, hearing that she was ill, I called at her old adobe home. A nurse received me, saying that she was going out for a short while; but her patient had requested that I be allowed to visit during this time.

Dr. Light lay in bed, her face white and drawn. "Hi, Frank!" she greeted me cheerfully. "Sit down!"

We exchanged pleasantries for a few moments. Then she said abruptly, "We know each other, don't we? Open the closet, and take out that old pair of boots in the corner. In one of them you'll find a bottle of bourbon. I can't get anything stronger, but this will help to give us a pleasant visit. What do you say?"

I didn't see Dr. Light again; she died shortly after my visit. I wish I had known her better. She was undoubtedly one of the best doctors of the time in New Mexico, a brilliant woman, a great humanitarian, and a tragically lonely soul whose need for love and understanding had never been fulfilled.

23

Smokey's Burned Feet

(Editorial—September 13, 1951)

W E folks are funny people.

You can tell us that last year two hundred thousand forest fires burned fifteen million acres of forest land in the United States. You can quote us such statistics till you're blue in the face. You can preach us sermons on fire hazards till you're hoarse as a hoot owl. And none of it will do any good.

But simply, silently, show us Smokey; and his burned feet will speak louder to our heads than statistics, and more directly to our hearts than sermons.

Smokey is the bear cub with burned feet who was picked up last year on the big Capitan forest fire in New Mexico, and sent to the national zoo at Washington.

This year, through a cooperative arrangement between the Forest Service, Post Office Department, and the Advertising Council, Inc., every mail truck in the United States will carry posters of Smokey and a plea for greater care with fire.

We may not read the plea, but it's a cinch we'll read the meaning of Smokey's burned feet.

24

The Regional Imperative

(Speech presented at the final session of the "Sundays in Tutt Library with Frank Waters Symposium" sponsored by Colorado College, Colorado Springs, on July 28, 1985)

Introduction

I THINK no one is immune to a faint flutter of butterflies in the pit of his stomach when he returns to that particular spot on Earth where he had his beginning. This region, from its short-grass plains to its western mesa and mountain slopes below its majestic peak, is the one I am privileged to call my birthplace.

My pleasure in returning here to Little London, to my old neighborhood on Shook's Run, and to Colorado College, is enhanced by a warm welcome from this city, which certainly has grown up since I was a newsboy. This is a high honor indeed.

The purpose of my visit is, of course, to attend the last Sunday session in a series devoted to discussions of my various books. Such generous consideration of my writings I cannot properly acknowledge. I can only thank those skilled in the art and craft of literature who presented talks and papers. Most of them are old friends—Alex Blackburn, Tom Lyon, Charles Adams, John Milton, Marshall Sprague, Dean Glenn Brooks, and Janet Le Compte. I am especially grateful to my longtime friend Joe Gordon of the Southwest Studies Program, who hatched this Sundays series and somehow inveigled its notable speakers to contribute their own work. Lastly I am indebted to President Riley and Colorado College itself for sponsoring it.

So you see this program owes its life and interest to a wide range of individuals in and out of Colorado. I hope all of you have gained much from it. I know I have. The thorough going-over my writing has received has revealed to me shortcomings I never suspected; while my sights have been set high, my aim has too often been off center.

My feeling for this region suggests the subject of my talk, "The Regional Imperative."

Our Mother Earth

It is a truism that man was born of the Earth.

Both have a long biography; the life of our planet goes back 4.6 billion years, man's began about 3 billion years ago. Biologists tell us that life here began with the formation of organic molecules from the gaseous atmosphere that envelopes globular Earth. Photosynthesizing bacteria in the primeval oceans added abundant oxygen to the atmosphere. Then began the slow formation of individual cells and multicellular organisms, followed by that miraculous parade of plants and animals we call biological evolution, and by the first appearance of the human species.

Concurrently the planet Earth was also evolving into the geological conformation we now know, through cataclysmic changes, continents rising and sinking, and high mountains heaving up from deep sea floors. It seems that the evolution of Earth was synchronized with that of man. The transition of life from water to land marked one of the great stages in this long process. Yet all intelligent life forms, even whales and dolphins it is said, evolved on land and returned to the sea.

How alike they are, Earth and man! Each maintains an even body temperature and an equilibrium among the primary elements of water, air, earth, and fire. There can be little wonder that from ancient times man has considered himself the microcosmic image of macrocosmic Earth. Water is the main constituent in both their bodies; blood is man's liquid flow akin to that of water throughout Earth. Both flows are in tune with the phases of the moon and sensitive to the influences of all of the planets. Man breathes eighteen times a minute or 25,920 times a day. This relates him to the great 25,920-year cycle of the Precession—the time it takes for the vernal equinox to move through the circle of the zodiac. For every eighteen breaths man takes there are seventy-two beats of the pulse, just as the arc of the ecliptic moves exactly one degree every seventy-two years.

How then can we doubt that Earth, like ourselves, is a living organism pulsing with the same universal life? Since ancient times all of

Indian America has so regarded it, in contrast to Anglo America, which considers it merely inanimate nature available for exploitation. What a beautiful residence Mother Earth has been for all of her children, and how varied are the land masses of this only planet known to support life. Lofty rainforests, thick jungles, wide plains, rolling prairies: every continent, each area, has its distinctive rhythm, mood, and influence which reflect in the lives of its human inhabitants. The drumbeat of native Africa differs from that of Indian America; yet modified as they are by their locality, both echo the pulse of their common Earth.

The Regional Imperative

The ancient Incas who lived along the spine of the Andes Mountains believed that their primal ancestors were separated into small groups. Each group was placed in the direction of the area its future tribe would populate and given the distinctive dress its descendants still wear today. Such long traditions of man's allegiance to one small portion of Earth—which I call the regional imperative—were worldwide when mankind remained thinly spread in small, isolated groups. As these groups increased to clans, tribes, and nations, men no longer gave allegiance to Earth but to the great military empires, religious dynasties, or political governments that ruled their lives. Today the world's human population has increased to some five billion, and the regional imperative has changed to racial, religious, and national imperatives with their accompanying hundreds of warring factions.

These groups' common Mother Earth has borne the brunt of their economic, social, and military rivalries. We are seeing the destruction of vast areas on Earth's surface, pollution of its atmosphere, contamination of its waters, and among ourselves widespread crime, terrorism, revolutions, and the mounting fear of annihilation by global nuclear war. The world is not a pleasant or even a safe place to live anymore.

A Planetary Imperative

Mankind must realize that it cannot continue to be fragmented into the destructive social entities that demand sole allegiance, nor can it adhere to the regional imperatives that once bound each group to small homelands. Yet it does not appear likely that any legislative or military measures can end our divisiveness. It will take a full realization of our dire need, a new way of thinking, to unite us in one effort.

It seems essential that we, as one great body of humankind, take another step forward and regard the entire body of Earth as our one planetary imperative in order to save it from further ravages. In light of present political dissension and social upheavals, this enlargement of perspective might first appear to be a utopian pipe dream; but I think it is in the cards. Mankind has been forced to take many quantum leaps in the past; we and planet Earth will survive this catastrophic era together.

Our increasing explorations of space suggest another alternative: that we may be ready to abandon our planet for greener pastures on another undetermined speck somewhere in interstellar space. Science fiction and NASA have been enthusiastic about this idea. An astrophysicist at the Los Alamos National Laboratory has predicted that by the year 2050 a seed population of one million people will inhabit the reaches of the solar system, and that after five hundred years one trillion people will exist in space beyond the solar system.

I cannot believe mankind is ready to abandon this global home on which we began to evolve some three billion years ago. We are so integrated with it that we are carrying our planetary thinking and earthly conceits into space. Already we have taken golf clubs to the moon and are preparing to extend our earth wars into "star wars." We are still umbilically connected to our Mother Earth, no matter how far from it our machines may carry us.

Our expanding awareness of the nature of the universe seems to indicate that it is structured on one cosmic principle, from the galactic to the subatomic world of matter. Each molecule within the living body of Earth, and each cell within the living body of man, is said to be informed with some degree of consciousness contributing to their composite consciousness. If this is true, then all of our planets contribute to the unfolding consciousness of the solar system, and it in turn contributes to the consciousness of the galaxy enclosing it. Then, indeed, the great goal of all the interconnected living systems from cell to star is the eventual attainment of universal consciousness. In this transcendent pattern of evolution, we can perceive the gradual rise of Earth's inherent consciousness through its successive mineral, plant, and animal forms, each manifesting a higher stage. Upon us, Earth's highest developed life form now, rests the responsibility to perceive ever more clearly its ultimate cosmic function.

Man's own evolution is marked by neither his technological achievements, marvelous as they are, nor by the succession of ever larger societies, communist or democratic, but by periodic expansions of his human consciousness. Our evolutionary journey from molecules to cells, to composite organisms, and to human beings with cerebral intelligence has also been a rising movement toward ever higher consciousness. Today, I believe, we are beginning to experience another periodic expansion toward a psychic, universal consciousness that will supersede our rational, terrestrial mode of thinking: a quantum leap, as I suggested earlier, toward a new perspective inspired by a planetary imperative.

A New Perspective

Accepting the idea, the possibility, of a planetary imperative requires that we look at the world in a way new to most of us: with a holistic, geomantic, or cosmological perspective. Modern scientific studies tend to show a grid system or network of energy lines covering Earth. At the junctions of these lines are nodes of power comparable to acupuncture points on a human body. Many such sites are oriented toward the solstices and equinoxes, the planets and the stars. Their influences affect not only the magnetic currents in Earth's surface, but the mineral deposits and the waters below. The combined energy they release promotes our own development.

At such foci stand the sacred mountains of the world, widely regarded as depositories of cosmic energy. Pikes Peak here is such a font of power. To it in the past Indian tribes from the Great Plains and down from the mountains made annual pilgrimages. It was the beacon for the later, white "Pikes Peak or Bust" caravans that crossed the plains. Still later it marked a mecca for hordes of invalids who believed they would regain health from the region's pure air and medicinal springs.

On other such sites prehistoric peoples erected shrines and mazes, great stone circles, medicine wheels, temples, and pyramids. This is not a new way of looking at the relationship of man to Earth. It is really very old. The Chinese gave it the name we interpret as "geomancy," which referred to the divinatory art of reading a locality's topographical features in order to place man's structures in harmony with the forces of nature. They knew it as *feng-shui,* "wind and water," and the lines of energy were *lung-mei,* or "paths of the dragon." The British now call Earth's energy lines "ley lines," and on their patterns ancients built megalithic monuments like Stonehenge.

Similar energy channels in Mexico, called *trazos,* oriented ancient ceremonial centers, temples, and pyramids. Even the great metropolis of prehistoric Mexico, Teotihuacan, and the Mayan religious city of Palenque, were laid out as geomantic or cosmological paradigms. There are many other examples in Egypt, Peru, and elsewhere of this phenomenon, which Maurice Freedman called "mystical ecology" in his 1969 presidential address, entitled "Geomancy," before the Royal Anthropological Institute in London.

The common purpose of the ancient builders was to achieve harmony with the natural forces of Earth and sky. Their ruins today still visibly express the world view of their vanished civilizations. We can be properly impressed by the divinatory art that enabled these architects to align their temples and cities with astronomical, mathematical, and calendrical precision to topographical and planetary positions. But the modern visionary pioneers who have carried forward and developed the ancient geomantic concept are equally impressive.

Early among them was Georges Ivanovitch Gurdjieff, who established in France a school of the mystical teachings of Central Asia. In his doctrine of "reciprocal maintenance" he grouped all modes of existence into a series of energies or essences ranging upward from formless energy, through Earth and its plant, vertebrate, and human forms, to finally the supreme will and consciousness. Each class of energy fed on that preceding it and in turn fed its successor.

Teilhard de Chardin, a Catholic priest, advanced the now-famous theory that a "noosphere," an envelope of thought or a planetary mind, would eventually surround Earth once mankind's consciousness became unified and expanded. Since Chardin's death in 1955, Oliver Reiser, a physicist, has reportedly developed Chardin's theory. Reiser has postulated the existence of a psi or paranormal field of knowing, which is the equivalent of Chardin's noosphere, and which functions in conjunction with the Van Allen radiation belts surrounding the globe. This bipolar field is something of a planetary cerebral cortex; its two hemispheres correspond to the halves of a human brain.

How interconnected everything is! The left lobe of the human brain, as Robert Ornstein has written in *The Psychology of Consciousness,* controls the right side of our physical body and our rational thought processes. The right lobe is connected to the left side of the body and directs our intuitive and spiritual insights. Ornstein's neurological explanation can be stated more simply: philosophy since the time of Pythagoras has been based on the principle that in each of us there are two selves. One, the outer persona or personality, is oriented to the material world of appearances, of things. The other is an inner self with an apperception of the universal realm of divine reality.

These bipolar tensions have also split world mankind. Western civilization is dominated by the rational intellect, which is chiefly concerned with constantly increasing our material wealth, while the East traditionally has been more devoted to religious pursuits. Reconciliation of these opposite polarities would integrate us collectively as well as individually. A common imperative effort to preserve the global Earth from further destruction may well unite us all on a higher level of consciousness. Could this eventually lead to a postulated planetary mind consciously functioning as a part of a universal process of still greater integration?

How nebulous, incredibly vast, and immeasurably lengthy such an evolution of Earth and man appears to our puny, limited minds! Yet the trend of thought manifested by so many intuitive spokesmen points the general direction we are already taking. More and more of us will follow the trails they are blazing, impelled by the dire necessity of changing our mode of thinking in this tragic era of world turmoil. Hence it seems to me that a planetary imperative, with its cosmological perspective, is an inevitable step forward. Curiously enough, it validates the regional imperative of ancient small societies. For in achieving harmony with their immediate environment, they also attained a measure of integration with the world outside. As we know, the whole is in every part.

Regional Writing

These rather abstract and probably too expanded thoughts recall to me the specific subject that has brought us together: regional writing. It has long been the custom of the Eastern literary establishment to look down its nose at regional novels, especially those of Western writers, as being provincial, naive, and too narrow in points of view. John Milton in his *South Dakota Review* has been jousting against this prejudice for many years. Yet I think such criticism is sometimes justified. Too often regional writers paint only "local color," being too close to the trees to see the forest.

Nevertheless, regional writing is the common denominator of all literature. Certainly a writer must know who he is, what he comes from, how he stands in relation to his own region, but without confining himself to these limits of his awareness. His stance should provide him a glimpse of the horizons beyond. A regional novel, if it fulfills its highest function, is also universal.

I have never objected to being called a regional writer. This is my stance. Here my roots go deep. Yet in my attempts over the years to fulfill, in some measure at least, the true function of regional writing, I have often recalled an outing with my high school physiography class here in Colorado Springs. We met at the old Busy Corner downtown, rode the streetcar to Adam's Crossing, and spent the afternoon digging sharks' teeth out of limestone outcroppings. We needed no lecture to explain their meaning. It was apparent in a single tooth held in a sweaty palm. In a flash of comprehension I could see sharks and strange fish nosing at the streetcar windows: Adam's Crossing, Pikes Peak above, and all America itself washed by the engulfing waters of a timeless time. This was no longer a separate and isolated little vicinity, but an indistinguishable undersea part of a whole, vast world mysteriously undergoing another cataclysmic, evolutionary change. Such are the nebulous roots of feeling, deeper than thinking, that nurture in a regional writer a fuller realization of his place and time.

Change, constant change, is the one great theme in the history of Earth and its human family. There have been many changes here in my hometown, some of which, I think, have not been for the better. There will be more, as everywhere. The world is now undergoing the greatest cultural change since the beginning of the Christian era. Let us believe that it will reflect our growing universality of thought and unity with the enduring Earth.

25

Work, Sex, & Society

(Editorial—October 25, 1951)

I N a talk at Los Alamos last week, Dr. Donald Powell Wilson called America the only neurotic nation. He traced the growth of our neurosis to such factors as "moral legislation" and resulting gangsterdom and crime, and the prevalence of "Horatio Alger" ideals that can be realized by only a few.

His advice was: "Life is work, sex, and society; if you adjust properly in all three areas, you need never worry about insanity or neurosis."

From behind our obscure, battered, rolltop desk, we are a little worried about this rather glib formula. Somehow it seems to us that there must be a little more than plenty of work, sex, and social contacts to give our lives direction, meaning, and a sense of inner security.

Affluent gangsters often work quite hard in organizing and supervising their far-flung crime rings. From the photos of their glamorous mistresses, and their reception by respectable neighbors, they evidently also have made excellent adjustments in the areas of sex and society.

On the contrary, the late Mahatma Gandhi did very little work in the acceptable sense; he abstained from sex; and he removed himself as far as possible from all society.

The difference between this great leader of mankind and any influential TV gangster is, of course, a factor that is not mentioned by Dr. Wilson. A spiritual factor that is simply a deeply felt or dimly perceived sense of relationship to something beyond the work-sex-society scope of our world existence.

It need not be scientifically defined. For it has been apperceptively felt by all primitive peoples since the beginning of time, and it has given rise to the profound truths of Navajo ceremonialism as well as to the great creative structures of Christianity.

Without it, although we are "properly adjusted" to the "areas" of work-sex-society, humanity—as well as each individual—will be bound in a neurosis of frustration.

26

El Crepusculo

(Essay)

FROM the fall of 1949 to the spring of 1952, I edited the Taos weekly newspaper, *El Crepusculo.*

The paper was a descendent of the oldest newspaper in New Mexico and the first printed west of the Mississippi. It was established in Santa Fe in 1834 by Antonio Barreiro, a delegate to the Mexican Congress. He named it *El Crepusculo de la Libertad,* "The Dawn of Liberty," a *grito* for relief from Mexican dictatorship. Only four numbers were issued, and in 1836 Padre Antonio Jose Martinez moved the press up to Taos. The Padre is still the most controversial figure of his time. He was not only a priest, but a politician and a revolutionary. Defrocked and excommunicated from the Church, he continued to officiate as a parish priest and publish pamphlets and school manuals.

The first major issue of the modern *El Crepusculo* appeared September 29, 1949, on the eve of the annual San Geronimo Fiesta. This fiesta derived from the ancient harvest festival of the nearby Indian pueblo of San Geronimo de Taos. Name saint of the Pueblo, San Geronimo—or Saint Jerome—was born in Dalmatia early in the fifth century, a famous scholar of his time.

A San Geronimo Historical Supplement to this issue of the paper, most of which I wrote myself, recounted all this history, both Spanish and Indian, for the benefit of our Anglo readers. It also set the tone of *El Crepusculo* as conserving the heritage of Taos's three cultural groups during the region's continuing growth.

This was a big axe to grind for a new small weekly. There had been a number of successive small newspapers printed in either Spanish or

English during the past, the last of which was *The Taoseño,* whose owner was on the verge of going broke. Then appeared Edward C. Cabot of the historic Cabots of Boston. I had met him some time before when he and his first wife, a Lowell, had spent the summers here in a fine old adobe west of town. He had now returned with his second wife, intending to settle permanently in New Mexico and engage in a business venture of some sort. My suggestion that he buy and publish the failing *Taoseño* appealed to him and his wife. His purchase of the paper was settled while I was in Los Angeles, and I returned to work for him. The historic *El Crepusculo* was revived as the name for the weekly.

Cabot was assuredly one of the strangest oddballs in this New Mexico community of Indians, Hispanics, and Anglos. I have unkindly caricatured him in my novel *The Woman at Otowi Crossing,* but I think my exaggerations were not too unfounded. He was short and plump, with a dead white pallor on his face that never betrayed an expression, and always dressed in severely cut suits, starched white shirts, and black shoes. Manifesting his innate sense of superiority, he never spoke first to anyone he met, nor permitted anyone, not even his wife, to precede him through a doorway. I must confess that I never liked him.

From the start we ran into trouble. The Publisher, as he liked to be known, was easily influenced, knew nothing about publishing, and being endowed with great finances, hired almost everyone who came looking for a job. Spud Johnson, a great friend of us both, he named editor. Spud, though a good journalist and humorist, was too hesitant to manage affairs; he left it to me.

Another new staff member was Mrs. Gertrude van Tijn, a courageous Dutch woman with a fabulous background. Caught in the Nazi roundup of Jews in Holland, she had secretly worked for the underground, was detected and sent to a concentration camp in Germany. From this she miraculously escaped, recovered later in Israel, and was then sent to China to work for UNNRA. Finally, she came to Taos to regain her physical and mental health. Cabot hired her to write a column of world news. He then hired another newcomer to town, Abel Plenn, to write a similar column. Plenn had written a notable book on the tragic conditions in Spain, *The Wind in the Olive Trees,* and was politically acute. He immediately leased a large house, and began to demand Mrs. van Tijn's copy as mere research for his own column. Every week she came to the office in tears, and the rest of us were greatly upset.

It was finally agreed that Plenn should be fired. But by whom? I declined, not being the editor. Spud refused. And the Publisher, who had hired him, was not up to it. When Plenn received written notice and stalked into the office to confront him, Cabot ran into the back shop and hid under the press, leaving his wife, Charlotte, to dismiss him. Plenn then filed suit for breach of contract, demanding payment for the lease of his house, his salary for the period, and damages to his reputation. Cabot immediately paid off in full in order to avoid publicity. Mrs. van Tijn thereafter wrote her excellent column for several years and remained a close friend of mine until her death in Oregon in 1974 where, almost blind, she had gone to live near her daughter.

With these inter-office squabbles *El Crepusculo* faced another major challenge. A new competitive paper, the *Taos Star,* put our little weekly to shame. It was financially well backed and presented an imposing format—standard seven-column size, printed on glossy paper, with good layout, photographic coverage, and reportage. An excellent newspaper, it was edited by Charlie du Tant, a superb professional newsman and an old friend of mine. Its policy was to encourage the modernization of Taos, its battle cry Progress at any Price.

It was evident that *El Crepusculo,* in attempting to preserve the heritage of the region's three cultural groups, was facing a long uphill fight.

That fall the Cabots returned east for the winter, where he owned large houses in both Boston and Washington, D.C. Spud obtained a leave of absence and was taken by friends to spend the winter in Mexico. In deference to Cabot, I carried Spud's name as editor on the masthead, waiting for Cabot to authorize me to use my own. He never did, but late in March I received a telegram from him saying Spud had written him asking for a definite statement that he was still wanted on the paper. Charlotte suggested that he be given a separate department on the paper. Both wanted to know if I had any objections. I wired back that I had no objections to his contributing a weekly column or article if he would not be called upon to collaborate on editorial policy and management. I then belatedly put my name on the masthead as editor.

This arrangement worked out well. Spud sent me from Mexico periodic feature articles of great interest. In recent years he had written and printed on his own small hand press a tiny weekly resumé of local events entitled *The Horsefly*, illustrated by his own woodblocks, most charming and amusing. Soon after he returned home in the spring, as did the Cabots, his "Horsefly" was added as a page to *El Crepusculo*, a welcome addition.

Every month that winter I sent Cabot a full report of our progress, with suggested ways to reduce operating costs and increase circulation. To these he never replied. I didn't understand why until he returned, evincing his displeasure. He wasn't concerned about putting *El Crepusculo* on a paying basis; he wanted to use its annual deficit as a tax write-off.

I continued to build up the paper: increasing the standard seven-column pages to fourteen or sixteen, with 49 percent advertising, and a circulation of three thousand including subscribers throughout the United States and several foreign countries.

What a trying and yet exciting winter it was for me. The old flatbed press often broke down; the Linotype was always squirting lead, necessitating hours for repair. There was no folding machine. We had to fold by hand the printed sheets as they came off the press. I was never able to leave the shop until midnight on press day, walking home in freezing cold through the unlit plaza and street, through the dark snowy wilderness that is now a public park, to fall into bed exhausted. But what a sense of achievement we all felt—the greatest reward of small-town newsmen; we had finally put to bed another issue of *El Crepusculo*.

The staff in the front office included several notable characters who covered all of our three racial groups with their different languages, traditions, and customs. Joe Fulton was our top-notch reporter for the major English section. He loved people, knew everyone in town, and possessed a file-cabinet memory. If there is anyone capable of writing the intimate history of Taos in that period, it is Joe.

The Spanish section of two pages was edited by Felix Valdez, who like his father before him had worked on previous papers. A little, courtly man, he was an authority on the Spanish language, both as spoken in Spain and the current idiomatic Spanish of New Mexico. He possessed an uncounted store of old proverbs and folk beliefs, and was especially adept at reporting *velorios* with a literary flourish. For his section we obtained cartoons drawn by J. W. Marquez, a young man from a mountain village who had wandered into the office after taking a correspondence course. His weekly cartoon "Pepe y Pancho" portrayed two characters speaking in old colloquial Spanish, and depicting the simple, seasonal life of his mountain village.

For Indian coverage we received a weekly column from both Taos Pueblo and Picuris Pueblo. Spud's "Horsefly" provided a page of humor, and Gertrude van Tijn's world news a digest of what was going on in the world outside. To counteract the *Star's* photographs of distressing car accidents and scenes of murder, I began the custom of featuring on the front page a scenic photograph of the mountains or the Rio Grande, a huge Penitente cross, sacred Blue Lake, or a hedge of wild plums in blossom.

My own chores were varied. I helped Joe with spot news, wrote feature articles and book reviews, edited all copy, read galley and page proofs, and spent Sundays writing two or three editorials.

Tension between myself and Cabot began when he settled permanently in Taos, building a new modern house, and spending every day in the office. Publishing *El Crepusculo* now began to give him a sense of status, an itch for power, a feeling that through it he could mold public opinion. He began to give me illiterate editorials, which I threw into the wastebasket.

One of them created a rumpus. It demanded that the whole German race be obliterated as a result of the Nazi atrocities. I refused to publish it, and Spud and Mrs. van Tijn agreed with my rejection. Charlotte was indignant; she reminded me that I had no business refusing the publisher of a paper, which he had bought and was wholly financing, the right to express his own views. The editorial was not printed, but it left a bad taste in all of our mouths.

From time to time Cabot also sent to my desk atrociously sentimental poems written in ungrammatical English. I referred them with deplorable tact to Charlotte, who in turn gave them to Spud to rewrite. We had moved into larger quarters, and Spud was in the office continually, writing and setting up his "Horsefly" with Charlotte. More and more the Cabots relied upon him for support, and to rewrite their occasional editorials, poems, and articles. So gradually there developed a noticeable rift between the Cabots and myself

A clear break came when I was invited to speak at a Newspaper Week conference held at the University of Colorado on May 12, 1951. As we put *El Crepusculo* to bed on Wednesday night, and my talk was scheduled for Saturday, I was free to drive up to Boulder in my pickup.

There was a good gathering of outstanding journalists in the country, including Edward J. Meeman, editor of the *Memphis Press-Scimitar,* popularly known as the "Man Who Put the Crimp on Crump" by breaking the power of the Boss Crump political machine in Tennessee; and George Ver Steeg, editor of the *Pella Chronicle,* who had won two trophies for the best weekly editorial page in Iowa.

The title of my own talk was "The Newspaper and the Adhesive Past." In it I emphasized that *El Crepusculo* was a modern weekly newspaper whose avowed function was to report current news. Yet the region it served held three cultural groups, Indian, Hispanic, and Anglo; and some of its traditions and customs stemmed back to the era before American occupancy. Hence we could not completely ignore this long past which still clung to the coattails of modern progress.

I quoted an interesting example. A man had been killed on the highway by a hit-and-run driver. He could not be identified, being known only as a sheepherder who always referred to himself as "El Tocallo." In despair his neighbors came into our office to ask the help of Felix Valdez, editor of our Spanish section. Felix was equal to the occasion, saying that the full name of El Tocallo was El Tocallo de la Muerte, "The Namesake of Death." He also added that according to tradition, death was often referred to as La Madre Sebastiana. With this clue, the victim was finally identified as Sebastian Romero.

The talk was well received and reported, with favorable accounts appearing in *Publishers Weekly* and the *Printers Exchange Digest.* But when I returned to work on Monday morning, proud of having gained *El Crepusculo* wide notice, Cabot refused to comment. He was angry because he had not been invited instead of me, nor had I taken him with me.

From then on the situation grew more intolerable. The financial backers of the *Taos Star* went broke and Charlie du Tant took it over on a shoestring basis. When it became obvious that he could not make expenses, he sold it to Cabot and moved to Santa Fe as Governor Mechem's secretarial assistant. The acquisition of much of the *Star's* physical plant, one of its staff, and many of its subscribers and advertisers increased Cabot's growing itch for power. It was not enough to mold public opinion through *El Crepusculo.* Every day he invited local politicos to spit on the floor beside his highly polished black slippers, surreptitiously giving them rolls of bills while he expostulated on every subject under the sun. I began to suspect that he was preparing to put in his bid for election to the state legislature.

Joe had retired from active service in the Air Force, but was in reserve status. He was finally called back for duty and resigned from the paper. His absence as reporter created a serious loss. There was no one to fill his shoes. Cabot and I seldom spoke to each other; and he, Charlotte, and Spud never included me in their low-voiced discussions of whom they might obtain to replace him. One of Spud's friends was finally hired. This presented new problems. He was a newcomer who knew few people in town, and his copy required my copious editing. His resentment of this was backed by the Cabots. It began to be evident that a final break between the Cabots and myself was due.

My demise as editor-in-chief came in the spring of 1952. I came to my battered rolltop desk early one morning to find a letter firing me on the grounds of incompetency. I telephoned the Cabots immediately, but they had left town for several days. So I packed up my things and went for a vacation in Mexico. When I returned home, I sent in an application for an Atomic Energy Commission job in Los Alamos, giving *El Crepusculo* as a reference. Cabot replied that he did not recommend me for employment. Nevertheless, I was hired by the Los Alamos Scientific Laboratory as Information Consultant and spent three years working in Los Alamos and in Las Vegas, Nevada, during the atomic tests.

The anticlimax to *El Crepusculo's* brief splurge was not pleasant. Cabot was elected to the state legislature at obviously great cost to him, and was never reelected. He sold the paper to the publisher of the *Santa Fe New Mexican,* who changed its name to the *Taos News.* Cabot and Charlotte were divorced. He then married a local Spanish girl, formerly a waitress whom he had always tipped with a dime from his leather pocketbook. This third marriage estranged him from former friends. He never spoke to anyone on the plaza. As he began to succumb to his fatal illness, he confined himself in his home except at noon. Then he would come to El Patio to drink beer at the bar, never speaking to anyone, never looking up from his glass. Despite my dislike for him, I felt sorry for this scion of a noble family who had come to such a dead end.

In retrospect now, years later, I must freely admit the justification of his own viewpoint. He had bought *El Crepusculo* outright, as well as the defunct *Star,* investing a great deal of money in their purchase and operating expense. The paper offered the first opportunity in his life to voice his repressed ideas and feelings. But over its editorial policy and reportorial direction, he had little control. It was usurped by a hired editor. He could not even publish his own poems without having them given to someone else to rewrite. Nor could he publish all his views on public matters without objections, and this he needed in order to advance his political ambitions. If Cabot wanted to use *El Crepusculo* as an expression of his ego, there was no doubt that I used it to express my own feelings for the land and its people.

Yet the paper was a novel endeavor, which in its short life benefited the community and aroused considerable interest outside. With good reason. Since its passing I know of no other like it. The day of small, local, independent newspapers is over. Most are being taken over by large national publishing chains. Wherever you go, you see in them the same syndicated political opinions, the same syndicated columns and features, the same advertisements of national chain stores and manufacturers. Their modicum of local news is aimed toward supporting the business community and garnering more advertising inches. This, as they say, is "the name of the game."

The crepuscular life of *El Crepusculo* began at a time when Taos itself was beginning to outgrow its boots as a backward, impoverished village. It was entering a new era of modernization and rabid commercialism that would transform it into a town like any other—devoid of its former color and charm, exploited by an influx of real estate hustlers and chain business stores of every kind. Its historic adhesive past was losing its glue and becoming unstuck.

Charlie du Tant of the *Taos Star* had sensed the change of wind. But *El Crepusculo,* in attempting to preserve the traditions and values of the past, was out of tune with the times and bucking the inexorable march of progress.

We should have known its fate from its name. For *el crepúsculo* means the crepuscular light not only of dawn but of evening. How much fun we had, though, in its twilight hour!

27

Pikes Peak by Barrow

(Editorial—March 23, 1950)

LAST week a fellow pushed a wheelbarrow all the way to the top of 14,110-foot Pikes Peak. He was forty-nine years old, and it took him five days.

This noteworthy accomplishment follows the even more epoch-making feat of another fellow who, some years ago, pushed a peanut with his nose to the summit of America's favorite mountain peak.

It seems as if there ought to be some kind of a conclusion, lesson, example, moral, or pertinent remark to be drawn from this valiant expenditure of time and energy. But after scratching our head for too long already, we're durned if we know what it is.

28

Frank Waters Park Dedication

*(Speech written for the dedication of Frank Waters Park
in Colorado Springs on April 27, 1991)*

MIDDLE Shook's Run Neighborhood Association, Vice Mayor Leon
Young, City Council, and the People of Colorado Springs:

It is difficult to express at long range my regret at not being able to
be here this morning for the dedication of this park on the site of my
early steps. I'd have preferred to thank you in person for the honor of
having it named for me, and for the pride I now feel.

No other person can better convey my feelings, however, than Professor Alexander Blackburn. He is a literary scholar of wide repute, an
editor, an author whose appraisal of my own writings will soon be
published—and a dear friend who knows my thoughts and feelings.

My grandfather Joseph Dozier settled here along Shook's Run in
the 1870s and built this ungainly big house at 435 East Bijou Street to
house his growing family of six girls and a son. My mother, Onie,
moved into a house of her own for a time. Yet none of them quite out-
grew the clan nest, returning to it for the birth of every child. So I too
was born in the big front bedroom on the second floor.

My father, Frank Jonathon, died when I was twelve years old. My
mother; my younger sister, Naomi; and I then moved back into the old
house on Shook's Run to live with my grandparents. The neighborhood had long been familiar to me, my first little world. From Bijou
Hill on the west to the high embankment of the Santa Fe Railroad to
the east, it seemed a world complete in itself.

On the corner of Corona and Bijou stood the small grocery store
owned by grumpy Mr. Bryce and his sweet little wife who always gave
us a dill pickle from the barrel. Shook's Run was a deep gulch through

which ran a small stream from which we picked watercress. Children sorted the neighborhood families into those who wouldn't let you jump their fence or step on their lawn and those who gave you an apple or a cookie.

More interesting were the regular visitors from the world outside. On snowy mornings the Pan Dandy Bread wagon, drawn by a spanking team of mares, stopped in the street long enough for me to hitch my sled behind it for a fast ride to school. During the summer we waited for the Iceman to come, carrying from his wagon a huge block of ice to put in our ice box, and giving to us children chips of ice to suck through our handkerchiefs. The Knife-and-Scissors Sharpener with his portable grinding wheel. Indian Joe, the vegetable huckster in his wagon. And from the alley in back, the shrill cries of the Rags, Bottles, and Sacks Man making his rounds.

The girls and boys in my class at Columbia School were another assortment whose peculiarities it didn't take long to learn. A tall, black-haired boy was a whiz at arithmetic while I was a numbskull, but we became partners in several escapades. His name was Charles Hathaway. We became chums and went through school together. He eventually directed the apportioning of monies to all the schools in the state of Colorado. He now lives in Denver and we are still friends.

Columbia School was a long walk up Bijou, through the underpass of the railroad embankment, to El Paso Street, then north and west to a two-storied red brick building on the edge of the prairie. It was here, in the eighth grade, I first saw her. The new girl who had just entered school. Leslie Shane. She looked up to meet my stare, and in that instant it happened. That single glance revealed for me a strange truth and a mystery never since explained. My soul rushed out to her in a flood, as if I had long awaited her coming. Yes, children fall in love as well as grownups, and with as deep feelings.

Leslie was a small girl with apricot-colored hair, a pale face covered with freckles, large brown eyes, and a snub nose. She seemed the most beautiful girl I had ever seen. Bashful as I was, I began to walk home with her. She lived with her parents and younger sister on top of Bijou Hill, a block west. That October she consented to go with me to our class Halloween party.

"Why don't you just drop by on your way?" I suggested. "There's no need of me climbin' the hill just to come back down."

"I guess that'll be all right," said Leslie.

I didn't tell anyone at home I was taking Leslie to the party, but on the night of the party I waited anxiously till I heard a loud knocking on the front door and rushed to open it. Standing before me was Mr. Shane, grinning good-naturedly. "Well, young man!" he roared. "I've brought your girl here for you to take to the party. But you make sure that you bring her home. Understand?" He pushed Leslie over the threshold and walked away.

Leslie came in to meet the family at the supper table. Mother was dutifully shocked at my lack of gallantry in not calling for Leslie, but Leslie was not embarrassed. And I did walk her home in the dark in the middle of Bijou Street.

My class graduated from Columbia that year, and entered high school just three blocks from home. This ended my daily walks with Leslie, and I saw her seldom. A short time later Mr. Shane moved his family away—where, I didn't know—and I never saw Leslie again.

All these persons and dozens more I haven't mentioned—the odd assortment of neighbors and tradesmen and school classmates and yes, the two friendly ghosts, the Kadles, who haunted our house—left on me imprints that I've carried long after I've forgotten their names. Despite our over-the-fence spats, I loved them all. It seemed to me then, as I've said, that we were somehow interconnected in a small closed world. Now I'm learning that all of us in this larger planetary world are similarly interconnected in a global pattern of relatedness and mutual dependency.

So in dedicating this park on Shook's Run, I feel as though we're remembering all of those who gave it life.

29

Safe and Sane Fourth

(Editorial—July 5, 1951)

I F we're lucky, this week's issue will be out in time to warrant a plug for a "safe and sane Fourth."

It was many years ago that we first heard this phrase. Papa sold Mama the idea. Mama sold us. We agreed to accept ice cream and cake instead of the usual batch of fireworks.

All went well until noon. Firecrackers popped all around us until the neighborhood supply ran out. We began on our ice cream and cake in safe and sane peace.

Then some miner's kids got hold of several sticks of dynamite. They went off with a bang on the side of the railroad underpass, just as a buggy was going through. The horses bolted, throwing a woman out of the buggy. Careening down the street, the wheels caught on a patch of wooden sidewalk. We heard from our front lawn the crash of the buggy on the hotel porch, the screaming of horses entangled in the traces.

Then suddenly from the underpass opposite us came running one of the miner's kids covered with blood: a flying piece of metal dyna-mite cap had cut an artery in his arm. While he was bloodying up the kitchen during emergency treatment, more neighbors arrived carrying the woman thrown out of the buggy. Her parasol was smashed, her head had gone through the crown of her picture hat, and one stay had popped loose from a torn corset.

Papa's dire predictions on the folly of a noisy Fourth had been well demonstrated. But unfortunately the excitement had raised in our small animal breasts the craving for still more. Nothing could appease it. Our two patients, recovering on the front lawn, had emptied the ice-cream freezer and the cake box. There was nothing left for Papa that evening but to walk to town and bring back a bag of pinwheels and sparklers to restore the family equilibrium.

Like him we still believe in a safe and sane Fourth, especially in this later era of mechanized destruction. But this rambling has gone on long enough. We have got to get busy if we are to buy a bottle or two of whiskey and a case of beer, step on the gas, and hurtle off at a seventy-five-mile-an-hour clip on a crowded highway to spend this safe and sane Fourth of July in a tinder-dry forest that will explode with mountain-size fireworks at the first spark from a cigarette.

30

The Horses

(Essay)

No sketches of unique personalities I have known would be complete without some notes on a few horses I have owned. Each had a distinct character of its own, and all of them spoke for the spirit of the living land.

There must be enough Indian in me to feel that every man's land should have a horse on it. This Indian feeling, I must admit, has far outstretched all sensible bounds. Every reservation is full of unused worthless broomtails, half-starved on the overgrazed land. A man would be better off if he got rid of his bunch and brought in a few good animals he could use. But no. An Indian has got to have horses, the more the better, to show his social standing; or perhaps merely because he loves their movement in the static landscape. This latter feeling may partly explain why I have always kept a few horses on my own small pastures. It is a great pleasure to observe their conformations, their superb movements, their habits and feeding.

They may have a deeper appeal. The horse is the oldest existing mammal; man is the youngest. Does this suggest the reason for Indians' deep veneration of the horse? In Navajo and Apache myth and ritual the gods in the upper world owned horses long before they were given to man below. They were created for him from all the elements of the earth. A cornstalk was used for the spine and legs, which is why the skeleton of a horse is jointed like a cornstalk. The powers of rain, hail, whirlwinds, stars, and the rainbow were imparted to give life. They were colored according to the four directions—white for the east, blue for the south, red for the west, and black or spotted for the north. How beautiful and powerful they were, and how peculiarly

American. We are told that they first appeared here in this ancient New World as the tiny primitive Eohippus, then migrated to Asia over a now vanished land bridge. It is believed that they were tamed by nomads on the steppes of central Asia. Eventually fully developed horses reached Europe, and in historic times were brought back to America by Spanish explorers. Whatever their history, they seem to have been one of the last wild animals to be domesticated. Horses still reflect their wild heritage, the unpredictable moods and enduring strength of the earth itself.

Every cowpoke warns that it is folly to make a pet of a horse. You have to break his spirit from the start, riding him hell-to-breakfast for all his bucking, and mastering him completely. I don't hold with this cowboy stuff. Although it may be true of cold-blooded animals, it doesn't work with warm-blooded horses, who will kill themselves or their riders before their spirit can be broken. Several cowpokes absolutely refused to mount our Thoroughbred mare. Hazel Hoffman, who bred Thoroughbreds on her Rocking Horse Ranch, always maintained that a horse was ruined if it were ever allowed to buck. A colt must be broken to halter and saddle by long, patient, and gentle handling.

Aside from our pleasure in riding and watching them, our horses became intimate family members. Here are a few of them.

Rocket

Rocket was Janey's favorite horse. In 1946, before we were married, she had owned a great stallion named Rock whom only she could ride. To replace him, she bought a filly colt named Rocket. She was a registered Thoroughbred, brown, spindly, with great soft eyes. When she was a two-year-old, we took her to Albuquerque to be trained for the track. She had massive sculptured hindquarters, a deep chest, and long, thin running legs with long pasterns that gave spring to her stride.

How she could run! But one afternoon when the trainer was away, the Spanish exercise boy put her in a run when cold, then jerked her up sharply. This gave Rocket a splint, ruining her off foreleg. We could never run her, or even ride her after that, for she would suddenly stumble and throw the best of riders.

I went broke in 1948 and left for California, while Janey went to work for Mary Jane Colter, interior decorator of the Fred Harvey hotels. Before leaving, she gave Rocket to a horse lover in Farmington to keep in his own small band. A year later we both returned to Taos. Janey, pining for Rocket, took off for Farmington to get her back. She returned with distressing news. The man to whom she had entrusted the care of Rocket had been a deputy sheriff who followed the practice of stealing silver and turquoise jewelry from drunk Navajos. Fired from his job, and unable to feed his horses, he had turned them loose on the southern edge of the Jicarilla Apache Reservation.

We immediately hired a cowpoke with a pickup and drove back to Farmington. The ex-deputy took us to his wife's isolate trading post near the reservation to spend the night. In the morning we set out to find Rocket. The band of horses had gone wild; there was no tracing them. But once a day, we were told, they came to a waterhole a few miles away. Here we waited and finally caught Rocket when she came. She was so starved her ribs stuck out. Her mane and tail were matted and full of burrs. Dysentery had stained her back legs yellow. And in the right side of her jaw there was a hole oozing pus where she had been shot with a .22 rifle.

A hot-blooded horse can't be treated like an ordinary cold-blooded cow horse. It goes crazy when manhandled. So it was a job roping her and getting her into the pickup. Then she tried to jump over the side and got caught, hanging over the rail. It was a wonder she wasn't killed. But we brought her back to Taos and turned her loose in the pasture behind Nicolai Fechin's studio, which I had rented. From that day on, it was impossible to load her in a truck or horse-trailer.

From my land at Arroyo Seco, the Quintanas brought down a huge stack of hay at which she could stand all winter, and daily I gave her a feeding of warm mash. How wonderful it was to see Rocket improve. Her barrel chest filled out and deepened, her muscled hindquarters became a sculptor's dream, and her brown coat grew glossy. The hole in her jaw still oozed pus and blood. So in the spring I got two men to take out the impacted rifle bullet and the tooth it had infected. One of them was young Walton Hawk, the son of Bill and Rachel up on Lobo who was beginning practice as a vet; the other was Aloysius Liebert, an old reliable standby.

That spring Rocket foaled a palomino we named Star, and we bought to join them a little white mare named Cry-Baby, both of which I will describe later. Then in the fall we took them—Rocket, Cry-Baby, and Star—up to our place in Seco. Occasionally we rode

Rocket in the big pasture, but gave it up; she was too fast and likely to stumble. Nor could we take her out on the reservation or up into mountains. She spooked at the smell of a bear, a noise in the brush, and then there was no holding her.

Janey played a game both mares loved. Dressed in her leather chaps, her apricot hair flying, she would run Cry-Baby in the back woodland—around the chokecherry thickets, through the aspen grove, and across the clearing, in a great circle. Rocket followed with pounding hoofs. And then the chase back through the open pasture to the house! Rocket's long thin legs were like pistons driven by her powerful hindquarters. You could hear the thunder of her hoofs out on the road; she seemed to shake the very house. Cry-Baby could not keep up with her.

Rocket was seldom aroused like this. Like all Thoroughbreds, she would poke along like an old plow horse most of the time. But I loved to watch her grazing. Under her glossy coat her muscles stretched, bunched, rippled like water. She loved company, loved to be petted, and would stand at the back fence waiting for attention.

She was sick only once, evidently with colic. Trinidad, an Indian friend, told me that the spring change of temperature of the water in the stream had made her sick, a common occurrence. To cure her, he instructed me to burn some old greasy rags, then stamp out the flames and hold the rags to her nose for her to inhale the fumes and smoke. I did so, and in a little while Rocket regained her feet and walked out into the pasture.

Cry-Baby bullied her, eating her own grain quickly, then stealing Rocket's. Rocket didn't protest. Her dependence on Cry-Baby was like that of a child on a grownup. When I saddled Cry-Baby and rode off, Rocket would stand at the fence and whimper until we returned. One afternoon I heard her pounding up the pasture and neighing wildly until I came out of the house. She then turned and ran back a ways, waiting until I caught up with her, then running farther back. I followed her all the way to the back woodland to discover that Cry-Baby had broken through the fence and couldn't get back again.

It took time to learn Rocket's nature. It was that of a loving, unspoiled, high-spirited child. She was trusting and gentle, with lovely manners, great courage, and pride of breeding.

And yet there was in her a stubborn indomitableness and a streak of wildness that would suddenly erupt without provocation.

I used to think it rather sad that Rocket's world was restricted to my small acreage. Yet I have realized how diverse it was, containing a long open pasture, a virgin wilderness of lofty cottonwoods and aspens, tangled thickets of wild rose, plum, and chokecherry. She was not restricted to this. Her world embraced the flanking mountains, the hanging stars, all nature of which she was a part. In her lifetime she fulfilled her maternal function by foaling two colts.

Her end came suddenly, early one March while I was staying in Taos. In the evening Mr. Quintana came down from Arroyo Seco to tell me that Rocket was off her feet, a bad sign. There was no vet practicing in town, so I telephoned Aloysius Liebert. There was no answer. I went on to Eve Young-Hunter's, who had invited me to dinner, and continued to telephone. Her maid, Tavita, also called several of his neighbors, but he could not be located. Without staying for dinner, I drove out to Hazel Hoffman's Rocking Horse Ranch. Thinking that Rocket might have a bowel obstruction, she looked up the remedy in *Capt. Hayes Veterinary Notes for Horse Owners:* an enema with warm soapy water, and a dosage of castor oil and glycerin. I then drove up to the Quintanas, my Seco neighbors.

It was now nine o'clock and all the Quintanas were in bed. Aroused, Mr. Quintana said Rocket had got back on her feet and wandered off into the back. Bolivar, his son, had just driven in, and walked over to my place with me. The night was cold and the ground covered with snow. Cry-Baby and the other horses we found in a corner of the orchard, but no sign of Rocket. By the dim light of a lantern we traced her steps across the open pasture to the tangled wilderness area in back.

Here we gave up the search. It was impossible to get the Quintanas out of bed, to heat water and carry it back to the woods in deep snow, and to administer an enema by the light of a lantern and a flashlight—if we could find her. Moreover, my intuitive feeling told me that Rocket had forsaken her companions—something she never did—and gone off alone to die.

All nature confirmed this feeling. There was an eerie feeling of sadness, of tragedy, in the air. The stars, close and bright in the black sky, glittered with preternatural awareness. The snow packs on the peaks and the snow on the ground gave off a queer muted sheen. And the silence spoke loudest. The whole thing got me: gentle Rocket hiding out there in the dark woods alone, knowing that her time had come. Accepting the mystery of death, I drove back to town.

Early next morning—Sunday—I returned to Seco. Mr. Quintana had got up at sunup and found Rocket dead. I went over to see her. She had come out from the woods and was lying in the pasture, face to the mountains. What the cause of her death was, I don't know. Her coat had no sweat stains; there was no sign of agony, of struggle. Her heart had simply stopped beating. I closed off the pasture from the other horses; and as it was impossible to bury her in the frozen, snow-covered ground, I asked Mr. Quintana to get a team and drag her body back into woods and cover it beyond the reach of coyotes.

She was twenty-one years old, and this had been her home for fifteen years. The sun was coming out over the mountain peaks and the church bells in Arroyo Seco were ringing for mass.

Cry-Baby

If Rocket by temperament was Janey's horse, Cry-Baby was peculiarly mine. She was a small white mare, at once cantankerous, stubborn, and loving. I often thought she should have occupied a couch in the office of a Jungian analyst, who might have reconciled the many quirks in her complex nature.

Janey and I bought her from Jack Denver in 1949 when we were living in Ralph Meyers's old place, across from the Anderson sisters' ranch near Los Cordovas. Her mother was a famous bucking horse used in many rodeos; and whenever she was let out of the chutes, her colt used to cry for her. Hence the cowboys called her Cry-Baby. Obviously she had been mistreated, for she was always difficult to catch and handle. One could assume that she was a cold-blooded cow pony, a bronc like her mother. But I was told she must have had a strain of Arabian to give her such a beautiful conformation and indomitable spirit. The theory holds some water anyway. All the mustangs or broncos of the Southwest are descended from the Spanish explorers' Arabians, which escaped and founded herds of wild horses.

The first time I rode her was across the mesa to the gorge of the Rio Grande through the vast expanse of sagebrush. I saw then how neatly she picked her way and how untiring she was. In 1951 when we opened the house at Arroyo Seco, I brought her up with us.

Cry-Baby always gave us trouble. One could never walk up to her with rope or halter, even hidden under one arm. She had to be chased and cornered. Then she would turn her back and kick. There was a virtue in this. When I was away, none of the neighbors' children, who I am sure came to ride her, could get close to her. Mr. Quintana hayed her, but was afraid of her. She was the uncontested boss of the other horses. It was she who always was their watchdog: warily keeping an eye out in all directions, intuitively sensing any possible danger, the approach of a stranger, the scent of a bear coming down for choke-cherries.

Cry-Baby's instinct could be relied upon. Shortly after I brought her up here, I rode her up to the base of the mountains and cut through the reservation on an old trail that was blocked farther on by the fallen wires of a barbed wire fence. Cry-Baby balked. I foolishly did then what a rider should never do. I switched her over the wires instead of getting off and leading her. She of course cut a forefoot just above the hoof. Blood was pouring from it by the time I got home. With Janey's help I sewed up the cut with thread soaked in iodine, and put her in the colt corral where she couldn't run until the cut healed. This experience taught me a lesson.

Janey had better luck one day when Cry-Baby balked with her. She had ridden up the trail that led into a wild pocket canyon in the side of El Salto, the refuge of a few brown bears, deer, large striped-tail raccoons, coyotes, and other wild animals. Abruptly Cry-Baby stopped. Janey refused to be dominated by her mount. She spurred and whipped Cry-Baby, who refused to budge. Then Janey happened to notice the overhanging branch of a large pine just ahead. On it she could make out a tawny animal with a tuft on its switching tail. It was a mountain lion waiting to jump down on her when she rode underneath it. Luckily, she turned Cry-Baby around and rode back home.

Cry-Baby was sick only once, with a rasping cough I could hear from the house. Out in the pasture with the other horses, she couldn't graze. In misery and desperation she'd run back to the barn for relief, and here the cough would drive her back into the pasture. After trying all the remedies suggested to me, I drove to the vet hospital in Santa Fe and brought back several bottles of Theratuss, an antihistaminic cough syrup. It was impossible to force it down her throat; she would rear up, buck, kick, and scream. Finally, I soaked oats with the syrup and tied and haltered her until she ate them. At last she recovered.

The death of Rocket left Cry-Baby desolate after their years of close association. Fortunately Ann Merrill's daughter Lolly brought up her horse, Tommy, to keep for her and to provide company for Cry-Baby.

Tommy was a powerful, brown quarter horse who had been "cut proud"—only one testicle having been removed. From the start they hit it off. Periodically, Tommy tried to mount Cry-Baby. It didn't work. But Cry-Baby didn't mind. She had foaled two colts and seemed uninterested in his masculine attempts. Nevertheless, she accepted his male prerogative; he bossed her as unmercifully as she had bossed Rocket. Yet as a wise old soul, she exercised over him a peculiarly female domination. Between them grew a love such as I've never seen manifested between horses.

Tommy, being male, was adventurous. He was always getting out. A horse, supposedly, never crawls under a fence. Tommy, however, would find a loose wire in the fence, put his neck underneath it, and come through. One day he was missing. A second day. A third day. Cry-Baby was wild with anxiety, crying for him in the back pastures, racing up to the barn. My neighbors and I hunted for him all over Arroyo Seco. Finally, one morning Salomé Duran shouted to me from next door. Tommy and two Seco horses were coming down the road. They had gone into the mountains for a spree, and getting hungry, they were coming back. I ran out, snubbed him with my belt, and led him out to the pasture.

Cry-Baby was waiting for him. Tommy, proud of his adventure, acted like any male. He simply stood there to be admired and welcomed home. Cry-Baby gave it to him with a dance such as I've never seen. She whinnied and neighed. Ran around and around him, kicking up her hind legs, bucking, and prancing. Nuzzled him. Tommy endured it patiently until she was tired out. Then he gave her a nip, and they wandered together out into the back pasture.

Riding Cry-Baby was never mere sport nor exercise for me. It simply took me out of myself, much like my moment of morning silence. I never put a bit in her mouth, using only a hackamore. When I didn't ride her bareback, I used an English saddle, for I disliked heavy Western saddles. We had grown so accustomed to each other, we were both at ease; and she settled into her usual lope the minute we entered the big open reservation. This gait was broken periodically by a gallop and a walk. She loved to gallop. No matter how tired and winded she was, her wonderful spirit would have urged her on until she dropped; I had to watch her carefully. But we both liked her lope best. Reins loose, easy in the saddle, I reacted instinctively to whatever she did; and she adjusted her lope to accommodate me.

During our long rides through the reservation it always happened, and she seemed to feel it as well as I. We fused into one, and together into all that wildness and beauty of sagebrush, mountain, earth, and sky. There was no differentiation, no sense of movement; all seemed caught up in one timeless unity marked only by the silent, slow, and steady heartbeat through us all. A feeling I never experienced on another horse.

Her end came on a bright June morning in 1971. I saw her peacefully grazing in Salomé's pasture when I was taking my early morning walk. An hour later Salomé came over to say she was dead. I could hardly believe him, and rushed out to see her. She had come back to her own pasture and quietly lain down beside the fence, legs under her, as if for her usual morning nap. She still looked asleep. She was twenty-nine years old, and this had been her home for twenty-two of them.

I hastily closed the gate to Salomé's adjoining pasture where Tommy was standing. All morning he stood there at the fence, unmoving and silent, while Celestino Quintana dragged her body away for burial. I was unable to watch him. Then I went out and opened the gate.

There began now a hellish period that lasted days and nights. Tommy, neighing for Cry-Baby, raced continually from the far back Acequia Madre to the barn and back again. I could hear him calling for her at dawn, still hear him calling at night. His agonizing grief at her absence tore at my heart.

In desperation I bought another mare in an attempt to alleviate his loneliness. She was an unusually large, big-boned sorrel named Betsy. It took them a long time to adjust, but gradually he assumed his male dominance and taught her all the confines of her new home. Yet the rapport, the peculiar love that held Tommy and Cry-Baby together, did not exist.

A remark once made by Frank Dobie might serve as Cry-Baby's epitaph: "A man who had known a good horse in his life would remember her as he would a calm mother, or a stately tree amidst all life's flickering vanishments."

The Colts

It happened in the spring of 1951 when I was renting Tinka Fechin's pasture and living in Nicolai's studio. One early Tuesday morning I went out to see how a Jersey calf had got into the pasture with Rocket.

At second look it seemed more like a jackrabbit mounted on stilts. Then I tumbled.

It was a new palomino colt: fully formed, with long straight legs, and sharp little pointed hoofs; already walking, switching its white flag, and nervously eyeing a magpie's taunts—and yet only a couple of hours old. One of nature's miracles no less! Excited and elated, I went down to *El Crepusculo* and wrote an editorial: "Tuesday Morning Miracle."

Rocket's new filly was bright as gold, with a single white spot on her forehead. Janey named her Star. She was spoiled from the start by Tinka Fechin and everyone who saw her. Hazel Hoffman showed me how to halter-break her by means of a marvelous trick. A rope was looped around her hindquarters, and the loose end was passed through her halter. Whenever I pulled forward on the halter, Star balked and pulled back. I then let the rope looped around her behind suddenly go, and Star tumbled on her rump. After that she never balked again.

Later, when we brought the horses up to Seco, Frank Samora, our Indian standby who had trained horses for Captain O'Hay, came up to break her. Star wouldn't be broken gently, and we didn't want to break her spirit by rough handling. So she grew up into an unreliable, willful, spoiled debutante. But she was very fast.

Sometime later Janey took her down to Tucson where she was visiting her mother, intending to race the horse at Rillito, a small hometown track limited to local owners of horses. Star was boarded there to be trained by a fine old man, whose name I can't recall. He owned two or three animals, and his highest ambition was to win a race with one of them. He looked after Star like a mother, teaching her innumerable tricks: to bow, kneel, and pull a handkerchief out of one's pocket. His training of her to run was not so successful, although she filled out, developed muscles, and became truly beautiful. The great day came for the heat in which she was entered. Janey and the old man beamed with pride when she was led to the starting gate. And then, from the starting gun, Star showed her true colors. She had no competitive spirit like her mother, no will to run. To her, the race was a game in which she could make a grandstand play in front of the shouting spectators. A spoiled, beautiful show-off. She finished last with plenty of energy still to toss her head and endeavor to prance a little. That, thank goodness, marked the end of Janey's ambition to run a horse on the track—an expensive hobby for poor pikers. Later that day, I'm glad to say, one of the old man's horses won a purse.

We brought Star back to Seco and kept her for a couple of years, where she loved to show off her tricks and to march proudly in local parades. I do not wish to denigrate the lovely spirit, proud nature, and great beauty with which she was endowed. She amply fulfilled all the dictates of her own destiny, despite the criticisms of some of us, to the pleasure of us all. Rocket, I think, would have been proud of her. We finally sold her to the historic Star Ranch in Colorado Springs. There she was valued as a gaited saddle horse, an outstanding parade horse, and one with countless tricks.

Cry-Baby's colt Ocote was also, strangely enough, a palomino. He was sired by the Quintanas' young stallion. Unlike slender, ladylike Star, Ocote was sturdy and dependable as his father. As we had too many horses to support when he was weaned, I gave him to the Cottams. Louie Cottam was an old friend of mine, former superintendent of the Kit Carson National Forest, who had retired and was living nearby with his wife and daughter, Barbara. They had several horses and ample pasturage, and I knew Ocote would have a good home.

A couple of years later I arranged a pack trip to Blue Lake, above the Sacred Mountain, for the director of the New York foundation sponsoring my research for *The Book of the Hopi*. Frank Samora at the Pueblo was engaged to guide us; and needing another packhorse, I borrowed Ocote. The long, steep trail, rising to almost thirteen thousand feet in altitude, was most difficult. It was necessary to stop often to breathe the horses, especially Ocote, for sturdy as he was, his golden coat was dark with sweat. Said Frank, "Now he's finding out for the first time what work is!" Lesser horses have died on this long, severe trip, but Ocote had Cry-Baby's stamina and spirit.

Sometime afterward Barbara gave Ocote to her uncle and aunt, Bill and Rachel Hawk, up on their ranch on Lobo Mountain to keep for a while. They were old hands with horses, but Ocote foundered. His death saddened me, as selling Star never did. He was a true son of the earth.

We had other catch-colts which we sold or gave away. We also had Armstrong, a burro. He was brought up here by Ann Merrill's young daughters when they could not take care of him. From my early days in Cripple Creek, Colorado, I've always loved burros, who were called

"Pikes Peak Canaries." And Armstrong was a character, indomitable and unique. All the horses of course snooted him completely. He could graze with them, but was not accepted as a member of their family. In the summer he found his own place in the shade, beneath the cottonwoods near the house, and here he would stand alone, turning up his own nose at any horse who approached.

A "short and simple animal of the poor," mild and meek as he was, Armstrong came very much to life when his outgrown hoofs needed trimming. Neither I nor my neighbors could touch his feet. A burro's small sharp hoofs are as fast in striking out as a rattlesnake and as deadly. Finally Carlos Trujillo, an excellent hand at horses, came from San Cristobal. Within ten minutes he had tied all of Armstrong's feet with an ingenious network of rope, allowing him to work on the burro's hoofs: a good example of what a master of his trade can do. We later gave Armstrong to a nearby family with another lonely burro.

Beauty

Beauty shamed me. A travesty of her name, she was a white stocky mare between twelve and fifteen years old, with big feet, a slight drag in her off hind leg, long eyelashes over her incurious big eyes, and a voracious appetite.

She had been bought for Rose's small daughter, Mindy, to ride. Mindy was city-bred. She disliked the country, preferring to stay in town, which offered more amusements.

So I brought Beauty up to Seco. The other horses treated her like a peasant, refusing to let her in the barn with them in the summer to escape the flies, or to feed in the winter. Beauty accepted her role calmly, following them all day in the fields, never asserting herself.

She had her virtues. Unlike high-strung Rocket and spooky Cry-Baby, she was easily caught and handled. With her strong body, she sturdily carried a big western saddle, and made a good spare riding horse. Stolid and patient, she was a true peasant, a part of the earth. Late one June, however, she developed diarrhea. It would clear up and then return. The local vet informed me that she was not absorbing water because of some injury to her tissues, and he could do nothing for her. I then sent her down to the Large Animal Veterinary Clinic in Santa Fe, which had facilities for treating her. Dr. Blach kept her there for three weeks. During this time he put her on a diet, gave her enemas, and forced a charcoal compound down her throat. Finally, he sent her back with the discouraging news that her chronic diarrhea was impossible to stop, and that I should feed her timothy hay with a cellulose mixture he recommended.

Beauty arrived looking more dead than alive: badly gaunted, backbone and ribs sticking out, her long eyelashes turned white, and a dull, unseeing look in her eyes. I penned her in the corral, feeding her as instructed. She touched nothing, simply standing head down, oblivious to the world about her.

There is something about a sick animal that tugs at the heart, and Beauty's years of docility and humbleness seemed condensed now into her abject stance. Ashamed now of having ignored her enduring patience, I realized that man had done all that could humanly be done for her. She belonged now to the living land. So I opened the gate and gave her back to nature—to her familiar pastures, to the brooding mountains.

Beauty was in no hurry; the look of death was still in her eyes. She hesitantly ambled down to the empty barn, then slowly trudged out to join the other horses in the pasture. Not grazing, but looking as if she were accustoming herself to life after a living death.

Gradually she pulled out of it. But in December when the snows came, I noticed that her stools were getting looser again, and that she was voraciously hungry all the time.

Despite the fact that I gave her all she could eat, her backbone began to ridge, her hindquarters grew thin and bony, and she died in February.

As I recall these and other horses like Shorty and Blackie, it seems that I have accentuated here the worry and sadness caused by their illnesses and deaths. Actually their illnesses were rare. Their health reflected their green grass, good alfalfa, fresh running water, and pure mountain air. I loved their clean, sweet smell. I was aware of how healthy they were when Louie Cottam brought up one of his horses, Lobo, to rest after months of working for the Forest Service. The gelding's eyes were dull, his coat was matted. His entire body was so permeated with sweat, dust, stale hay, and impure tank water that he stank to high heaven. My horses avoided Lobo for days. But gradually he lost his obnoxious smell, his eyes cleared, his coat took on a sheen.

All my horses were creatures of habit. I knew where to find them almost every hour of the day. They had their places for morning and evening grazing, for their midmorning nap and night's sleep. Herd animals, they loved the company of their kind and also of human beings; they stood nearby whenever I was patching a fence, or followed me wherever I walked. Yet they were not completely domesticated. They stood in the barn only during summer afternoons to escape the flies. In winter cold, even during blizzards, they stayed out in the open pasture where they could be aware of approaching danger. It was this constant wariness, this streak of wildness, that made them so unpredictable. They spooked easily; one could not make a quick movement, and always had to watch their ears. This quality led me to a closer relationship with the wild creatures of the animal kingdom. It seems to me that no one who has ever doctored a horse can kill a deer, and proudly carry it home on the hood of his car with its throat slit open and bloody entrails hanging out, as evidence of his great "sport."

My few horses, then, helped to put me in closer touch with the wildness of the living land. A silent communication grew between us. I could not at first understand how they silently called me from the house when anything was wrong or they needed immediate attention; nor how when I wanted them and they could not be seen, they trotted out from the woods. Then I began without question to rely on their intuitive calls and responses. This involved of course the mystery of silence, in which all we children of our Mother Earth speak in a common tongue.

31

Tuesday Morning Miracle

(Editorial—April 26, 1951)

TUESDAY morning as usual we sleepily went to whistle our brown mare in from the back pasture. For the first time she high-hatted us. She was too engrossed in what seemed to be a Jersey cow that strangely had got through the fence from somewhere. At second look it seemed more like a jackrabbit mounted on stilts. Finally we tumbled. It was a new Palomino colt.

Fully formed, long straight legs, sharp little pointed hoofs, already walking, switching its white flag, nervously eyeing a magpie's taunts—and yet only a couple of hours old.

It beats the devil how things like this happen so neatly and perfectly. Man can invent a cumbersome, complex Linotype machine, and be amazed that it works despite the constant metal squirts and breakdowns. But when you first see something like this newborn colt, there's nothing to be said. It's one of those rare moments when for a split second you feel the swish of air from the wings of the Holy Ghost, and you know you are standing in the presence of a miracle.

With the nearest vet seventy-five miles away, we had been worrying about the event for months. It just shows how much overemphasis we all can put on manmade machines like a Linotype, but how quickly we can be snapped back into place by one of nature's miracles of life.

32

The Guru and the Fox

(Essay)

BESIDES my horses, several cats and dogs have given me companionship and enriched my life. One of them, years ago, was Bimmie, a champion collie that Janey, my second wife, had brought back from England. Another was Missie, a shepherd, with whom I experienced a curious empathy. She slept on the floor of my bedroom. Just as I was ready to turn off the reading lamp, she came to the bed, stood up, and embraced me. The gesture somehow frightened me, it carried such emotional intensity. Another dog was a spaniel named Little Wolf which belonged to Eliseo, our Indian neighbor whose summer house was on the reservation across the road. She kept coming to my house, and periodically I took her back. When she became pregnant, Eliseo prepared for her a bed underneath a tree where she could give birth to her puppies. Yet on the day of their birth, she waddled down to my adobe.

I made her a comfortable bed of old matting and a Navajo blanket in the hall. But that night she indomitably insisted on sleeping beside my bed as usual. Here she gave birth to seven puppies. What a mess and smell they made! I moved them all, mother and puppies, to the spare bedroom, and cleaned the floor so I could sleep in my own room. They remained for a couple of weeks, during which I fed them and let Little Wolf out for exercise.

I then dutifully drove her and the puppies back to Eliseo's summer house on the reservation. He was not concerned about their welfare. Fall had come, with cold weather. He promised to take them down to his house in the Pueblo for the winter, and to give me one of the puppies next spring. What happened was tragic. He became bored with Little Wolf; she was too expensive to feed. So he gave her to the animal shelter. The puppies he set loose.

Two of the cats were Smokie and Blackie. Both were Persians, with long hair; one smoke-gray and the other jet-black. They slept inside the house at night, but I left the window open so they could roam outside during the day. What curious, lovable little cats they were.

Yet none of these pets during their brief times with me aroused the admiration and love I felt for my horses, those constant companions of many years. Not until recently, after I was married to Barbara and living during the winters in Tucson, did two later small pets—a cat and a dog—touch me deeply. Different as they were, they became a part of our lives, evoking a joy by their presence and an anguish at their death I'd not felt before.

Snowbird

Snowbird came to us in Taos one October evening in 1980. We had attended a dinner given by Paul Vassallo, head of the University of New Mexico library, at Casa Cordova in Arroyo Seco. After dinner all of the guests came up to our house for coffee. One of them, a woman dressed in a full-length white mink coat, picked up the cat and held him in her arms. How beautiful he was, snow-white, with long silky fur! Barbara fell in love with him at once, and wanted to adopt him. The woman was quite agreeable. The cat was not hers; she had no idea where he came from. She had simply found him outside the restaurant when she came out.

I immediately objected, "Not another cat to take care of." For we were already taking care of a little yellow cat named Marmalade while Jongewards, our winter housesitters, were away. So the guests carried him back to the restaurant on their way home. Barbara went down later, but was unable to find him. Then somehow he came back to us the next morning, and we brought him down to Tucson for the winter.

Barbara gave him the name of Snowbird, which winter visitors to Tucson were called. Often she called him "His Majesty." He played the role well, making himself lord of the house and garden. I began to love his gentle nature, his staunch little soul. I can still see his silky white body curled up in a chair. Lying feet up on the couch with Barbara stroking his soft belly. Crouching on the windowsill in the bedroom to greet the morning sun and to put the day to bed. He loved us, too, and taught us much. Our "little silent Guru," as Bob Kostka called him.

In May we drove him back with us to Arroyo Seco to spend the summer. How wonderful it was for him—a bigger house, large lawn, and open pastures behind. In August Barbara had to return to school in Tucson, and the Jongewards left on a trip to Canada. I was left alone with Snowbird and Jongewards' cat Marmalade. He was a tough little thing, as plebian as Snowbird was aristocratic. I fed them both, breakfast and supper. Whenever Marmalade tried to steal Snowbird's meal, Snowbird simply backed away, nose up. So I began to feed them separately.

After supper the three of us spent the evening together. Myself reading on the couch, Marmalade and Snowbird lying on opposite chairs. How different in appearance and character they were! Marmalade scrawny, scarred from many battles, given to wandering up into the mountains; and always hungry. And Snowbird, beautiful and fastidious, showing a curious mixture of all cats' independence and his dependency upon me. I kept wondering where he had been born, who had owned him, and whether he had been lost or abandoned in Arroyo Seco. At bedtime I let Marmalade out to sleep in the hay as usual, and Snowbird came to sleep on the foot of my bed.

For six weeks he was my only constant companion. He anticipated my habits exactly. Jumping off the bed in the morning, waiting at the bathroom door for me to shower, waiting in the bedroom while I dressed, then waiting till I fed him and let him outdoors.

Where he went every day I don't know. But late in the afternoon, or when it began to rain, I called and he came bounding back like a leopard. Then one rainy day—September 16 it was—he didn't come back when I called. All evening in the dark I walked out to the orchard, in the fields, on the road, looking for him and calling. Finally I went to bed, propping the back door open. Then, past midnight, I was awakened by a familiar thump. Snowbird had returned and jumped in bed with me. How happy I was that he'd found his way back home at night!

All next day he slept as if exhausted. But I couldn't keep him shut up in the house. So on Sunday morning I let him out into the warm sunshine. He didn't come back that night although it was raining. I left the door open again. Long after midnight a clatter in the kitchen awakened me. Surely Snowbird had returned again. But when I got up, I discovered that a young skunk had come in and was ravaging the garbage pail. What a job it was to get him out of the house! Fearful that forcing him would cause him to let loose a barrage, I kept gently urging him with a broom to the open door. Then I had to clean up the mess on the floor.

Where was little Snowbird all night long? Out in the cold and rain, without food and water for twenty-four hours? Sick with worry, I went out early in the morning. There I saw him, a white blotch crouching outside the corral fence. When he didn't answer my call, I knew something was wrong. His body was thinner, his glossy white coat bedraggled, his pointed ears and nose without their pink coloring. Was it that day and night he had picked up the virus of his disease? Where and how? Why had not Marmalade, roaming the entire neighborhood, also been infected? I carried Snowbird into the house, and tried to give him food and water. He refused it.

On Monday morning I drove him to the vet. He gave Snowbird a blood transfusion and sent blood samples to the laboratory. The report came back that Snowbird had developed leukemia, a fatal disease, and was given only two weeks to live.

On Saturday morning Barbara arrived to drive back with me to Tucson. It was her birthday, a joyful day darkened by the news that her little beloved Snowbird was doomed to die. We ordered the vet to give him another blood transfusion, which would give him the strength to endure the long drive back to Tucson next day. If we could only get him back to familiar surroundings, and give him good food, care, and love, for his remaining days with us! And with this, our prayerful hope for a remission of his disease.

Snowbird stood the trip beautifully—the long drive, change of altitude, and the hundred-degree heat after cool Taos. And then he stepped into familiar home surroundings as if he'd never been away. His first day here was worth all our worries.

His stay here extended to two weeks, three, and four. Barbara fed him raw beef and chicken livers. He ate well, rambled around the house, enjoyed being let out into the garden to watch and chase the quail and birds. We began to hope the ravages of his leukemia had been stopped.

Then on Friday, October 23, Barbara and I left for the Gaspard showings in Santa Fe and Taos, returning on Sunday. Barbara's young niece stayed in the house while we were away. When we came back, she said Snowbird had eaten well on Saturday, but Sunday he had refused food and water. He was lying in the dining room, and didn't respond to us. Nor did he later come into the bedroom to jump up on the windowsill to usher in the night and to sleep at our feet.

Did our absence make him so lonely he wouldn't eat? Did it hasten the advance of his illness?

On Monday morning he still wouldn't touch food or water; and when Barbara left for school, he went to lie in the spare bedroom, an unusual place for him. He was so bloodlessly white; all the color had drained from his ears and nose. I felt frightened, and about 3:00 I carried him out into the garden. He rested a few minutes, then walked to the bird bath and stood up. I lifted him to drink a swallow. Then he went to lie down under the olive tree, paying no attention to the birds above. This was Snowbird's last peaceful hour on earth, and I'm so glad he had it.

I know now that he was dying, but waiting until Barbara, the one person he loved most, came home. She arrived after 4:00 p.m. She carried him inside the house, tried to get him to eat something. But he only tried to throw up from an empty stomach. So we carried him outside again to lie on a soft bathroom mat. Instead, he went to lie down beside the low wall of a flower garden. His legs were unsteady; he staggered. Then we knew, bursting into tears. And now there came from him little wracking cries of pain. I knelt beside him, stroking his wasted body. Barbara, with more courage than I, telephoned the Animal Control Center that we'd be there before it closed at 5:00.

So we drove there, Barbara holding Snowbird on her lap, trying to comfort him between his cries of pain. His eyes had a far-away look, the look of death. The pink had drained from his ears, lips, even his gums. So we gave him up to the attendants at the Center. One of them, a young Hispanic, said compassionately, *"Esta bueno."* I might have taken his body home, had I been alone. But Barbara, who loved him so, said no. We couldn't have dug a grave in the rocky ground deep enough to be safe from coyotes and dogs. So we left him, our beautiful Snowbird, to be mercifully severed from his distress and pain.

It was just a year since he had come to us, just five weeks from the day I took him to the vet who gave him only two weeks to live. What a great gift these five weeks, this year, had been. He gave us his full love and devotion, as we gave him ours. He enriched our lives, our silent little Guru in the mortal shape of a snow-white Himalayan cat, embodying the spiritual essence in all of us. And he has left us enduring memories of his snowy beauty, his gentleness, and his stout little spirit.

Zorro

We were so distressed and lonely after losing Snowbird that Barbara bought a shelty or Shetland sheepdog from a breeding kennel. Like Shetland ponies, they were small in size, resembling diminutive collies. This one, like a collie, was tri-colored with red highlights, a white chest, and little white legs. His registered name was Demon, quite unsuitable. We finally gave him the name of Zorro, meaning Fox in Spanish, for in looks and coloring he indeed resembled a little fox.

He was about four years old, and much of the time had been confined in the customary cage sixteen inches on a side. The topnotch breeder, a woman named Jean, was fond of her dogs and took the best of care in raising them. But her main concern was grooming them for show, seldom allowing them out in the sun for fear they would lose their color. When she sold Zorro to us, she assured herself that he would have a good home, receive a proper diet, and be given a similar small cage. Against our better judgment, therefore, we bought at the airport a small carrying cage in which he was to be fed and locked in at night. Immediately we realized this was ridiculous. We let him have full run of the house. Then Barbara fenced in the garden in back, made a gate between it and the driveway, and even laid a red outdoor carpet in the patio so he wouldn't catch cold when lying on the concrete outside.

How strange it must have been for our beautiful little fox to have a house and garden to roam in! A whole new expanded world. And how high-strung and nervous he was, at first trotting around ceaselessly on his little quick-stepping white legs. It was difficult to get him to eat. Barbara would sit on the floor with his plate, patiently enticing him. Or she would take his plate into the bedroom and lie on the bed resting until he finished it in silent companionship. We often had trouble getting him to go out into the garden. He wanted to hide in the bedroom closet, whose small closed confines perhaps reminded him of his years in a cage. Nor would Zorro ever let us catch him. Whenever we put a hand to him, he would shy away. Yet, unbidden, he would jump up on our laps.

That he was so neurotic made little difference to us. His very quirks endeared him to us. He was so shy, beautiful, and sensitive, we loved him. Every day Barbara brushed his long silky hair. In the evening she would put a leash on him and take him for a walk. He would heel and sit, but never would he obey the summons of "come." At night he slept on the floor beside our bed, where Barbara could reach down and touch him. He was her red Little Fox.

In January I underwent surgery for a hip joint replacement. When I came home from the hospital, I was confined to the house, learning to walk with crutches. As Barbara was away at school all day, Zorro and I were left alone to keep each other company. Our routine was simple. I put him out in the garden and set his breakfast plate on the red carpet in the patio while I stayed in the house to work. Zorro meandered around, ignoring the birds and the quail feeding on the ground near him. A gentle little soul, he had no hunting instinct. Not for weeks did he bark at a neighbor's dog passing by, then rushing furiously at the fence. This to me was an excellent sign, showing that he now regarded the garden as his own property.

After lunch I let him in to lie on the bed beside me while I took a nap. He didn't want to go out afterward. He was lonely. So I let him stay inside. When I worked at the typewriter, he would sit beside me. Or if I was reading in a chair, he would suddenly jump into my lap, snuggling down with his pointed nose thrust into my armpit. Then in mid-afternoon I put him out again. He would pace up and down in front of the driveway gate, waiting for Barbara's arrival.

During those months alone with him, I thought about his many quirks, his shying away whenever we put out a hand to him and yet jumping up into our laps, his contradictory independence and trustful dependence upon us. Did he still retain the instincts of his breed as a Shetland sheepdog, used to herd flocks in open country, after being confined in a cage most of his life? How was his life with us, experiencing a new larger home and meeting new people, affecting him? Such questions can't be answered. An animal lives in a world apart from man, as I knew from my horses. One can begin to relate to them only by intuitively divining in their individual character the one essence in all of us. So it was that I began to understand little Zorro as he sat in my lap with his nose poked into my armpit. His warm, silky body communicated to mine his gentleness, trust, and loneliness, without the need for words. I understood him then, whatever his breeding and upbringing, as a little boy at heart, in a strange, new and expanded world. I loved him, and I was responsible for his death.

On Saturday morning, March 20, when I opened the driveway gate to the garden after feeding the birds, Zorro slipped out between my feet. I was not aware of it, didn't know he was gone until Barbara called. Once before, he had slipped out the front door one evening. Barbara found him far out in back, in the dark, and brought him back. This morning she at once went out in robe and slippers to find him. From eight in the morning till ten, she trudged through the desert greasewood on the slope of the mountains. She soon found him, but he wouldn't allow her close enough to touch him. At times she sat or lay resting on the ground while he frisked about nearby, nosing everything excitedly.

Finally, hot and thirsty, he followed her home. Worn out, she came into the house for his water dish and dog treats, hoping to lure him back into the garden through the open gate. Chuck Adams and Bob Blanchard from Las Vegas, Nevada, had arrived for a visit. Ignoring them, Barbara went outdoors again to coax Zorro, who remained just out of reach in the unfenced front yard.

Suddenly we heard her wild, hysterical cry of horror—an agonizing cry that will forever ring in my ears. Zorro had run across the road to get back to the desert, was hit by a motorcycle, and killed. Barbara had seen it; I know it will live in her memory with all its torment. Her beloved Little Fox! I knelt down beside his still body, picked him up in my arms, and carried him back to the house. Then with Chuck and Bob, I drove him to the Animal Control Center to be cremated—the same place to which Barbara and I had taken Snowbird last October.

Zorro had come to us only five months before, and now he had left us. Why had this dreadful accident happened? I felt guilty because his death was the result of my carelessness. And yet it contained an element of inevitability. Zorro's small world of a closed cage had expanded when he came to us, to the freedom of a house and garden. This was not enough. His walks with Barbara had showed him the driveway outside the gate, the road in front, and beyond it a still larger, unknown world. He was loose on the open expanse of desert rising into the slope of the mountains above. A great, wide, wild world, and freedom to explore it. These last two hours of Zorro's life were his supreme adventure, the superb climax of his emancipation from the neurotic repression of his natural instincts. He was himself, completely free at last. How wonderful that he had them.

No wonder he refused to be caught and returned to a small garden. So he had crossed the road again to get back into the best of all worlds. At just the moment a motorcycle was passing. Zorro's sheepdog instinct asserted itself. Just as his ancestors had been trained to rush at and snap at a sheep straying out of the flock, Zorro rushed at the motorcycle. Barbara saw it swerve out of the way. But Zorro rushed at it again, was hit and killed. The accident was not the driver's fault, as she told him; he drove away, leaving us to confront the bitter tragedy of Zorro's death.

These are surmises, mere excuses perhaps. They don't alleviate the enduring anguish Barbara feels. Nor the guilt I feel for letting him out, I who loved him so. I can still feel his silky hair, little pointed ears, and tiny white feet, as he snuggled on my lap, nose into my armpit. His little trot around the house will always be trotting into my dreams.

Zorro, our Little Fox! Only for five months had he filled our loneliness, but how much love and joy he had given us. Then he returned, like Snowbird, to the vast wellspring of all our lives. And so we must acknowledge the transcendental bond that links us all—men, animals, birds, trees, and stones. Only then do we realize what we really are. But still we grieve their absence.

33

What! No Street Cars Yet?

(Editorial—September 8, 1949)

In the 114 years that *El Crepusculo,* under its many names, has observed the goings-on in Taos, the period our town is now undergoing is one of its most peculiar.

It is a period of actual, necessary growth. It is also a time of empty posturing and wishful thinking—of what grandma used to call "button-stretching."

We are still seventy-five miles from the nearest railroad. We lack the water and coal for power necessary to convert the region into an industrial and manufacturing center. Taos probably will never be a thriving river port on the Rio Grande. But Taos is still one of the most unusual towns in the United States. It still possesses its own inherent and inalienable qualities, which have carried its fame to Europe.

Yet in this button-stretching period we are ignoring these real potentialities and craning our necks to see in the mirror a metropolitan Taos that exists only in our imaginations. We are trying like crazy to sell ourselves the illusion of Big Town Importance.

One result of these growing pains to which we have been treated lately is a journalistic gobbledygook not exceeded by the Hearst Syndicate. The birth of a baby down the road a piece is reported as a Special Dispatch from the Placita Correspondent. A snatch of Santa Fe gossip originating in the La Fonda bar is hailed as a Political Communique of the Capitol Bureau. And when our local photographer, Martin Shaffer, is rousted out to snap a picture, it becomes no less than an Official Staff Photo.

Under this button-stretching exaggeration the bickerings of the village council and the Taos Chamber of Commerce take on the gravity of the United Nations Security Council. We expect to see Mayor Pascual Martinez properly attired in bowler hat and frock coat, and are shocked to glimpse him still trudging around under his old Stetson. A housewife does not dare to dash to market with one Levi-leg rolled up to her knee without the possibility of setting a New Taos Fashion.

Heaven only knows where all this will lead to before the period is over. It may well be that out of our self-conscious metropolitanism, High Society will rear its ugly head, afternoon tea will become a necessity for all visitors to the Pueblo, and the conference table will replace the hitching post as the molder of public opinion.

Shades of Padre Martinez, our illustrious founder! Who are we kidding? Ourselves—the most of us simple folk who grub for the daily dollar with pencil or hoe, the many of us who still wear blankets, trudge in from the "suburbs" of Cordova, Cañon, and Llano Quemado on dirt roads, and still depend on outside two-holers? Or outside tourists and business prospects who upon arrival will indignantly demand, "What! No street cars yet?"

We are stretching at our buttons all right. But when they pop, *El Crepusculo* is going to duck behind its battered rolltop desk. We are for Taos's physical growth and mental expansion. But we believe this growth must be a development of its own unique and irreplaceable resources rather than a mushroom copy of all other towns standardized for merely more business at any price.

34

Prelude to Change

*(Speech delivered at the University of Nevada, Las Vegas,
commencement on May 23, 1981)*

PRESIDENT Goodall, Faculty, Graduates, and Students of UNLV, it is a great pleasure to receive an honorary doctorate from the University of Nevada, Las Vegas. I would like to acknowledge it, if I may, on behalf of the many books written under my name. For it seems to me that they did not come from me individually as much as through me from the powers that somehow direct the efforts and activities of all of us in our respective fields.

Meeting with you here this afternoon is an added pleasure. Las Vegas has been familiar and dear to me for many years. I lived and worked here thirty years ago—during the early atomic test series at Yucca and Frenchman's Flats, while I was associated with the Los Alamos Scientific Laboratory. I have also enjoyed a continuing relationship with this university through Dr. Charles Adams's teaching courses on my work and Dr. William Fiero's preparation of his multi-dimensional presentation of my book *The Colorado.* I must also acknowledge the help and encouragement given me by Dr. Craig Walton of the Department of Philosophy; Rita Deanin Abbey of the Art Department; Dr. Patricia Geuder, an expert in speech; and many other friends.

It seems to me that all of us here are strangely interrelated by our common dependence upon one universal creative force manifesting itself in many different ways. However, ours is a time which has lost sight of this inherent unity of all aspects of life. We are concerned only with its diversities—their contradictory aims and practices, their opposing modes of thought. We live today in a fragmented world.

Just how long ago we got into such a confusing world mess, no one seems to know. But about the turn of the century, signs of a brewing tempest were picked up by sensitive fingertips, as the great Greek novelist Kazantzakis wrote. H. G. Wells's *War in the Air* and Jack London's superb *Iron Heel,* for example, were both published in 1908, and both predicted the outbreak of World War I in 1913, missing it by only one year.

World War II followed, the wars in Korea, Vietnam, Cambodia, hot and cold wars and revolutions throughout the world. Fragmentation—the disease of our time, as Wendell Berry calls it. Fragmentation into separate and warring nationalities, races and racial minorities, political entities, religious creeds and sects.

More tragic is what has happened to us here in the richest and most powerful nation on earth. Excessively rationalistic and materialistic, we are dedicated to Progress at any price, to constantly increasing the Gross National Product. We are destroying the land, poisoning rivers, lakes, and the oceans, polluting the very air we breathe. In doing so, we have alienated ourselves from our Mother Earth and all the forces of nature. This has resulted in the fragmentation of our own natures—a rupture between our conscious and unconscious selves, our minds and hearts. Spiritually bankrupt, we are no longer in harmony with the source of life.

Clearly, what has been good for General Motors has *not* been good for us. The price we have paid for Progress has been increased mental illness, crime, vandalism, delinquency, drug addiction, and alcoholism. I don't need to elaborate this negative, dreary picture. Authorities in every field present the documented facts, and you are well aware of what is happening here in the land of the Hard-Way Eight.

It is impossible for anyone to foresee the end of this cultural decline. The most pessimistic herald a complete, disastrous collapse. The most optimistic believe that political, economic, and ecological measures will halt our present suicidal course. The majority of us look on helplessly, knowing that federal and state governments, multinational and agribusiness developers, will not do an about-face overnight. And we are too apathetic to rock the boat of our comfortable lives, to change inwardly.

But if at the beginning of this century, sensitive fingertips picked up the signs of a brewing, invisible tempest, so now many other fingertips are detecting a change in the wind. The signs of change may not be easily discernible, but they are everywhere. More and more families are moving onto small farms to grow their own food and live simply. Young people are rejecting the doctrines of the outmoded Establishment. Western scientists are becoming more receptive to the ancient religious beliefs of the East. Paranormal experiences of every kind are becoming common. Earth itself is erupting with signs of inner unrest.

Notable too, I think, is the recent widespread interest being taken in the religious beliefs of our American Indians after a century of neglect. In their ages-long reverence for Mother Earth as a living entity, and their respect for all her other children—the four-legged and the winged, the pine and the stalk of corn. Theirs is a spiritual ecology we have yet to achieve by recognizing man as an inalienable part of a universal unity that cannot remain fragmented if he is to endure.

And he will endure despite all trials and tempests. Like the American Indian. Like the coyote who has not been obliterated despite the guns, traps, and poisons of State Game Departments. Like the ocotillo and greasewood, which survive months of terrific heat on waterless deserts.

Behind all these signs of change, we can believe there lies a new pattern about to unfold, dictated by cosmic powers that govern the life of mankind, all nature, the universe itself. The governing higher powers and their transcendental laws are beyond our comprehension. But we can vaguely perceive that their thrust is generally creative, always toward establishing unity of the self and harmony with the whole.

There seems to have been in the past a marked correspondence between zodiacal cycles and the changes in earth and mankind. Former civilizations have risen and vanished in great cycles of birth, death, and transformation. But man alone does not control the destinies of peoples and nations by legislation or armed might. Forces outside him influence events. As Schwaller de Lubicz records, a new period is always preceded by preparatory events—seismic movements, climatic changes, and finally by the spirit that animates man, giving birth to a new state of thought.

These expansions of human consciousness appear to follow the organic pattern of all Creation. They do not take place gradually, but periodically in cycles that coincide with great cosmic cycles. For man's evolution comprises more than the physical evolution of his bodily form, more than his own evolution of material means to support his daily needs and desires for food, comfort, and entertainment. The only true measure of his evolution is the enlargement of his consciousness.

Hence we can, I believe, view this negative era of fragmentation as a period preliminary to the unfolding of a larger pattern of creativity. Another expansion of our own ever-evolving consciousness.

How fortunate, how exciting it seems to me, that we are living today! Experiencing the last phase of our dominating rationalistic and materialistic Western culture. And standing on the threshold of the most drastic change since the beginning of the Christian era. The stars above assure us this is so, auguring a still greater universal change. They herald the end of our present 2,000-year Age of Pisces—the twelfth and last age in the zodiacal cycle. And with this, the end of the greater 26,000-year cycle of the Precession of the Equinoxes.

Since earliest times, man has been aware of the drastic changes accompanying these astronomical cycles. It may be interesting to note that the ancient Mayas of Mexico believed that there had existed four previous worlds. Each had been successively destroyed and replaced by another. The lifetime of each the Mayas astronomically and mathematically computed to be 5,200 years. Hence the duration of the four previous worlds and their current Fifth World totaled 26,000 years— the exact length of the Precession of the Equinoxes, which I have just mentioned. More curiously still, the Mayas projected the beginning of their Fifth World—which is also the world or era we are living in today—back to 3113 B.C.; its end they projected to 2011 A.D.

What an astounding prediction to have been made by a supposedly uncivilized people a thousand years before Columbus's alleged discovery of the New World!

I have not pulled this out of a hat as a strange, amusing oddity of ancient human thought. For it is echoed today by our contemporary Indian pueblos in the Southwest. The Hopi Prophecy has lately gained wide notoriety. It predicts our world will soon be destroyed because of the very evils now besetting us—crime, corrupt materialism, and violation of our earth. And still more curiously, many current scientists are predicting cataclysmic changes about 2000 A.D.

Personally, I don't believe a dire catastrophe will overtake this planet. I prefer to regard the successive mythical worlds of the Mayas and Hopis, the Zunis and Navajos, as dramatic allegories for our consciousness—ever expanding in rhythmic cycles that effectively relate our inner lives to our outer world.

If these myths are truly symbolic of such growth, this pivotal hour on the World Clock will mark not only the death but the transformation and expansion of our current limited beliefs. The change will not be completed overnight, perhaps not even in a century. But it is already under way within us.

The individual—each one of us—is supremely important as the Net National Product, the enduring human capital remaining after the transient profits of the Gross National Product have been squandered. So I hope that especially those of you who are graduating from this university today will leave with a sense of partaking in this growing inner evolution of mind and heart—this prelude to change manifested in outer material form.

35

The Chokecherries Are Ripe

(Editorial—August 30, 1951)

THE chokecherries are ripe.

This is not news to that strange and migrant sect of professional fruit pickers working northward through the plums, peaches, and apricots in the hot, rich valleys of California to the famous apple orchards of Washington. Those hardy apple-knockers, able to pick their two hundred boxes each from dawn till dark, would turn up their noses at our little clusters of wild, native fruit.

But the chokecherries are ripe, and that is news to all our neighbors and friends. In pickups and old jalopies they bump up the rough country roads. Whole picnic families scatter into the upper valleys and the thickets along the mountain streams.

For along the water courses, in remote pastures, the chokecherries grow thickest and biggest. Blood-red clusters drooping from their fragile stems against the pine-forested horizon. Beset by squawking magpies and tiny yellow finches, surrounded by growths of prickly wild rose and scratchy scrub oak. You have got to work to get at them. And you have to work harder to fill up a pail.

Maybe that is why gathering chokecherries is such a picnic outing in these Indian Summer days for all of us—Indians in their Monkey-Ward blankets, Spanish folk in Levis, and Anglos in their oldest catch-as-can get-ups. It's been a traditional outing as long as we can remember, and probably will be until the thickets finally retreat over the horizon from plow and axe.

If anything tastes better during a long snowy winter than dark red chokecherry jelly, its flavor sharpened by a pinch of garlic, we can't think what it is during these clear, mild days when the chokecherries are ripe here in New Mexico.

36

The Mesoamerican Calendar

(Essay)

THE mystery of time has never been solved, but the passage of time as we conceive it has been marked since man's earliest days. From the first primitive observances of the periodic change of seasons, of sunrise and sunset, to later calendars and electronic clocks, man has attempted to record the flow of time and to understand its ordering of the universe.

A far different conception from our own linear view of it was held by the Nahuas, Mayas, and other segments of the great Mesoamerican civilization that existed in the New World during the first millennia preceding and following the beginning of the Christian era. Its resplendent achievements in art, architecture, and hieroglyphic writing command today worldwide admiration and study. Scholarly researchers have unearthed the jungle-covered ruins of its great cities and pyramid temples, its tombs and walls of fresco paintings; they have deciphered glyphic inscriptions, and revealed details of the people's life. The Mesoamerican Calendar of this high civilization is its greatest achievement; but as it is a mental construct rather than a visible object, it has drawn less general interest. One of the most comprehensive time-reckoning systems ever known, it reveals a consummate knowledge of mathematics, astronomy, astrology, and symbology, illumined by a guiding religious principle.

The Calendar has long held a strange fascination for me, as for many other laymen. My interest was first aroused in 1970 when I received a Rockefeller Foundation grant for research in Mesoamerican culture and religion. For six months I traveled throughout Mexico and Guatemala, visiting all major archeological sites and studying ancient and modern literature at the national museum in Mexico City. The result of my research was published in 1975 under the title *Mexico Mystique: The Coming Sixth World of Consciousness*. The subtitle derived from the Mayan belief in four previous worlds, the present Fifth World, and another yet to come, all of which I interpreted as allegories for mankind's successive stages of consciousness. An astrological appendix to the book was prepared by Roberta S. Sklower, giving the planetary positions at the beginning and end of the Mayan Fifth World, our present world.

This first personal interpretation of the Mesoamerican or Mayan Calendar brought me in touch with Jack L. Ryan, a devoted student of Americana. He had made many trips to Mexico, and for years he had been making an obsessive study of the Calendar. With his remarkable knowledge of mathematics, astronomy, and astrology, his studies embraced a universal scope. We began to work together.

My *Mexico Mystique* was followed in 1981 by my book of essays *Mountain Dialogues*. In it I recorded Ryan's hypothesis of the origin of the Sacred Calendar, one of the four major calendars that comprised the great Mesoamerican calendar system.

Just when or where this Mesoamerican Calendar originated is unknown. It seems certain that the Olmecs on the east coast of Mexico originated the dot-and-bar system of counting and recording time. It employed only three symbols: a dot for the number one, a bar for five, and a stylized figure for zero.

So little is known about the Olmec culture, it invariably carries the adjective "mysterious." Its lifetime is believed to have extended from 1100 B.C. to 400 B.C., and it is considered the mother culture of all Mesoamerica because its influence spread so far and endured so long.

The Zapotecs at Monte Alban in Oaxaca adopted the Olmec dot-and-bar in their system of chronology, using a name-glyph instead of the symbol for zero. On one of their stelae is inscribed the oldest record of writing. The date is 644 B.C.

By the first century A.D. the Toltecs had erected the massive Pyramids of the Sun and the Moon at Teotihuacan in Mexico, establishing it as the metropolitan center of Mesoamerica; and to the south the Mayas were founding their first pre-Classic cities. The Mayas, adopting the Olmec counting system, initiated a method of place-value notation, placing their numerals in a vertical sequence with the higher values at the top. Their system was vigesimal, increasing in units of twenty.

The comprehensive Mesoamerican calendar system, as perfected by the Mayas, comprised a set of time-reckoning cycles or calendars: the Long Count, Solar, Venus, and Sacred cycles, as well as a Lunar cycle of 29.5 days.

The Long Count was a count of the number of days that had passed since their present world had been created. This date of 13.0.0.0.0 recorded that thirteen bak'tuns of 400 years each had elapsed since the end of the last Great Cycle of 5,200 years. The unit for computation in this era-based calendar was 360 days, a tun, with its multiples:

20 tuns	=	1 k'atun or 20 years or 7,200 days
20 k'atuns	=	1 bak'tun or 400 years or 144,000 days
20 bak'tuns	=	1 pic'tun or 8,000 years or 2,880,000 days
and so on up to		1 alau'ton, some 64,000,000 years.

The Solar Calendar or "Vague Year" of 365 days, the *haab*, was composed of eighteen months of twenty days and an extra period of five days called the *Wayeb* (resting days) by the Mayas, and the *Nemontemi* by the Nahuas or Aztecs. These additional five days resulted from the fact that the exact length of the Solar Year was one-fourth day longer than 365 days. Hence the Mayas added the extra period at the end of every five years, while we today intercalcate one day every fourth year or Leap Year. Each of the Maya months and days was named and added to the Long Count number, such as 13.0.0.0.0 4 Ahaw 8 Kumk'u (August 13, 3114 B.C.).

The Sacred Calendar, the Mayan *tzolkin* and the Nahuatl *tonalamatl*, was the cornerstone of the entire calendrical system. It was a cycle of 260 days consisting of groups of twenty days each bearing a name or day-sign combined with a number progressing from one to thirteen. Thus the first day-sign *cipactli*, "crocodile," was assigned the number one, and so down to the day-sign *acatl*, "reed," which bore the number thirteen. The fourteenth day-sign *ocelotl*, "jaguar," took the number one again. With this permutation system, a day with the same name and number could reoccur only every 20 × 13, or 260 days. Beginning a new cycle, it was endlessly repeated without regard for any natural time periods.

The Venus Calendar attests to the religious significance of the planet to ancient Mesoamerica. The Nahuatl myth equates with it the great figure of Quetzalcoatl, who upon leaving earth went underground in the west and, after a sojourn in the Land of the Dead, rose in the east as the morning star, Venus. So does the *Popul Vuh* myth record the apotheosis of the Maya twin brothers into the Sun and Venus.

These separate calendars meshed with superlative precision. Of primary importance was the meshing of the Solar Year Calendar of 365 days with the Sacred Calendar of 260 days. The two calendars coincided on the same day every 18,720 days, or 52 years. This cycle was called the Calendar Round. At the end of each, the Aztecs, fearing the world would be destroyed, extinguished their fires, broke their cooking pots, lamented, and fasted until the danger of calamity had passed.

The interlocking of the Venus Calendar and the Solar Calendar was based on the observance that the synodical period of Venus was 584 days and that of Earth 365 days. Their relationship reflected the ratio five to eight, for Venus made five revolutions and Earth made eight before they coincided at the end of 2,920 days. Hence the number five was an Aztec symbol for Venus, Quetzalcoatl, and the Fifth Sun, World, or Era.

To mesh the Venus Calendar with the Sacred Calendar, it was necessary that the beginning of the Venus cycle, the day 1 Ahaw, the day of Venus, occur within the 260-day Sacred Calendar. Hence the calculation was made that sixty-five revolutions of Venus and 146 cycles of the 260-day Sacred Calendar would coincide on the day 1 Ahaw, at the end of 37,960 days or 104 years. The calculation tables in the *Dresden Codex* took into account the fact that the synodical periods of Venus did not average exactly 584 days, but 583.92 days. This small accumulated error they balanced by a correction of eight days at the end of the fifty-seventh revolution in order to retain the day 1 Ahaw as the beginning of the cycle.

So accurate were all these calculations that the cycles of the three main calendars—Solar, Sacred, and Venus—coincided every two Calendar Rounds or 104 years of 365 days.

The Lunar Calendar was also correlated to the Sacred Calendar. Figuring a lunar month to be 29.5302 days, the Mayas adopted a cycle of 405 lunations, or 11,960 days, which coincided with forty-six Sacred Calendar periods.

It is useless to speculate how these ancient priest-astronomers, without telescopes or measuring and computing apparatus, could have achieved with such remarkable accuracy this complex calendar system. More incomprehensible has been the invention of the Sacred Calendar, the heart of the entire system.

The origin and purpose of its 260-day cycle is not known. It measures no natural time span, and may not properly be called a calendar although it is still used as a divinatory almanac by Highland Maya tribes. Various theories have been offered to explain it: that it represents the period of human pregnancy, or the interval between the zenithal transit of the sun at the latitude of fifteen degrees north. All such explanations have been rejected as implausible.

Jack L. Ryan, already mentioned, offers a new hypothesis which was published in my *Mountain Dialogues*. It need not be fully repeated here, but its premise is simply stated.

The Mesoamerican Calendar was a reformulated holdover from an incalculably older calendar that existed when the earth experienced a faster-moving solar year of 360 days. The originators of this first archaic calendar, whoever they were, based it on the wobble in the world's terrestrial axis which caused it to describe a small circle around the pole of the ecliptic. Moving one degree every 72 years, it completed one rotation every 9,360,000 days or 26,000 years of 360 days. This time, taken by all the planets in the solar system to return to their original positions, is known today as the Precession of the Equinoxes.

Then, at a date not yet known, there occurred a slight but significant deceleration of the earth's axial spin. One degree of the circle of the ecliptic no longer measured 72 years, but 72.222. The solar year was lengthened from 360 to 365 days.

To reconcile the difference, the prehistoric astronomers invented the 260-day cycle of the Sacred Calendar, 36,000 of which would equal a precessional period of 9,360,000 days ($360 \times 26,000 = 260 \times 36,000 = 9,360,000$).

They also adopted 25,920 instead of 26,000 years as the precessional period, so that every 72 years the arc of the ecliptic moved exactly one degree. This adjustment totaled 9,331,200 days instead of 9,360,000. Hence they inaugurated the 365-day year. This reformation of the archaic or antediluvian calendar solved many problems. For the 18,720-year (52×360) period of one calendar, and the 25,920-year (72×360) period of the other, converged at the end of 336,960 days.

As mentioned, the later historic Mayas' basic unit for their Long Count of millions of years was the 360-day tun; and all its increasing periods—the k'atun, bak'tun, pic'tun and so on—were multiples of 360. Ryan's theory satisfactorily explains why the Mayas ritually retained the prehistoric 360-day year, while their secular solar year comprised 365 days.

Nevertheless, his explanation raises many unanswered questions.

Who were the originators of the prehistoric calendar? When did the change of the length of the solar year from 360 to 365 days occur? And why did the Mayas of the early Christian era ritually retain the archaic 360-day year?

These unanswered questions involve a consideration of the four-world cosmological concepts of Mesoamerica, and the catastrophes that successfully destroyed them.

Belief in four previous worlds was not unique to Mesoamerica. It is found in the writings of Hesiod, the Greek historian; the religious texts of Zoroastrianism in Persia; the Hebrew Cabala; and Hindu and Tibetan Buddhism. Still today it is a basic tenet in the religious ceremonialism of the Hopis, Navajos, and other Indian tribes in the American Southwest.

Mesoamerican myth records the existence of four previous worlds that were successively destroyed, being supplanted by the present Fifth World, which will eventually suffer the same fate as the others. The *Popul Vuh,* the Sacred Book of the Quiché Maya, specifically describes the destruction of these previous worlds: the First World by jaguars, representing the element earth; the Second World by air; the Third World by fire; and the Fourth World by water, a great flood.

The Nahuas' mammoth basaltic disk weighing twenty-four metric tons, commonly called the Aztec Calendar Stone, pictorially confirms the *Popul Vuh* text. Each world, epoch, or lifetime they called a "sun." The four previous suns are represented by the square panels around the center carving. The First Sun was Ocelotonatiuh, Sun of the Jaguar, inhabited by giants who were devoured by jaguars. The Second Sun was Ecstonatiuh, the Sun of Air. Its deity was Quetzalcoatl in his role as God of Wind, and the world was destroyed by cyclones. Quisuito-natiuh, the Sun of Fire, was the Third Sun, whose deity was Tlaloc, and it was destroyed by a fiery rain. The Fourth Sun was Chalchi-huitlicue, named for the sister of Tlaloc, whose inhabitants were drowned in a diluvial catastrophe. In the center of the great stone is portrayed Tonatiuh, the fifth and last sun, destined to be destroyed by earthquakes.

Here we will take a look at some modern views of the catastrophe that apparently accompanied the change in length of the solar year, necessitating reformulation of a prehistoric calendar and marking the end of a previous "world." Cosmic disruptions have repeatedly changed the surface of the earth. Whole continents have sunk beneath the waters. Lofty mountain ranges have risen from deep sea floors.

Floods have submerged plain and desert. Many causes for these crustal changes have been proposed—shifts in the earth's orbital axis, diastrophism, and the movement of tectonic plates. None of them has satisfactorily explained what caused the worldwide legendary Flood, or when it occurred. Yet the memory of it is preserved in the myths and legends of peoples everywhere, and embodied in our unconscious today. The Catastrophe. The great Deluge. The Flood.

The first known historic account of it was given to the Greek sage Solon when he visited Egyptian priests about 590 B.C. They related that there had existed an immense island or continent situated in front of the Pillars of Hercules. Then had come violent earthquakes and floods that submerged the continent beneath the sea about 9500 B.C. Solon's account was passed down to Plato, who finally related it in his dialogues *Timaeus* and *Critias* about 355 B.C. This is the earliest recorded account of Atlantis.

Unproven, often derided, the theory of the existence of Atlantis has endured for 2,400 years. Over five thousand books have been written about it. If this establishes its psychological significance, many other sources have developed reasons for believing in its physical existence.

Esoteric schools include Atlantis in a global pattern of four successive continents that served as evolution centers for mankind: the Polarian, Hyperborean, Lemurian, and Atlantean. Carl A. Zapffe in his *New Theory for the Great Ice Ages* presents the thesis that a major catastrophe accompanied each of the four great ice ages, and that they coincided with the formation of the four successive continents of esoteric theology. The last one, the Wisconsin glacial age, had four stages, the final one being the Mankato Maximum specifically dated at 9564 B.C. Its accompanying catastrophe coincides with the one that sank Atlantis in 9500 B.C., as recorded by Plato.

R. A. Schwaller de Lubicz in his prodigious three-volume study of the ancient Egyptian Temple of Luxor refutes the assumption of orthodox Egyptologists that Egyptian history began in 2750 B.C. He asserts that the civilization of Egypt was founded as early as 36,000 B.C.; that it did not develop gradually, but was inherited from a still earlier, vanished civilization. He also held the belief that the Sphinx was eroded not by windblown sand, but by a great flood.

Another seeming confirmation of the Atlantis myth was given by the noted psychic Edgar Cayce. In his "life readings" of some seven hundred people over a period of twenty-one years, he recounted the catastrophes that finally sank Atlantis in 10,000 B.C., sending thousands of its inhabitants to Egypt, Europe, Yucatan, and Peru.

Such dates for the sinking of Atlantis bring us back to the Nahuatl and Mayan Fourth World which was destroyed by water, a great flood. Why the Mayan date of 13.0.0.0.0 was selected as the beginning of the last Great Cycle of 5,200 years, and the base from which all other dates were reckoned, is not known. It seems most probable that it was conceived as marking the end of the Fourth World and the creation of the current Fifth World.

Numerous scholars over the years have worked out correlations with our present Gregorian calendar. J. T. Goodman in 1905 established the date as 3113 B.C. Juan Martinez Hernandez, Yucatan archeologist, corrected it by one day in 1918. And in 1927 J. Eric S. Thompson of the Carnegie Institute further corrected it by four days. The combined Goodman-Martinez-Thompson correlation was accepted as the most accurate. Their date was August 12, 3113 B.C.

Apparently it was not the start of the Mesoamerican Calendar, for thirteen bak'tuns of four hundred years each had already elapsed, and inscribed stelae show dates within bak'tun 7. Hence Morley, Thompson, and Coe believed that the Long Count was begun in that period. A definite fixed point in cyclic time, 13.0.0.0.0 was the zero point from which the Mayas projected dates farther into the past and the future.

Herbert Spinden's correlation sets the date at October 14, 3373 B.C.—one cycle of the 260-day Sacred Calendar earlier. And the German scientist Otto Muck, inventor of the snorkel and guided missile rocket, using Spinden's correlation, calculated that the Mayan calendar was begun in 8498 B.C. and that the current Great Cycle began 5,127 years later in 3375 B.C.

Obviously, then, the sinking of Atlantis about 9500 B.C. could not have been concurrent with the destruction of the Mayan Fourth World about 3113 B.C. Which one coincided with the great Deluge? When occurred that change in the world's axis resulting in a longer year of 365 days, and what people originated the archaic calendar of 360 days, ritually adhered to by the later Mayas? A dark shadow envelopes these two dates and the time between them. If it bears the shape of a vanished civilization, it may be the projected image of our imagination, but we cannot be too sure. We know too little about this dark period of antiquity.

A few events confirm the significance of the Mayan date of 3113 B.C.

Ixtilxochtitl in the sixteenth century of the Christian era concluded from his study of antique Nahuatl sources that the Fifth World was created in 3245 B.C. According to ancient texts in India, the conjunction of Saturn and Jupiter in 3102 B.C. caused the great Deluge, and the *Bhagavata Purana* states that the Hindu cycle of Kali-yuga began in 3101 B.C. The first dynasty of Egypt began about 3200 B.C. The Chinese calendar was begun in 3082 B.C. And Nineveh was founded in 3100 B.C., marking the beginning of the Sumerian civilization.

Ryan in his study reveals a remarkable similarity between the Mesoamerican and other ancient calendars.

The Babylonian Calendar was based on a precessional period of 25,920 years, divided into a zodiac of twelve houses of 2,160 years. This was evidently a reformulation after the Flood, for the preceding Sumerians retained the same number of days, 9,460,000, as in the Sumerian archaic calendar (360 days $\times$ 26,280 years = 365 post-flood years $\times$ 25,920 = 9,460,000 days).

An interesting study was made by Maurice Chatelain in 1975 during his research on Babylonian cuneiform tablets in the Nineveh library. He found that the huge number of days in 246 Babylonian precessions of 25,890 years was the exact multiple of all the planetary conjunctions and revolutions during 240 precessional cycles of 25,890 years, the basic constant of the life cycles of the solar system. The Mayan Great Cycle of 5,163 years reflected 260 Saturn-Jupiter conjunctions, the same number as the days in the Sacred Calendar. Chatelain then found that the last Saturn-Jupiter conjunction in 3141 B.C. approximately coincided with the last Mayan cycle of thirteen bak'-tuns. On this basis Chatelain figured a Mayan Great Cycle to be 5,163 years, divided into thirteen bak'tuns of 19.86 years, and each k'atun into twenty tuns of 363 days.

The Hindu-Chinese precession was 25,200 years. The beginning date of their calendar is believed to be 10,602 B.C., occurring at the beginning of the zodiacal age of Leo. This places the cusp at 8502 B.C., approximating Muck's date of 8498 B.C. (10,602 − 2100 = 8502 and 3373 + 5125 = 8498).

The archaic Egyptian Calendar was evidently based on a precession of 26,280 years. It was divided into twelve mansions of 2,190 years, or eighteen Sothic cycles of 1,460 years. The Zodiac of Denderah apparently began in the zodiacal sign of Leo, registering the entry of a new cycle between 10,950 B.C. and 8,000 B.C. in Cancer. The Coptic papyrus *Abou Hormeis* of the ninth century A.D. indicated that the Deluge took place when the "Heart of the Lion" entered the first minute of Cancer.

The archaic Mesoamerican Calendar, as we know, was based on a precession of 26,000 tuns or years of 360 days, reformulated to 25,920 years. This divided into a zodiac of twenty houses of 1,296 years each. Ryan finds many points of convergence. The Mesoamerican Calendar at the end of eighteen Calendar Rounds or 336,960 years converged with thirteen Babylonian precessions; and sixty-three Mesoamerican precessions and sixty-five Hindu-Chinese precessions converged at the end of 1,668,000 years. The first triple convergence of the Mesoamerican, Babylonian, and Hindu-Chinese calendars came at 3,276,000 years; and the final quadruple convergence (including the Mesoamerican variant of "Vague Earth Years" of 365 days) at the end of 58,968,000 years.

These similarities seem to confirm the hypothesis that all known calendrical systems derived from one common source—a calendar originating in an unknown civilization that had existed before the length of the solar year changed. What its purpose was in projecting time in great cosmic cycles far into the future is not revealed by the Mesoamerican Calendar. We can accept its cosmology only on its own terms despite our attempts to reconcile them with our modern beliefs.

Much has changed since I began to study the Calendar. The dates of the last Great Cycle of 5,200 years have been revised by a later correlation to August 13, 3114 B.C., and December 23, 2012 A.D. And the view of Morley and Thompson that the Mayas were a peaceful people dedicated to their art and religious philosophy has been supplanted by a far different picture. Scholars in the fields of archeology, ethnology, iconography, epigraphy, and art have deciphered glyphs revealing dates and dynasties, names of Mayan kings. What emerges is a record of a great population supporting about forty city-states warring with each other. Their primary purpose was to capture prisoners for torture and sacrifice matching, if not exceeding, that of the gory Aztecs. This starkly realistic picture is presented in the beautifully illustrated book *The Blood of Kings,* by Linda Schele and Mary Ellen Miller.

Text and photographs of Mayan carvings, sculpture, and paintings amply document their conclusion that the letting of blood was the mortar of Maya civilization. Bloodletting was carried out not only on captured prisoners of war. Voluntary drawing of blood from kings and their wives and nobles sealed all ritual events. As explained in the text, the purpose was to document royal bloodlines relating kings to their divine ancestors, the gods, thereby proving their right to succession and insuring continuance of the world.

Schele points out that the symmetry of the Long Count replicates that of the Sacred Calendar cycle of 260 days. There are twenty cycles of thirteen bak'tuns in the Long Count, just as there are twenty day-names and thirteen numbers in the Sacred Calendar. But after the completion of thirteen bak'tuns or 5,200 years the count reverts to 1 bak'tun again, instead of continuing by pic'tuns or twenty bak'tuns. Hence the same date occurs in mythical time and historical time, showing that the gods and human kings were essentially alike, and events were the same. A constant repetition in cyclic time.

True as this picture may be, it is only the dynastic view of the Mayas' ruling elite, expressing their divine right to accession. The larger Mesoamerican perspective is of course found in the Mayan *Popul Vuh*, the Aztec Calendar Stone, and other records. They too show cycles of time, but not constant repetition of temporal patterns. They record successive stages of mankind's evolution through worlds symbolized by earth, air, fire, and water.

Accompanying the professional study of the entire Maya civilization in recent years, the Calendar's projected date of 2012 for the end of the present Fifth World has aroused wide public interest. The publication of *The Mayan Factor* by José Argüelles met the demand. The picture it drew of the Mayas was completely opposite to that presented in *The Blood of Kings*, published almost simultaneously. Argüelles accepted the Mesoamerican four-world concept as literally true, but added new dimensions of his own. His imaginary premise stated that the planet Earth was passing through a galactic beam—a passage requiring 5,200 years and coinciding with the Mayas' Great Cycle beginning in 3113 B.C. and ending in 2012 A.D. At its end Earth would emerge from its present planetary stage of consciousness into full galactic consciousness, a belief similar to that developed in my own book *Mexico Mystique: The Coming Sixth World of Consciousness*, published eleven years before.

But Argüelles expanded this into a hypothesis that had no documentation nor attribution. To guide mankind in making the conversion from the Fifth to the Sixth World, he asserted that a group of Outer Space beings possessing full galactic consciousness was sent to

Earth from their star bases on Arcturus and the Pleiades. Arriving in Central America, they became known as the Mayas. Here they established the brilliant Classic Maya civilization that existed from about 300 to 900 A.D.

By 830 these Outer Space beings had concluded their mission, according to Argüelles. Having left records of their work and their prophecy in art, hieroglyphic writing, and the phenomenal calendar, they returned to Arcturus and the Pleiades. It is true that scholars today cannot account for the Mayas' sudden and mysterious abandonment of their splendid cities and the collapse of the Classic Maya civilization.

Argüelles's book assured an end to our world's wars and revolutions everywhere, terrorism, crime, starvation, disease, and despoliation of the planet itself. Hundreds of people acclaimed the book's imaginative prediction that humanity had only to wait until 2012. It would then be endowed with higher consciousness, and a new beneficent world civilization would replace our present materialistic economic structure and quarreling political regimes. The time was only twenty-five years away. So the "Harmonic Convergence" took place, when groups of believers assembled at various locations throughout the world to hail the coming change.

The Mayan Factor is a most imaginative book. To me it seems more Argüelles than Mayan. I find it difficult to believe the Mayas were Outer Space beings sent from distant stars. It is easier to accept Schele and Miller's view of the Mayas as human beings with a bloodletting obsession despite their great achievements. Yet the myth they left behind them rests on a belief in great cosmic cycles of time that are now regarded as either repetitive or transformative. From their records both the Nahuas and the Mayas seem to have regarded these as transformative stages of mankind's evolution, as previously discussed.

Change, constant change appears to be the law of life. Nothing is forever static and nothing remains the same. Laurette Sejourne, an archeologist who directed major excavations at Teotihuacan and whose perceptive interpretations were criticized because they were based on psychological and psychical grounds, viewed Mesoamerican belief from this higher level. She observed that the Nahuatl concept of movement or change is the fundamental motivation of all life. It is symbolized by one of the major hieroglyphs and day-signs, *ollin*, movement. It comprises simply four circles or petals placed around a central circle, all sometimes enclosed in a square or circle. It symbolizes the four quadrants of the universe, the four primordial elements, the four worlds or suns, with the Fifth Sun as their synthesizing center. The Fifth Sun is the Sun of Movement.

Leon-Portilla explains that the Nahuatl words for movement, heart, and soul have a common root. Hence the synthesizing center of the Fifth Sun was the soul of man. Here the moving thrust of evolution took place, a process whose only measure was man's ever-expanding consciousness.

The cosmography and cosmology of these worlds or stages must surely reflect a psychic foundation. Their quadruplicate structure shows a fourfold mandala form, an archetypal symbol of psychic wholeness. As such, it presents an image of Mesoamerican thought. Writes the analyst C. G. Jung, "Careful investigation of the unconscious shows that there is a peculiar coincidence with time, which is also the reason why the ancients were able to project the succession of unconsciously perceived inner contents into the outer determinants of time." This may explain the Mesoamerican four worlds as an unconscious concept of psychic wholeness translated into physical form.

The Mayas' projection of successive worlds in time and space was based on their phenomenal knowledge of astronomy and astrology. Their study of the stars is validated by modern astrology. According to astrologer Liz Greene, "the solar system is a living energy pattern mirroring the energy pattern of the individual human psyche. The same forces are manifested simultaneously in both at every moment, reflecting their interconnectedness."

The Mesoamerican Calendar's projections of more cycles far beyond the Great Cycle lead us to expect a continuing change in the ordering of both the planets and our human psyche.

Thus far we have considered a far distant past suggested by Ryan's postulation of an archaic calendar based on the great precessional cycle of 26,000 years of 360 days. There then occurred a deceleration of the Earth's axial spin which changed the precessional cycle to 25,920 years and the solar year from 360 to 365 days. The later Mayas ritually retained the prehistoric count, but adopted the later count.

The Precession is still for us the basis of our measurements of temporal time. Any change in it, for whatever reason, is certain to affect all our time-reckoning systems. It is astronomically apparent that 2012, the end of the Mayas' last Great Cycle, approximately coincides with the end of the present precessional cycle of 25,920 years and the last zodiac cycle of 2,160 years, the Age of the Fish. Surely one might expect a corresponding change of some kind in the world and the life of mankind.

Man is ready for a change. Our present world civilization is in an advanced stage of collapse. Political, economic, and social systems are breaking down with no rational means of control. Yet man's mode of thinking is beginning to change. We are entering a period of transition, seeing the world and ourselves differently, adopting values ignored by our materialistic and excessively rational civilization. This transformation is taking place internally, preparatory to the external transformation of the existing political and economic systems. The result will be the virtual creation of a new world equivalent to those successive worlds of Mayan myth.

The rulers of the Maya city-states, according to Schele, were less concerned with possible human and social changes than with maintaining their divine right of succession in repetitive cycles of time. The priest-astronomers, however, raised their sights higher. The great Mesoamerican Calendar, reformulated from a prehistoric calendar, reflects a projection of changing but ordered astronomical cycles far into the future, with corresponding changes in the Solar System.

The major part of Ryan's study comprises extrapolation of these cycles, presented with astronomical charts, mathematical tables, and computational analyses. In his illustrations, he first pictures the Aztec Calendar Stone, showing the antediluvian precessional period of 26,000 years divided into five Great Cycles of 5,200 years, believed to be the duration of each of the successive worlds, as we know. He shows each of these Great Cycles subdivided in turn by the Mayas into four periods of thirteen bak'tuns of 400 years, the last ending in 13.0.0.0.0, the beginning of the Fifth World.

He then illustrates the Mesoamerican zodiac obtained by dividing the corrected post-precessional period of 25,920 years into twenty houses of 1,296 years. In contrast, the ancient Babylonians, who also used an ecliptic-centered astronomy, divided the same precessional period into twelve houses of 2,160 years.

Ryan also shows these zodiacal periods as they occur within the five calendar periods of 5,184 years.

Next, projected outward from the basic Calendar Round of 52

years are nine great cycles or rounds. They embrace the synodic periods of all the other planets in the Solar System known to the Mayas.

Mercury	117 years
Venus	585 years pre-Deluge calendar
	584 years post-Deluge calendar
Mars	786 years
Jupiter	400 years
Saturn	375 years

Their significance becomes apparent when we remember that the 52-year Calendar Round marked the time when the Solar Calendar of 365 days meshed with the Sacred Calendar of 260 days, and these two calendars coincided with the Venus Calendar every two Calendar Rounds, or 104 years.

The first of the projected great cycles, the Minor Venus Year, comes as the completion of eight Calendar Rounds, or 416 years. This period of convergence was monumentalized in the Pyramid of Kukulcan at Chichen Itza. Each of the eight side-sections was faced with fifty-two stone slabs, comprising 416 years. Each of the four staircases contained ninety-one steps; and with the addition of the top platform the total amounted to 365, the number of days in the Vague Earth Year.

In the second great cycle, the Major Venus Year, Mercury and Mars are synchronized with the above convergences. It occurs after the passage of eighteen Calendar Rounds, 936 years.

The third, the Great Venus Cycle, comes after 3,744 years. It embraces four Major Venus Cycles as well as nine Minor Venus cycles. Their ratio, four to nine, is the same as that between Venus and the Sacred Calendar before the Deluge: ($4 \times 585 = 9 \times 260 = 2,340$, the Mesoamerican Constant). With it is reconciled the new number of Venus revolutions, 584 ($585 \times 2,336 = 584 \times 2,340 = 1,366,560$ days).

Here on the great time scale emerges the full scope of Mesoamerican thought. It reflects the world's ages-old belief in a divinely ordered universe. The seeming purpose of the Calendar was to reveal the times when all the planets, one by one, were to be synchronized in harmonious phase relationship.

The fourth cycle, round, or time wheel is called the Great Calendar Round because it contains 360 Calendar Rounds of 52 years each, 18,720 years. As each time wheel embraces 360 of the former unit, the

Calendar Round represents an indicator of one degree in a full-circle cycle. In this great Calendar Round, Jupiter comes into line for the first time, leaving only Saturn still unaligned.

The Minor Venus Year Round at 149,760 years is followed by the Major Venus Year Round at 336,960 years. This latter time wheel marks the great convergence of the preceding five cycles, when eighteen Great Calendar Rounds coincide with thirteen precessions of 25,920 years. Their 13:18 ratio replicates that between the *tzolkin* and the tun—260:360.

Wheel Seven (Great Venus Cycle Round) at 1,347,840 years is followed by Wheel Eight (Great Calendar Round Cycle) at 6,739,200 years, which marks the conjunction with 260 precessional periods.

The Colossal Round, the last of the nine, is measured at 485,222,400 years. It embraces 9,331,200 Calendar Rounds of 52 years, the kernel and starting cycle of this phenomenal time system. And here at last recalcitrant Saturn is aligned with all the other planets in one harmonious, universal order.

Wheels within wheels. Great cycles of time spreading outward from a temporal center to an unimaginable future. Every detail meshes, coincides, synchronizes in absolute precision—cycles, planetary conjunctions, calendars, convergences, mathematical ratios—into an interconnected whole confirmed by a guiding religious pattern.

Ryan comments, for example, that the aggregate total revolutions made by each planet up to the last cycle can be numerically reduced to the number "nine." The Mesoamericans believed there were nine hells below the earth and thirteen heavens above. In the various heavens traveled the moon, sun, and Venus. The highest heaven was the Place of Duality, the abode of Ometeotl, the supreme Nahuatl deity and ruler of the universe. Does this suggest an evolutionary progression of life from the lowest hell to the divine level of the highest heaven?

A similar evolution and progression was developed in the teachings of Central Asia expounded by Georges Ivanovitch Gurdjieff. He taught that all modes of existence in the universe can be grouped in ten "essences" or energies ranging upward from formless energy, through Earth, man, and the planets, to the divine cosmic consciousness, that "Endlessness" symbolizing the supreme creative force of all life. This "chain of worlds" links our Earth, moon, sun, and planets with the "Absolute." From each of the known planets, we on Earth are receiving physical and psychical influences. To these Gurdjieff adds two undiscovered planets beyond Pluto and two more spiritual planets, from which we are already receiving influence.

Gurdjieff clearly states that the entire universe is structured on one cosmic principle from the galactic to the subatomic worlds of matter, which is replicated in man's own consciousness. Our planet Earth, solar system, and galaxy are living bodies, each progressing through the same stages of development.

The ultimate stage of Earth's ever-expanding consciousness may have been glimpsed in a well-known theory of the French Catholic priest Teilhard de Chardin. He envisioned an envelope of thought or a planetary mind, which he called the "noosphere," eventually surrounding Earth once man's collective consciousness has expanded to a cosmic level.

How nebulous, incredibly vast, and far in linear time such a possibility appears to our puny, limited minds! Yet human history does not follow a straight-line evolution from primitive societies to the proud apogee of modern Western civilization. Previous civilizations achieved heights of conception and execution our own today have not attained. Like all organic growths, civilizations experience birth, growth, and death. Alternating cycles of mankind's polarity to rational and to intuitive modes of thought take place periodically. But the high level of consciousness some of them attained is preserved in the hermetic records they have left.

The Mesoamerican Calendar is such a record. "There is nothing," wrote Laurette Sejourne, "that would help us penetrate deeper into pre-Columbian thought more than exact knowledge of the temporal cycles within which the universe, having sounded a common note, advances a step further toward ultimate freedom."

Jack Ryan's projections of this masterpiece give new insight. Combined with his proposed study of the early Toltecs of Teotihuacan near today's Mexico City, his work if completed may be the most comprehensive record yet of ancient Mesoamerican thought, for this metropolis was the heart of a holy empire whose religious ideology spread throughout all Mesoamerica. Comparable to Rome, Mecca, and Alexandria, Teotihuacan was the birthplace of the Quetzalcoatl religion and of Nahuatl culture. No other structures in the New World equal its own, with their enormity and austerity. Measurements suggest that the city was built on a preconceived plan, a scale model of Earth itself.

I myself am still wandering in the labyrinthian implications of the Mayas' projection of cycles of time extending to 485,322,400 years. Time to me is still a mystery. Modern science now considers time as combining with space in a space-time continuum that is a factor of human consciousness. Neither time nor space is measurable and limiting. They do not separate us, but unite us in a state that is motionless and boundless.

This current Western belief appears somewhat similar to the ancient doctrine of the Eastern religious philosophy known as Shakta Vedantism. Time, it asserts, has no beginning or end, no breaks or stages. Called *Parakala,* it has two aspects. It may be statically condensed into the moment, *now.* And it may expand dynamically into the boundless continuum, *everywhere* and *always,* which is Duration involving past, present, and future. Space like time has the same twofold aspect, shrinking to a center, *here,* and expanding in a limitless continuum, *everywhere,* its involution and evolution being the pulse of life itself.

According to both views, the mystery of time can be solved only by understanding the greater mystery of the human consciousness that perceives it. And human consciousness is ever expanding, widening our perspective and giving birth to other views. It reaches farther outward than the planetary cycles measured by the Mayas and the computer limits of modern astronomy, deeper inward in the human psyche than modern depth psychology. Human consciousness, more significantly, embraces a gradually unfolding spiritual realm. It seems to me that mankind's comprehension of this is the measure of all our attempts to solve the mystery of consciousness. These attempts are highlighted by the Mayas' conception of time and space. With unbelievable audacity, they grasped by means of their known observable world the evolutionary attainment of divine universal order. In their effort we find man's eternal questing spirit, which links us with this inspired people of the past.